School Choice in the Real World

School Choice in the Real World

Lessons from Arizona Charter Schools

EDITED BY

Robert Maranto
Scott Milliman
Frederick Hess
April Gresham

Westview
PRESS

A Member of the Perseus Books Group

Copyright © 2001 by Westview Press, A Member of the Perseus Books Group

First published in 1999 in the United States of America by Westview Press, 5500 Central Avenue, Boulder, Colorado 80301-2877, and in the United Kingdom by Westview Press, 12 Hid's Copse Road, Cumnor Hill, Oxford OX2 9JJ

First paperback printing 2001.

Find us on the World Wide Web at www.westviewpress.com

A CIP catalog record for this book is available from the Library of Congress.
ISBN 0-8133-9820-7 (pbk.)

The paper used in this publication meets the requirements of the American National Standard for Permanence of Paper for Printed Library Materials Z39.48-1984.

10   9   8   7   6   5   4   3   2

*To our parents, who knew the value of a good education;
to our children, Anthony and Darby, who deserve
the best education possible; and to a teacher, Ellen Lucius,
who has provided a quality education to her students.*

Contents

Part One
Theoretical and National Perspectives

Part Two
Social Scientists Look at Arizona Charter Schools

Part Three
Practitioners Look at Arizona Charter Schools

Part Four
Lessons

Tables and Figures

Figures

Acknowledgments

This volume could not have progressed without the backing of many individuals and organizations. Most important, the Bodman Foundation generously funded much of the research reported here. In addition, the College of Business at James Madison University provided crucial institutional support in the form of a research leave and computer time for one of the editors. The Curry School of Education at the University of Virginia gave additional support for two other editors.

We wish to thank Cathy Murphy, acquisitions editor of the Westview series on education, for her constant encouragement and always sage advice. We also wish to thank our very accommodating and knowledgeable production and copy editors, Lisa Wigutoff and David Toole, who made the editing process bearable. Two anonymous, hardworking reviewers developed suggestions that were difficult to implement but certainly improved our "baby." In addition, the editors of this volume were blessed with contributors who brought their work in on time, and in good order. The remaining flaws are ours alone.

We are also grateful to a number of the analysts of and "players" in Arizona charter school policy who were nice enough to provide information, including Doug Pike of the State Board for Charter Schools, Mary Kay Haviland of the Arizona Education Association, Lori Mulholland of the Morrison Institute, Jaime Molera of Governor Hull's staff, and Eddie Farnsworth of the Arizona Charter Schools Association. These people taught us that Arizona is a state where policy makers make a point of urging researchers to interview *their opponents*. If only Washington could work that way!

We wish to thank the hardworking teachers from Arizona and Nevada who took the time to fill out our teacher surveys. A number of outstanding public servants from the Arizona Department of Education took the time to provide information and explanation, including Mary Gifford, Lyle Skillen, John Eickman, Jonathan White, and especially Michelle Carter, who worked hard to find the data we needed. Perhaps more than anyone, Barbara Fontaine answered our questions, often for the fourth or fifth time, and never lost her patience with the interlopers from back east. Barbara's knowledge is second only to her dedication to the education of Arizona's youth.

Finally, our greatest thanks must go to the charter school entrepreneurs and teachers, particularly Carol Sammans and Ann Peshke of Edupreneurship and Merrill Badger of Pine Forest. We can only salute their commitment to their students. Thanks to their ilk, we are optimistic about the future.

Robert Maranto, Scott Milliman,
Frederick Hess, April Gresham
CHARLOTTESVILLE, VIRGINIA

Acronyms

ACU	American Conservative Union
ADE	Arizona Department of Education
AEA	Arizona Education Association
AFT	American Federation of Teachers
AFT	Arizona Federation of Teachers
AIMS	Arizona Instrument to Measure Standards
ANOVA	Analysis of Variance
ARS	Arizona Revised Statute
ASA	Arizona School Administrators
ASBA	Arizona School Boards Association
ASBE	Arizona State Board of Education
CPA	Certified Public Accountant
CQ	*Congressional Quarterly Weekly Reports*
CRS	Congressional Research Service
ED	Department of Education
EPA	Environmental Protection Agency
ESEA	Elementary and Secondary Education Act
FALA	Flagstaff Arts and Leadership Academy
FY	Fiscal Year
GAO	General Accounting Office
HMO	Health Maintenance Organization
IDEA	Individuals with Disabilities Education Act
JTPA	Jobs Training and Partnership Act
LEA	Local Educational Authority
MPCP	Milwaukee Parental Choice Program
NAEP	National Assessment of Education Progress
NCTM	National Council of Teachers of Mathematics
NEA	National Education Association
NPR	National Performance Review
NSEA	Nevada State Education Association
PCS	Public Charter School
PPEP TEC	Portable Practical Educational Preparation Training for Employment Centers
PPOR	Per-Pupil Operating Revenues

SBCS	State Board for Charter Schools
SEA	State Education Agency
TEA	Tennessee Education Association
USFR	Uniform System of Financial Records
USFRCS	Uniform System of Financial Records for Charter Schools

1

Real World School Choice: Arizona Charter Schools

ROBERT MARANTO, SCOTT MILLIMAN,
FREDERICK HESS, APRIL GRESHAM

A National Controversy

In the last ten years, issues of choice in education have grown dramatically in prominence. Debates about school charters and school vouchers elicit high passion, meaning that much of the debate about charter schooling and school vouchers leans toward the emotional rather than the empirical. Choice proponents believe that vouchers (which parents could use at private schools) or public charter schools (which compete with and are independent of local school districts) will solve perceived education woes. Choice opponents fear that such drastic reforms raise serious concerns about equity and accountability, while promising nothing traditional schools do not already offer.

Although polls find that the public generally favors school choice in the abstract, the margins of support are often narrow and depend on the exact plans described. Policy makers are similarly divided: Republicans typically support more school choice, whereas Democrats are divided about or simply opposed to such choice. In 1998, public referenda on school vouchers were hotly contested and defeated in California and Colorado, but more such proposals are sure to surface in other states (Cookson 1994; Henig 1994; Feistritzer 1996; Doherty 1998; Milbank 1998). This book explores the implications of one key form of school choice—charter schooling. The authors explore the issue primarily by considering charter schools in Arizona, a state that provides the most promising laboratory currently available.

Charter schools are public schools that have been freed of many state restrictions, are independent of traditional local school districts, and actually compete for students with traditional public schools. Although schemes proposing vouchers for private schools attract most of the attention in the choice debate, charter schools are far more popular and widespread. As of October 1998, thirty-three states and the District of Columbia have passed charter legislation. Although charter schools exist in more than half of the states, Arizona contains nearly one out of every four charter schools in the nation, and nearly one of four Arizona public schools is now a charter school (Center for Education Reform 1998). As the authors in this volume detail, because the barriers to entry are sufficiently low and the number and variety of charter schools sufficiently high, charter schools in Arizona present something new: the first system approaching comprehensive school choice in the real world.

This volume brings together both social scientists and education practitioners to give the first published account of the Arizona charter school phenomenon. The authors focus on how choice has affected Arizona public education as a whole. We are particularly interested in why Arizona has the nation's largest charter sector, how that sector grew (and whether growth is likely to continue), how charter growth has impacted traditional district-based schools and how districts have reacted, how charter schools differ from district schools, and how (and whether) charter schools are held accountable.

The primary purpose here is to present information that will help parents, teachers, school administrators, charter operators, policy makers, and taxpayers across the United States better understand how charter schools operate in practice and how they can affect a state's educational system. We will not try to convince the reader that Arizona's charter system is good or bad. We are far more concerned with helping readers to understand the complexities and potential consequences of charter school reform. Toward that end we have assembled essays that speak to various challenges, successes, and intricacies characterizing the first five years of the charter school experience in Arizona.

In this volume we do not attempt to provide a comprehensive survey of the critical issues in charter schooling. Such an effort is more than can we could competently address here. School choice raises an almost endless array of concerns, from the purpose of schooling and the equity of educational provision to the efficiency of educational services and the appropriate ways to evaluate school performance. Special education, how choice affects funding equity, and desegregation are just some of the important issues that we cannot address, due to limits of time and space. We do not imply that these issues are less relevant than the points explored here; rather, we simply recognize the finite capacity of any single volume to address an overwhelming number of issues competently. We are particularly interested in how charter schools emerged, why they have grown, the kinds of challenges that growth has posed to public authorities and traditional public schools, and how that growth has affected teachers and administrators in the schools.

The data examined here should be regarded as suggestive, not conclusive. The Arizona charter program is only five years old, involves only a small portion of the state's total students and teachers, and has been evolving over time. There is no way to use existing evidence to understand fully the ways in which charter schooling will play out over time. Changes in the structure of schools, the tastes of parents and students, the makeup of public school personnel, the statutory environment, and related elements of schooling may produce new and unexpected impacts in the long term. Our intention is not to provide precise estimates of how charter schooling affects education; we are more concerned with enriching and helping to structure a debate that often pays only glancing attention to the nuanced effects of school choice.

Finally, as with so much of public policy, the issue of school choice is at its core a normative one. It comes down to the role that one believes education should play in American society. All the evidence in the world may not convince someone that their faith in the market or in democratic processes is misguided. We are not seeking to convince either adherents or opponents of charter schooling; it is our hope that this volume instead will help to elevate the discussion of school choice and will raise more subtle points that may have received insufficient consideration in the policy debates.

Competing Claims

To understand the centrality of the choice debate, two points are essential. First, public schooling is the most direct connection that most citizens have with government. Public schools educate, feed, and protect our children; affect the value of our homes; and help shape our shared values. Primary and secondary education are the leading expenditures of state and local governments. Altogether the United States spends more than $300 billion a year on public elementary and secondary schools to educate nearly 50 million children (National Center for Education Statistics 1998).

Second, there is widespread dissatisfaction with the performance of American public education. Since at least the publication of *A Nation at Risk* in 1983, public schools have been accused of having overstaffed central administrations, incompetent teaching, inadequate discipline, high costs, and, perhaps most importantly, lax academic standards. Politicians of both parties have responded with a plethora of solutions: school building programs, higher requirements for teacher licensing, higher teacher salaries, school report cards, more rigorous curriculum standards, mandatory testing, and, of course, various forms of school choice (Smith and Meier 1995; Spring 1997; Clinton 1998).

Beyond the importance of public education and concerns about its performance lurk powerful material interests. Taxpayers naturally want to receive value for their money and often desire some say in how schools are organized and managed. Similarly, the business community has an interest in procuring cost-effective schools that produce disciplined, productive workers (Doherty 1998; Stone 1998). Meanwhile, the National Education Association (NEA) and the American Federation of Teachers (AFT), together representing roughly 2.5 million teachers, seek to improve the salary, working conditions, and security of members. These union goals can conflict with what others deem necessary to improve schooling. Although teachers' unions always back coalitions to increase school spending, they seldom join coalitions advocating changes in schooling (Lieberman 1997; Stone 1998).

Conflicts exist between those who fear schools are ineffective—taxpayers and business community members—and teachers' unions, which have a strong interest in maintaining the current system. Given the perceived success of privatization and deregulation in the past two decades, popular sentiment for applying those lessons to education has grown. Support for choice has grown particularly among minority parents, who are most immediately concerned about school performance issues. The most prominent critics of choice have been the unions and district school officials, but they have been joined by a wide array of communitarians, civil rights leaders, and suburban parents who are worried about undermining schools that they find satisfactory, or about the implications of choice for equity, access, and the teaching of common social values (Spring 1997).

A range of ideological groups want education to reflect their own societal goals. Whether of the left or right, groups that feel marginalized in public schools support greater choice of curricula (Spring 1997). These value-laden fights are more intense in education than in other areas of public policy, both because schools directly influence the development of people's children and because education directly touches the life of the local community. Finally, virtually all U.S. citizens have spent a great deal of time in classrooms. The experiences of people and their children shape perceptions of school choice and other education issues. Thus people are often passionate about schools because they are quite certain that they understand the problems (Tyack and Cuban 1995).

Just as the public and politicians are divided over school choice, so too are academics. Academic supporters of market-based reforms argue that choice will make schools more accountable for performance. Instead of attempting to follow ever-changing political mandates, advocates of choice expect that market-based schools will be free to govern themselves, define their own special focus, and win over a niche market. Rather than being "shopping mall high schools" offering a little of everything to all people, market-based schools would need to please only the parents who enroll their children.

There are two ways in which advocates expect choice-based remedies to improve schooling. Most commonly, advocates argue that introducing choice permits parents to choose schools appropriate for their child, increases parental and student commitment to schooling, and enables new quality schools to blossom. A second, less commonly advanced argument for school choice is that *if the choices offered are comprehensive enough*, markets will unleash competitive pressures and force all schools to improve. Rather than focusing on the improvement of education one school at a time, the *market hypothesis* expects competition to force the great mass of schools to improve by increasing the efficiency and quality of their educational offerings. In theory, competition between schools will drive failing schools out of business as they lose students, thereby gradually improving the educational system as a whole (Friedman 1962; Chubb and Moe 1990; Kirkpatrick 1990; Hill et al. 1997).

These claims have not gone unchallenged. Critics argue that school choice will increase segregation without improving student achievement, in part because parents will not base their choices on academic quality, but rather on racism or social status. Further, traditional school supporters believe that existing public schools already work better than pro-choice accounts suggest, particularly in ensuring diversity and uniform accountability. Choice critics suggest that governance or curricular reforms are much more likely to produce significant improvement than are market-based reforms, and that the "innovation" noted by charter supporters is much overblown. They fear that the freedom granted charter schools invites corruption. Finally, critics worry that even if charters improve education one school at a time, these isolated gains will do nothing for the students who remain in public schools, and that the outflow of talented students and teachers may actually leave the masses worse off than before (Smith and Meier 1995; Berliner and Biddle 1995; Henig 1994; Cookson 1994; Sukstorf et al. 1993; Witte 1998).

Why Study Arizona?

Many works have sought to understand empirically the impacts of school choice and the competing claims cited above, yet all these works have been hampered by the limited and controlled nature of existing choice options. For example, the works within Nathan (1989) tested the impacts of choice in magnet and open enrollment programs controlled by school districts, even though districts often restrict the range and viability of such options. Some of the most prominent works on school choice— Chubb and Moe (1990), Smith and Meier (1995), and Hoxby (1996)— compared public and private schools or else tested the impacts of private school enrollments on public education, extrapolating the impacts of more thoroughgoing choice from there. Yet access to private schools is limited by income and restricted admissions. Finally, the works within Peterson and Hassel (1998) tested the impacts of small-scale and limited charter school sectors, or of voucher programs limited to low-income families. Studying the impact of large-scale choice has been difficult because such schemes have not existed traditionally in the United States. Since the implementation of Arizona's 1994 charter school law, however, we, for the first time, have something approaching comprehensive school choice in an American context.

What do we mean by *comprehensive school choice*? A general definition might be that almost all parents have some choice of where to school their children. We suggest that four criteria help determine comprehensiveness. First, how many options do families have to choose from, and how extensive is that range of choices? (After all, if all the choices are similar, then choice does not exist.) Second, what percentage of families are financially able to send their children to a school other than their assigned public school? Third, what percentage of families find it *logistically* feasible to send their children to schools other than their assigned public school? Finally, how much competition between schools is engendered by choice (that is, do schools have an incentive to compete for students)? Notably, the existence of comprehensive choice does not mean that many parents will choose to use it. If parental satisfaction with district schools is high, it may be that very few parents will choose to opt out; thus the percentage of parents using choice is not a good measure of comprehensiveness. We find it convenient to think of choice as a continuum, with Arizona's system much closer to comprehensive choice than any other system now going.

Historically, choice has depended on a family's ability to cross geographical boundaries into a better school district or to send their children to private schools. In recent decades, magnet schools have also provided some choice. However, these options provide only limited choice. Few low-income families can afford private school tuition. Similarly, it is costly to change residences, and if the better schools are located in high-priced locations, as is often the case, low-income parents are at a serious disadvantage. Access to public magnet schools is not restricted by money but by institutional constraints: Relatively few school districts have magnet schools, and magnet schools often restrict admission to a select few (Maranto and Milliman 1996; Nathan 1996). Some districts offer parents a choice among public schools (open enrollment). In fact, Arizona districts have had open enrollment for some years, but this option is little used since it is not well publicized and since, in Arizona, the most desirable schools are in rapidly growing areas and are usually full. Further, in Arizona and nationally, districts tend to offer relatively homogeneous "choices."

In contrast, Arizona's charter system offers a choice between a number of different kinds of schools to a large and growing percentage of the population. As Bryan Hassel finds in Chapter 5, Arizona's charter school law is one of the most likely to introduce choice and competition into the public school system and to lead to charter autonomy, though one of the least likely to require charter accountability to oversight institutions. The Center for Education Reform, a national school choice advocacy group and research center, ranks Arizona first in the nation for the expansiveness of its charter school law. As of December 1998, 272 campuses operated across the state, with dozens more expected in 1999. Excluding Arizona, there is a mean of only 32.9 charter schools per charter state (Center for Education Reform 1998).[1]

As shown in Chapters 6 and 10, charter schools in Arizona provide a number of distinct options for parents, and these schools are fairly accessible as well.[2] Unlike private schools, they charge no tuition. Unlike magnet schools, Arizona charter schools are not allowed to restrict admission, so all families have access. Charter schools must accept whoever comes and hold a lottery if too many students apply. The vast majority of Arizona residents live within a half-hour commute of a charter campus, so it is usually logistically feasible to choose a charter—although relatively few charter schools provide transportation, so in some cases low-income families have limited access to charters. Still, access to school choice in Arizona is far greater than in other states, even if it is not yet complete.

A final contrast between Arizona charter schools and public magnet schools is that when charter schools lose students they are not buffered from the impact of market forces. In fact, all Arizona public schools lose the state per-pupil operating subsidy when a family sends its children elsewhere. Consequently, Arizona offers the best example of a school system towards the comprehensive end of the choice continuum.

President Clinton has called for the creation of 3,000 charter schools nationally by 2001 (U.S. House 1997; Clinton 1998). In early 1999, more than 1,200 charter schools were operating across the United States. Amazingly, Arizona has one fourth of this total. As is detailed in Chapters 6 and 8, Arizona's charters enroll about 34,000 students, which means that 4.4 percent of Arizona public school students attend charter schools; some local

school districts have lost more than 10 percent of their potential enrollment to charter schools.

Organization of This Book

The works in this volume offer the first published accounts of the Arizona
charter school experience, bringing together social scientists, policy makers, and practitioners in search of lessons for other states and for the U.S.
Department of Education.

We purposely sought a diverse collection of authors who have either
researched or experienced the impact of charters nationally or in Arizona.
The authors hold very different views of the promise of charter schooling,
so not all chapters agree. These conflicts reflect the current state of knowledge about school choice in Arizona, where there is much controversy. L.
Elaine Halchin in Chapter 2, Robert Maranto in Chapter 3, and Bryan
Hassel in Chapter 5 draw upon diverse theoretical perspectives from normative public administration theory, the Reinventing Government literature, and education literature, respectively, to provide a backdrop for Arizona's situation. History serves as the basis for the descriptive chapters
by David Leal (Chapter 4), Robert Maranto and April Gresham (Chapter
6), and Stephanie Timmons-Brown and Frederick Hess (Chapter 7). Four
chapters focus upon results of initial research studies in Arizona: Chapters 8 (Robert Maranto et al.) and 11 (Frederick Hess et al.) and Chapters
9 and 10 (Gregg Garn and Robert Stout). Two authors draw upon their
own experience as members of the political elite leading Arizona's charter school debates: Lisa Keegan in Chapter 12 and Mary Hartley in Chapter 13. In Chapter 14, Lee Hager writes from a traditional school perspective. Finally, in Chapter 15 Jim Spencer adds a personal touch to the book,
as he recounts his experience as a charter operator.

We have divided the book into three general sections: (1) broader approaches to school choice and charter schooling; (2) empirical examinations of the Arizona experience; (3) and first-person discussions of the
Arizona phenomenon from policy makers and school people. This volume uses Arizona as a lens through which to help the reader understand
the promise and the problems of school choice more fully.

For our discussion of Arizona to be most valuable, the reader needs a
general familiarity with school choice issues. Consequently the first third of
the volume, the background chapters in Part I, explores the nature of and
theories behind school choice generally and charter schools in particular.
The first two chapters present opposing perspectives from within public
administration literature. Education is the largest part of American public
administration, and reforms of government service generally affect educational policy. These two chapters ground evaluations of charter schooling

in contrasting theoretical frameworks. In Chapter 2, L. Elaine Halchin uses a normative perspective to examine a key question—whether school choice conflicts with our traditional democratic values. She considers the very nature of education as a good and asks whether that good should be public or private. Examining the roots of education as a public good, she points out that the Founders favored government control of education to avoid a host of ills, including religious persecution, inequality, and societal balkanization. The education of all citizenry leads to a better society; as such, education is a public good that should be publicly controlled and publicly funded. Halchin's conclusions that charters and choice-based education are a potential threat to democracy clearly contrast with Maranto's views in Chapter 3.

Robert Maranto combines organization theory with public choice theory to place Arizona's reforms within the context of an international movement to reinvent government by infusing choice into public services and using competition to improve public sector performance. Maranto summarizes criteria to judge successful public administration in a reinvented world, borrowing from two well-known models; he then applies those criteria to the Arizona charter school system. He hypothesizes that Arizona's school choice reforms are more likely to be implemented than previous education reforms because they defuse culture wars and conflicts over teaching methods by not imposing a single model of education. Unlike Halchin's historical and normative focus on democratic values, Maranto uses a results- and consumer-oriented approach, reaching a very different conclusion about charter schools' potential for helping American society. Such is the nature of the controversy over values facing education policy generally and choice-based approaches in particular.

In Chapter 4, David L. Leal offers a historical analysis of how and why Congress passed an appropriations rider in 1994 to subsidize the national spread of charter schools, and of how and why charter school appropriations have increased each year since. As a relatively small program supported by both Republicans and Democrats, the charter school appropriation has attracted little notice and garnered broad support from a variety of politicians who saw charters as able to serve diverse goals. Leal discusses the partisan divisions in the charter school debate and outlines provisions of the federal law that have sped the national spread of charter schools. Like the other writers in this section, Leal's focus is national; however, this chapter is a straightforward historical summary rather than a theoretical account.

Finally, in Chapter 5, Bryan Hassel draws upon the history of school reform and the education literature to present a theoretically based examination of the issue of innovation in charter schools, both nationally and in Arizona. He offers a framework for testing whether or not charters are actually more innovative than traditional schools and for distinguishing between charter schools as innovative policy and as innovative institutions. He concludes that charter policies are innovative, creative combinations of previous school reforms, but that actual charter innovation is much harder to determine. Using the three key aspects of potential innovation (autonomy, accountability, and choice and competition), Hassel finds that states' potential for innovation varies widely. He notes that Arizona's unique law tends to be high on autonomy and competition but low on accountability. In the end, actual charter innovation is an empirical rather than a philosophical or political question, a question that can be answered only through further research.

In Part II, social scientists conduct initial attempts to answer Hassel's call for empirical research in their examinations of Arizona charter schools. These chapters examine why the Arizona charter school law passed, how charter schools compare to district schools, how they affect district schools, how charter school accountability works in practice, how charter curricula compare to district curricula, and how Arizona teachers view the state's charter school law and other educational reforms. These chapters offer some of the first published research on Arizona charter schools, and thus present a first test of various claims about charters and their impact.

The researchers here employ a variety of methods to examine charters: interviews, surveys, public documents, and even observation of public meetings. Each method has its advantages and disadvantages; the differences in methodology complement, rather than contradict each other. The chapters investigate very different questions as well, ranging from testing claims about the innovation of charter schools' curricula to examining the potential competitive effects of charters on traditional public schools. In the conclusion to this volume, we take up these chapters and analyze the research studies and their implications, placing some differing research viewpoints in context and attempting to reconcile others. At this point we want simply to summarize the chapters in Part II.

First, in Chapter 6 Robert Maranto and April Gresham detail both the expansive Arizona law that permitted the rapid spread of charter schools and how the charter sector is changing. They find some evidence that the rapid growth of charters is slowing. They conclude from a brief comparison of Arizona charter and district schools that charters are newer, smaller, serve a different set of grade levels, and generally have higher teacher morale. This chapter provides basic background, including descriptive statistics about charters, and should be of most use to readers unacquainted with Arizona.

In another descriptive chapter, Chapter 7, Stephanie Timmons-Brown and Frederick Hess trace the emergence of legislative proposals and the eventual passage of the Arizona charter school law. They compare the charter proposals in Arizona and Nevada to explain why charter advocates enjoyed such success in Arizona, while faring far worse in demographically and educationally similar Nevada. Chiefly, Republican dominance of state government and the near passage of voucher legislation made even a strong charter school law an acceptable compromise to charter opponents in Arizona. The authors believe that comparisons suggest weak teachers' unions and Republican dominance as antecedents for strong charter school laws. Those readers wanting to know why and how such strong legislation emerged in Arizona but not in other states will find this chapter helpful.

In Chapter 8, Robert Maranto, Scott Milliman, Frederick Hess, and April Gresham use interview data—as well as data from a survey of 1,641 teachers in Nevada, Arizona charter schools, and Arizona district schools—to examine whether competition from charter schools pushes district schools to improve, as is predicted by the market hypothesis. They explore potential charter impacts on a number of dimensions, ranging from administrator effectiveness to teacher empowerment. Analyses suggest that schools and school districts with higher levels of competition did experience small but significant changes between 1994 and 1997, compared to other schools and school districts. They note that it is still too early to say that competition improves public schooling (though most of the reported changes appear positive), but it is useful to recognize that Arizona's public schools are reacting systematically to the presence of competition.

In Chapter 9, Gregg Garn and Bob Stout, using interviews of civil servants and key legislators, on-site monitoring reports, and analyses of financial and auditing records, examine one key facet of market-based theory by assessing the actual accountability mechanisms for Arizona charter schools. As Halchin notes in Chapter 2, accountability for education as a private good (choice-based education) involves parents gathering or receiving accurate information about various school options for their children and evaluating that information. Hassel mentions accountability as one of the three necessary components for actual charter school innovation and as the only component on which the Arizona law scores below average. Garn and Stout conclude that Arizona's bureaucratic accountability mechanisms are not working and, more importantly, that parental accountability is diminished by the poor transmittal of information from charters to statewide agencies, and thus to public records. The authors suggest policy changes to improve accountability. The research data from this chapter resonate with Hassel's concern about the Arizona law's poor accountability ranking (Chapter 5) and Hartley's frustration with the Arizona charter school system (Chapter 13). Although their research is exploratory, Garn and Stout note finding significant weaknesses in a standard market process: the collection and dissemination of information by traditional oversight institutions.

In Chapter 10, Stout and Garn test whether innovation, often noted by choice supporters as an inevitable consequence of a choice-based system, actually occurs in the curricula of Arizona charter schools. They analyze charter school applications and official reports and conduct several school site visits. The authors find no evidence that charter schools are inventing new methods of instruction. Again, their multiple methodology strengthens their research, though (as they note) findings must be considered tentative. Stout and Garn use a selective, qualitative, rather than quantitative, approach to classify several types of charter schools, ranging from conservative, content-centered classrooms to vocational-technical job training programs. Their classification is a helpful first attempt to categorize the variety of charter options, a variety consistent with Maranto's Chapter 3 prediction that charters will make a range of currently existing options more available to parents. Although by no means a definitive answer, their findings are consistent with Hassel's predictions that most (though not all) charters are not likely to have innovative curricula because they will want to appeal to parents. As Hassel points out, real innovation may not come in the curriculum, but in the governance structure, a possible area for future innovation research.

In Chapter 11, Hess, Maranto, Milliman, and Gresham present a descriptive, survey-based account of how teachers view school reforms, including charter schools. They point out that teachers are the ones who translate policies to the classroom, yet little is known about how they view various school reforms. Individual teachers may affect the charter movement in many ways: as potential charter operators, charter teachers, charter parents, and as educational professionals consulted by parents about charter opportunities. Accordingly, this chapter presents important exploratory work concerning whether teachers' expressions of their own personal opinions would help or hinder charter schooling. Hess and his colleagues compare how Arizona and Nevada teachers view charter schools and other types of school reform: statewide education standards, site-based management, merit pay, magnet schools, and vouchers. They find that teacher support decreases as the degree of change imposed by reform increases. Charter teachers were significantly more likely to support magnet programs, merit pay, charter schools, and even vouchers than either Arizona district or Nevada teachers. Length of service, school culture, union membership, and partisan beliefs help predict teacher responses on some (though not all) reforms. Interestingly, Arizona district teachers seemed more negative toward charter reforms than Nevada district teachers, but Arizona teachers who had applied for a charter job (or who knew someone who had done so) appeared significantly more favorable towards charters than those who had not.

Part III departs from social science research to give the perspectives of practitioners. This section includes the views of two of Arizona's most prominent education policy makers, a school official from a district heavily impacted by charters, and a charter school operator. These contributions round out the theoretical, historical, and research-oriented perspectives found in the first two sections of the book. Authors in the book's first two sections study the phenomenon of charters in Arizona; these people live it.

The first two chapters of this section are by policy makers and present an interesting contrast in their accounts of the charter school legislation, of whether the charter school experiment is "working," and of plans for future policies. In Chapter 12, Lisa Graham Keegan, Arizona state superintendent of public instruction, describes how Arizona's charter reforms started and where she sees them headed. Keegan helped craft the Arizona charter law while heading the house Education Committee and was then elected state superintendent of public instruction. She focuses on reasons for the charter school explosion, charter school benefits for parental empowerment, and charter school accountability. Keegan relies on market accountability rather than bureaucratic accountability for charters. She acknowledges the importance of giving parents an informed choice, pointing to statewide standardized testing and school report cards. There is an inevitable tension between charters' need for freedom to create and parents' need for accountability information, which often must be collected by state bureaucrats. Keegan clearly supports freedom more than bureaucratic accountability.

In stark contrast, in Chapter 13 State Senator Mary Hartley, Arizona's most prominent critic of charter schools, echoes Garn and Stout's accountability concerns even more strongly. These and other concerns prompt her to urge other states to avoid Arizona's example. Senator Hartley, a Democrat and charter skeptic, starts the chapter with her own history of the passage of the charter legislation and of Keegan's downsizing of the Department of Education bureaucracy. She describes the transportation funding controversy (also mentioned briefly in Chapters 6 and 15) and details the state's funding appropriations for charters, concluding that charters are better off financially than some traditional public schools. Next, drawing upon media sources and her own experience, she details key issues—including religious sectarianism and alleged discrimination against children with special needs—raised by the failings of some charter schools. Her observations raise serious equity and process concerns, echoing the normative public administration views of Halchin presented in Chapter 2. Hartley also notes instances of corruption, another concern raised by Halchin. In conclusion, Hartley recommends limiting the number of charter schools until more financial and educational accountability mechanisms can be tested and found worthwhile.

Chapter 14 offers the view of school-district official Lee Hager. Although acknowledging the common frustration of district schools at the lack of funding and respect accorded them by a Republican state legislature, Hager does not adopt the "us versus them" mentality so common in the charter controversy. From his long experience in traditional schools, he draws parallels between charters and previous reforms: home schooling and magnet programs. In response to each, traditional public schools initially reacted with anger at perceived attacks (and fear of diminishing resources), whereas reformers began with contempt for "the establishment" and an arrogant independence. Over time, both parties learned that they needed each other and that they had to compromise for the sake of the children. Hager ends with a description of the benefits of charter schools, envisioning a productive working relationship between charters and traditional public schools in the future. Hager's chapter complements Chapter 8, which examines the quantitative data concerning the competitive effects of charter schools upon a traditional district; Flagstaff's "school of choice" and Pathways programs represent attempts by a traditional district to respond to charter competition.

In Chapter 15, Jim Spencer describes how he converted his private Montessori school to charter status in order to expand. Since converting, Spencer has chafed under public sector reporting requirements, increased scrutiny, and the inability to select students who could best benefit from a Montessori education. At the same time, he would do it all over again, because "the pioneers tend to get all the arrows, but they also get to be the first to cross the Rockies and see the Pacific." Spencer's chapter shows how charter schools differ from private schools. Most notably, Spencer gives an operator's view of the difficulties in offering equitable education to children with special needs, a concern noted elsewhere in the book. Spencer's description of the greater constrictions placed upon a charter school where "everyone is watching you" is consistent with Hassel (Chapter 5) and Stout and Garn (Chapter 10), suggesting that actual innovation may be less likely to occur in charters than supporters suggest.

Finally, in the conclusion we attempt to tie together the competing chapters by laying out their agreements and disagreements, and by suggesting directions for future research. The conclusion focuses on the contested answers to five questions. First, are Arizona charter schools accountable? Second, are Arizona charter schools innovative? Third, are Arizona charter schools spurring district schools to improve? Fourth, and many would say most importantly, do children attending Arizona charter schools learn more than those at district schools? Finally, what impacts do charter schools have on equity?

Conclusion

This book is a first look at the first (fairly) comprehensive school choice system. Eventually, we will be able to reach more certain judgments about how charter and district schools compare in terms of academic achievement, innovation, accountability, equality, socialization, and parental and teacher empowerment. The question of which system is better, though, is not one that research alone can answer. Fundamentally, that answer depends on what "better" means and on the values that one holds most dear. For those who wish to empower parents and teachers to take charge of education, the Arizona model holds great appeal. For those who want all citizens to govern education through the political process, the Arizona model will always fall short. The most basic controversies over choice are normative and thus can be presented but not resolved. The research presented here helps to inform those interested in charter schools but does not end the debate. Only the democratic system can provide authoritative answers.

Notes

1. Indeed, even traditional charter school supporters such as Joe Nathan (personal communication, June 1998) and Ted Kolderie (personal communication, July 1998) argue that Arizona's system is so uncontrolled as to the number and type of operators that it is more akin to vouchers than charter schools.

2. Though, as will be explored in Chapters 6 and 10 and in the conclusion, there is a question of whether charters present true *innovations*.

References

Berliner, David C., and Bruce J. Biddle. 1995. *The Manufactured Crisis: Myths, Frauds, and the Attacks on America's Public Schools*. Reading, Mass.: Addison-Wesley.

Center for Education Reform. 1998. "Charter School Highlights and Statistics." December 1, 1998, URL: www.edreform.com/pubs/chglance.htm.

Chubb, John E., and Terry M. Moe. 1990. *Politics, Markets, and America's Schools*. Washington, D.C.: Brookings Institution.

Clinton, William Jefferson. 1998. "State of the Union Message." December 1, 1998, URL: www.whitehouse.gov/WH/SOTU98/address.html.

Cookson, Peter W., Jr. 1994. *School Choice: The Struggle for the Soul of American Education*. New Haven, Conn.: Yale University Press.

Doherty, Kathryn N. 1998. "Changing Urban Education: Defining the Issues." In *Changing Urban Education*, ed. Clarence N. Stone, 225–249. Lawrence: University of Kansas Press.

Feistritzer, Emily. 1996. *The American Teacher*. Washington, D.C.: National Center for Education Information.

Friedman, Milton. 1962. *Capitalism and Freedom*. Chicago: University of Chicago Press.

Henig, Jeffrey R. 1994. *Rethinking School Choice: Limits of the Market Metaphor*. Princeton: Princeton University Press.

Hill, Paul R., Lawrence C. Pierce, and James W. Guthrie. 1997. *Reinventing Public Education: How Contracting and Competition Transform America's Schools*. Chicago: University of Chicago Press.

Hoxby, Caroline. 1996. "The Effects of Private School Vouchers on Schools and Students." In *Holding Schools Accountable,* ed. Helen F. Ladd, 177–208. Washington, D.C.: Brookings Institution.

Kirkpatrick, David W. 1990. *Choice in Schooling: A Case for Tuition Vouchers.* Chicago: Loyal University Press.

Lieberman, Myron. 1997. *The Teacher Unions.* New York: Free Press.

Maranto, Robert, and Scott Milliman. 1996. "The Impact of Competition on Public Schools." Paper presented at the annual meeting of the American Political Science Association, San Francisco, Calif., September 2.

Milbank, Dana. 1998. "Schoolyard Tussle: John Kerry Takes on the Teachers' Unions." *New Republic,* December 14, 22–25.

Nathan, Joe. 1996. *Charter Schools: Creating Hope and Opportunity for American Education.* San Francisco: Jossey-Bass.

_____., ed. 1989. *Public Schools by Choice.* St. Paul: Institute for Teaching and Learning.

National Center for Education Statistics. 1998. *Digest of Education Statistics.* Washington, D.C.: U.S. Department of Education.

National Commission on Excellence in Education. 1983. *A Nation at Risk: The Imperative for Educational Reform.* Washington, D.C.: U.S. Department of Education.

Peterson, Paul E., and Bryan C. Hassel, eds. 1998. *Learning from School Choice.* Washington, D.C.: Brookings Institution.

Smith, Kevin B., and Kenneth J. Meier. 1995. *The Case Against School Choice: Politics, Markets, and Fools.* Armonk, N.Y.: M. E. Sharpe.

Spring, Joel. 1997. *Political Agendas for Education from the Christian Coalition to the Green Party.* Mahwah, N.J.: Lawrence Erlbaum.

Stone, Clarence N. 1998. "Civic Capacity and Urban School Reform." In *Changing Urban Education,* ed. Clarence N. Stone, 250–273. Lawrence: University Press of Kansas.

Sukstorf, Marla E., Amy Stuart Wells, and Robert L. Crain. 1993. "A Re-Examination of Chubb and Moe's *Politics, Markets, and America's Schools.*" In *School Choice: Examining the Evidence,* ed. Edith Rasell and Richard Rothstein, 209–218. Washington, D.C.: Economic Policy Institute.

Tyack, David B., and Larry Cuban. 1995. *Tinkering Toward Utopia: A Century of Public School Reform.* Cambridge, Mass.: Harvard University Press.

U.S. House Economic and Educational Opportunities Committee. 1997. Gerald Tirozzi, testimony before the Subcommittee on Early Childhood, Youth, and Families. 105th Congress, April 9, 1997.

Witte, John F. 1998. "The Milwaukee Voucher Experiment." *Educational Evaluation and Policy Analysis* 20: 229–251.

PART ONE

Theoretical and National Perspectives

2

And This Parent Went to Market: Education as Public Versus Private Good

L. ELAINE HALCHIN

Voucher and charter programs offer radical reform of American education, yet only two publicly funded voucher programs currently exist, and participation in each is restricted by means testing, limiting eligibility to low-income families. The Milwaukee program targets poor children in the inner city, and participation is further restricted by a cap on enrollment. Similarly, the Cleveland scholarship program gives preference to low-income families and is limited by the amount of money appropriated by the state legislature. These programmatic requirements restrict consumer participation by artificial means and hence limit the education markets in Milwaukee and Cleveland.

A much more inclusive form of school choice is found where charter schools exist side by side with traditional public schools. As found in Arizona, charter schools are not subject to limits on the type and number of customers they serve. Open to all and subject to an enrollment cap only to the extent that demand exceeds supply, charter schools offer school choice through an entire school district. The public schools do not retain a captive pool of students, as is the case in both Milwaukee and Cleveland. Whereas school voucher programs are unique for giving parents government funds to pay tuition at private schools, a system of charter schools is unique for opening up school choice to everyone—it is the most expansive form of school choice.

School choice strikes a chord with parents. On a practical, immediate level it puts into practice the belief that parents know what is best for

their children and that they will act appropriately on that interest in selecting a school. Greater parent involvement in education is laudable in
and of itself and can contribute to citizenship. Yet, although some applaud the ascendancy of the family over the state that this grant of authority offers, the implications of school choice for democracy and public
education warrant a more cautious response. The trip parents take to the
market to choose their children's schools might introduce or reinforce
the idea that education is a private good, an idea contrary to traditional
views of primary and secondary education as a public good.

This chapter will discuss the Founders' and modern political theorists'
conceptualizations of education as a public rather than a private good,
systematically compare the two approaches, and suggest ways in which
market-based education as practiced by charter schools in Arizona could
undermine the democratic polity.

Is Education a Public Good or
a Private Good?

The discipline of economics views education as a private good (Lamdin
and Mintrom 1997) or as a nonexcludable public good (Hyman 1993).
Douglas Lamdin and Michael Mintrom (1997: 213) argue that education
has the characteristics of a private good because it "is not non-rivalrous in
production (the marginal cost of education of additional students is not
zero) . . . and it is possible to exclude consumption."

This is a conventional method for assigning functions to the public or
private good category, but it is not the only one. Using the inherent characteristics of education to categorize it as a private good does not change
the polity's need for education. Applying the principles of excludability
and rivalry discounts or ignores the reasons for establishing education as
a public good in the first place. Education is not the same as public safety,
garbage collection, road construction and maintenance, and the regulation of food and drugs. These functions and activities make life safer,
convenient, and more pleasant. But they are not essential to the function-
ing of democracy. Education sustains democracy by producing an educated citizenry equipped to participate in self-government (Gutmann
1987; Henig 1994).

The political and societal validation of education as a public good occurred over many years. Guided by democratic principles and using
both government organizations and political processes, society determined that public education was needed to satisfy the public interest.
Opting for the term "public needs" instead of "public goods," Deborah
Stone (1988: 81) asserts that a democratic society has a legitimate right to

decide what functions are essential to the common good and hence are public needs:

> Those needs that a community recognizes as legitimate and tries to satisfy as a community might be termed *public needs*. The conception of public needs in real political communities is far broader, more varied, and tied to specific cultures than the economic concept of *public goods*. . . . In welfare economics, the inherent characteristics of goods determine whether they are 'public.' A lighthouse is a public good because it is in the nature of light signals to be visible to many users at one time and to persist even after being 'used.' By contrast, public needs are determined in a political process and have far more to do with people's ideas than with inherent characteristics of things. (italics in original)

This approach, whereby society expresses and acts upon its interests through political means and in the process decides which functions and activities are public goods, represents an alternative to the market method offered by economists. Although a widespread system of public education was not established until the twentieth century, the rationale and various plans for government-controlled schools were first discussed in the eighteenth century. Hence, we need to examine the origins of ideas about education and its relationship with democracy in order to understand the unique place of education in American society and why it is considered a public good.

Roots of Education as a Public Good: The Founders

Having recently won independence from Great Britain and having established a form of government never before implemented on such a grand scale, the founding generation gave careful consideration to what it would take for the new nation to survive. Although these men might not have argued necessarily or explicitly for public education—a system funded and provided by government—their reasoning finds expression today both in the arguments of political theorists who discuss the link between education and democracy and in the very existence of a public system of primary and secondary education.

Public education and democracy are joined in the ideas of several of the Founders. Thomas Jefferson and like-minded colleagues believed that the viability of the American republic depended upon the common people. Yet not just anyone was equipped to take on the demands and responsibilities of the public office of citizenship. Though he placed great faith in the common people, Jefferson also recognized the need to prepare them for citizenship, saying, "The qualifications for self-government are not innate. They are the result of habit and long training" (Jefferson, cited in Battistoni 1985: 62). Enlightened citizens were needed for democracy, and education was the means to produce citizens fit for the duties of self-government. But the founding generation had no model to follow (Pangle and Pangle 1993: 11). They had to fashion their own plan, and their ideas about education were informed by their understanding of democracy and what it required of citizens. Committed to avoiding contamination from European ideas and to crafting an educational plan suited to America, the Founders focused on a common theme: to develop "a distinctively American system of education" tailored to the needs, interests, and concerns of the new nation (Curti 1935: 47). A chief need was to create "a new unity, a common citizenship and culture, and an appeal to a common future" (Tyack 1967: 840).

Those members of the founding generation who believed that an enlightened citizenry was essential to the viability of the new nation and its continued success favored government control of education. First, government had a legitimate claim on an institution existing to serve the public interest. With the viability of the nation dependent upon its ability to produce democratic citizens for the present and the future, government could not be expected to entrust schooling to the private sector. Jefferson argued that "public schools aiming to serve the whole public must be under governmental direction and free from religious or sectarian or private control" (Butts and Cremin 1953: 93). Noah Webster and Benjamin Rush concurred that "the only social agency capable of creating an educational system was the government." (cited in Tyack 1967: 86–87). Second, given that many members of the founding generation believed in the necessity of universal education, awarding control to a neutral institution made sense. An institution open to all would not be bound by the dictates or beliefs of any one segment of society. Additionally, social divisions might intensify, and factions might be aided, if religious and private interests exercised control over schooling. By bringing together students from different backgrounds and fostering a common American understanding, language, and set of values, it was hoped that publicly controlled schooling could ameliorate the divisiveness of a diverse society. For these reasons, public education was needed to serve the public interest as a public good.

The connection between self-government and citizen education drove certain of the Founders' strong beliefs in universal education. If republican government in America was to survive and flourish, all future participants had to be prepared for fulfilling their obligations as citizens. Jefferson, possibly the most prominent advocate of universal education, was joined by John Jay, Benjamin Franklin, John Adams, James Madison, Benjamin Rush, and George Washington in supporting universal education at least at the primary level (Blinderman 1975; Butts and Cremin 1953; Meyer 1967).

The institution of universal public education would be hollow in the absence of financial support. The fear that not only individuals but also the nation would suffer politically and economically if people were denied schooling for financial reasons played a large part in the push for public support and public control of the nation's schooling (Butts and Cremin 1953), as did the nation's drive for egalitarianism (Pangle and Pangle 1993). Though separated by several decades from the founding generation, Thaddeus Stevens provided a succinct rationale for the public financing of education that surely would have met with their approval. Responding to those citizens who opposed paying taxes to support a service they did not need or receive, Stevens noted that, although there were some societal functions for which a portion of the population would not have "any direct personal use," these activities benefited the individual and society as a whole" (Stevens, cited in Butts and Cremin 1953: 203).

Even though some of the best minds of the day articulated the rationale for education, their ideas were not embraced by the polity as a whole. Their reasoning and concern for the nation were not enough to overcome a host of other ideas and social forces preoccupying American society in the late 1700s and early 1800s (Pangle and Pangle 1993). But concluding that Jefferson, Rush, and the others had failed would be a mistake. Their link of education to democracy would become the foundation of American schooling, but it would have to wait "until the changed conditions of life added their thrust to arguments and proposals for change" (Butts and Cremin 1953: 66).

The conditions of life *have* changed in the intervening years, and the founding generation's vision for education has been realized. Education has evolved into a public institution and a public good. The United States has a publicly controlled and financed system of universal education that helps to prepare future citizens for the tasks and duties of self-government. The link between democracy and education, a significant influence on the ideas of Jefferson and other Founders, continues to shape our understanding of those two institutions: "Education, in a great measure, forms the moral character of citizens, and moral character along with laws and institutions forms the basis of democratic government. Democratic government, in turn, shapes the education of future citizens, which, in a great measure, forms their moral character" (Gutmann 1987: 49). Traditional public schools satisfy "the state's need for an educated citizenry"

(Wise and Darling-Hammond 1984: 29) and are "a means [for democracy] to reproduce its most essential political, economic, and social institutions through a common schooling experience" (Levin 1991: 140).

Characterizing Education as a Private Good

The status of education as a public good, secured some time ago, was not questioned until recently. Now, the presence of charter schools could radically alter the way some people—parents in particular—think about education. Institutional arrangements suggest ways of viewing education, and schooling provided through a system of charter schools has the trappings of a private good. Government and the market are dissimilar ways of organizing human activities, because the polity and the market have different purposes, values, and operating principles. As a market-based education system, charter schools present education as a consumer good, with parents as consumers. The fragmentation of the school system, the weakening of the common school ethos, and explicit messages encouraging parents to shop around, all challenge views of education as a public good. In sum, the existence of charter schools could institutionalize education as a private good.[1]

How Do We View Education? Comparisons of Public Good and Private Good Conceptions of Education

Table 2.1 compares competing conceptions of education as a public and private good. This descriptive scheme illustrates how individuals view education and how those views suggest particular institutional arrangements and conditions. In his discussion of public goods, Albert Hirschman (1970: 105) provides an excellent example of how parents might treat education if they see it as a private good. When opting out of a public good is not accompanied by interest in improving the system from the outside, but rather is an effort to sever all ties, then the individual views the public good as a private good and treats it as such.[2] A related issue is the existence of a consumer mentality among parents who view education as a private good and ways in which this mentality might manifest itself.[3]

Table 2.1 catalogues individuals' preferences regarding education and suggests where those preferences might lead public education and democracy. Importantly, entries reflect tendencies or the dominant feature rather than the only feature. For example, schooling yields both social benefits and private benefits, but private interests predominate when an individual considers education to be a private good.

TABLE 2.1   Education as a Public Good and a Private Good

Attributes	Public Good	Private Good
Purpose	Social goals and benefits	Private goals and benefits
Locus of control	Public institution: government Professionals Centralized Role of government: fund and provide education	Private institution: family Parents and professionals Decentralized Role of government: fund education
Governance and accountability mechanisms	Democratic	Market
Institutional values and principles	Democratic	Market
Regulatory scope	Extensive Comprehensive	Minimal
Stakeholders	Society Community	Subset of community: Parents
Association	Public Universal	Private Selective

The Purpose of Education

We expect schools to fulfill "our personal goals as well as our social aims" (Johanek 1992: 140), a reasonable expectation since education generally includes a mix of public goals and private ones. Yet tension can arise over this issue:

> Education lies at the intersection of two sets of competing rights. The first is the right of parents to choose the experiences, influences, and values to which they expose their children, the right to rear their children in the manner that they see fit. The second is the right of a democratic society to use the educational system as a means to reproduce its most essential political, economic, and social institutions through a common schooling experience. (Levin 1991: 140)

The purpose of education in a democratic society is to develop deliberative or democratic character (Gutmann 1987), enabling individuals to self-govern. These social goals are driven by the desire to perpetuate democratic society. To do this, schools "provide students [from different backgrounds] with a common set of values and knowledge to create citizens who can function democratically, contribute to equality of social, economic, and political opportunities" and to "economic growth and full employment for the nation and its regions" (Levin 1987: 630).

Regarding private goals, schooling offers skills, knowledge, and opportunities to help an individual to become a productive and successful member of society. Schooling "enhances individual productivity and earnings; . . . seems to increase trainability, health, efficiency in consumption, access to information; . . . contributes to political participation and the inculcation of civic values; . . . [and] can contribute to social status, technical and cultural literacy, and promotion of family values" (Becker 1964; Haveman and Wolfe 1984). From this vantage point, where social mobility is preeminent, "education is not a public good but a private good" (Labaree 1997: 3). Parents who consider education a public good also want their children to receive the private benefits of schooling. Such parents might understand the value of education for society but are apt to focus primarily and perhaps exclusively on the private goals and benefits of schooling.[4] This perspective goes hand in hand with the desire for greater family control over schooling. For these parents, "to the degree that social benefits are deemed important, they are often viewed as the sum of the private benefits and their distribution" (Levin 1987: 629), a viewpoint that is shared by proponents of school vouchers (Levin 1991: 139) and also applies to charter schools.

Locus of Control

The issue of who has legitimate authority over primary and secondary education, and its corollary, the extent of government involvement, are closely linked to education's purpose and lie at the heart of characterizing education. Both the state and the family have legitimate claims on the education of children (Gutmann 1987), and "there is an inherent tension in American society and within the school system" between the two sets of competing claims (Holmes 1986)).

Parents who want to assert their rights over their children without government interference view education as a private good. Consonant with support for family dominance of schooling is the idea that some institution more responsive to parents than government should provide education, although government funding of education is acceptable. As with public education, teaching and staff professionals are involved in schooling, but their relationship with parents differ in perception, if not reality, from the traditional parent-teacher relationship. Educators are expected to be responsive and accountable primarily if not exclusively to the family, one benefit of turning education into a private good. Proponents of family control would applaud the education theory arguing that parents should control exclusively their children's schooling (Gutmann 1987). Unlike the public sector, authority and decisionmaking are decentralized because each family makes decisions for itself (Chubb and Moe 1990).

When education is seen as a public good, government, representing society at large, has a legitimate claim on the education of young people and hence have primary authority. The role of government is to fund and to provide education. While few people, if any, would argue against parental involvement, the key educational figures are teachers, school administrators, and district officials. Parents have less power than education professionals when education is viewed as a public good. Of course, locus of control is not an either-or proposition; it is a matter of degree. In practice, most parents probably would agree with Amy Gutmann's (1987) argument for the sharing of authority over education among the state, parents, and professionals.

Governance and Accountability Mechanisms

If education is a public good, governance and accountability are accomplished through democratic means. The distinguishing feature of democratic institutions and processes is that they involve a collective effort. The public interest is "the universal motivating principle." (Buchholz 1986: 80). Civic discovery (see Reich 1988), deliberation, negotiation, and compromise are some of the activities in which political actors engage. The governing process is open to all citizens, and all can use various participation channels to express their interests and attempt to influence their elected representatives. Accountability mechanisms enable constituents to check on the effectiveness of schools, their budget and expenditures, school activities, and student performance. School administrators and educators are accountable to local government and the public.

When education is conceptualized as a private good, governance and accountability are accomplished through market techniques and procedures. The distinguishing feature of the market is the invisible hand. "[The] preferences [of individuals] are aggregated by the market, and if strong enough relative to particular goods and services, they elicit a response from the productive mechanism of society to supply the goods and services desired" (Buchholz 1986: 73). Individuals (consumers) strive to maximize their utility. In addition to consuming the goods they purchase, individuals also engage in a series of pre-purchase and post-purchase activities. Unlike the democratic model, parents and students have a "more central and influential role" in a market-based education system (Chubb and Moe 1990: 32). Accountability exists in the guise of customer service and satisfaction mechanisms and is a form of results-based accountability. School officials are accountable to the parents of their students.

Institutional Values and Principles

As a public good, education operates, albeit imperfectly, under democratic values such as equity, justice, democratic accountability, security, representation, the public interest, and fairness. As a private good, market values include choice, efficiency, competition, productivity, maximizing one's utility, individual incentives, and effectiveness. In expressing a preference for one over the other (public or private good), a parent is intentionally or unintentionally also expressing a preference for a particular set of values. Coupled with the appropriate governing and accountability mechanisms, this expression establishes the rules of the game: how the decisionmaking process is conducted, who may participate, and how they may participate; how resources are allocated; what mechanisms for redress are available; and how participants may monitor the conduct of participating institutions.

Regulatory Scope

Public education carries a heavier regulatory burden than does private education. In the former, society uses education to help achieve other societal goals in addition to educating children. In its efforts to make society more equitable, public schools are regulated to ensure that they provide equal opportunities, resources, and access to students subject to inequitable treatment because of their gender, race, or disability. Other regulations involving, for example, accountability, the welfare of students, and the competency of educators, also are levied on public schools and school districts. Public education is subject to very extensive regulations; by comparison, private education is subject to minimal regulation. Parents who see that private schools are subject to fewer regulations than public schools and who prefer other features of education as a private good might come to the conclusion that education, regardless of its provider (government or private), should not be controlled by the government.

Stakeholders

Those who have a legitimate interest in the education of young people are considered stakeholders. This designation carries with it a passport to the forums where decisions are made about education. The question of who is rightfully considered a stakeholder depends on how education is viewed. Treating education as a public good means that all members of the community are legitimate stakeholders since "citizens have an important and common interest in educating future citizens" (Gutmann 1987: 67). To portray education as a private good is to limit stakeholders to a subset of the community, parents of school-age children. To open up the decisionmaking processes to the larger community would threaten family control and risk having family decisions overridden by others.

Association

Association, a child's contact with other students, has the potential to be universal and public when education is a public good. In a public school setting, parents do not choose with whom their children interact (except as noted below). Association is open to all. One of the benefits of education as a private good is that association is private or selective. One reason parents could prefer and seek school choice is that in choosing their child's school, they also choose their children's acquaintances and potential friends. School choice, whatever the particular mechanism, is the means for parents to restrict or direct their child's association with other students. Vouchers offer this opportunity, as do charter schools, magnet schools, and public school choice. Families also can opt for private associations for their children by sending them to private schools or moving to a different neighborhood.

Parents as Education Consumers

A consumer mind-set goes hand in hand with viewing education as a private good. Viewing, treating, and referring to parents as customers is what a voucher or charter program does. Implementation of a school choice program "establishes new relationships and new attitudes," according to David T. Kearns, former U.S. deputy secretary of education (Carnegie Foundation for the Advancement of Teaching 1992: 6). Changing to a market-based education system reconceptualizes parents as customers, alters the system's expectations of them, and shapes their expectations of the system and of education.

Because charter schools establish a market-based education system, parents are expected to act in ways calculated to serve their own needs and interests and those of their children. One major advantage supporters foresee is that parents who view education as a private good would be savvy, involved consumers. By substituting parental choice for government authority to assign children to schools, school voucher programs could make parents "effective market actors who actively compare the qualities of alternative schools and push for greater accountability at the neighborhood level" (Fuller, Elmore, and Orfield 1996: 11–12). Adapting the consumer decision process to the task of finding a school for one's child would result in the following steps.[5] Two parents recognize their child's need for a different or particular type of schooling. They obtain and evaluate information about the available educational opportunities and then apply to the "right" charter school. Throughout the school year they evaluate the school and their child's satisfaction and performance. An end-of-the-school-year assessment determines their overall level of satisfaction and whether to select the same school or explore alternatives for the next school year.

The positive outcome of consumer activities would not be limited necessarily to the satisfaction of having found the right school for one's child. Being able to choose their children's schooling could be the catalyst some parents need to venture into the civic arena (Barber 1984). Citizens must be able to think for themselves and have confidence in their own opinions. Charter schools represent an opportunity for parents to do just that and demonstrate government's confidence in parental self-government. In a school district that includes charter schools, parents would claim some of the power or decisionmaking authority that is now concentrated in the hands of government officials, and reliance on educational and bureaucratic expertise might decline.

It has been suggested that low-income families in particular would benefit from participation in a voucher program; this phenomenon also may hold true for families who live in a school district with charter schools. Low-income households are treated consistently as a dependent population by government, a designation that emphasizes their lack of political and economic power (Ingram and Schneider 1993). Government maintains a paternalistic attitude, but school choice could break the cycle and allow low-income families to make decisions regarding their children's welfare (Godwin 1993). It is not surprising that both parents whose children are enrolled in charter schools and their advocates would prefer the role and identity of consumer to that of dependent. The consumer role carries with it a more positive connotation and could benefit parents in other ways, too. Charter schools represent power by giving parents the authority to choose their children's schools. Parents have the power to make decisions about their children's schooling, and government could send the message that it trusts parents to make the right decisions for their children: an unfamiliar yet welcome position for families usually seen as dependents of government.

Yet inclusion is also a matter of concern for some people. A consumer mind-set could lead to or reinforce the idea that the only legitimate stakeholders in education are parents of school-age children. With their emphasis on family choice and individual prerogatives, and their corresponding silence on the possibility that public education serves a larger purpose for democratic society, charter schools could lend credence to the notion that only parents have legitimate interests in primary and secondary education. This notion runs counter to the view that public schools are an institution of democratic society and that "the entire citizenry, not just the parent body, has a legitimate interest in the character and quality of what goes on there" (Landy 1993: 38). It could also threaten the entire society's long-term financial support of schooling.

The institution of public education has been recognized by some people for its affiliation with civic values. Thomas Jefferson envisioned that establishing a system of local schools throughout the commonwealth of Virginia and entrusting them to the care of the local community would teach adults "civic-mindedness and collective self-reliance" (Pangle and Pangle 1993: 120). Charging a community with the collective responsibility of operating and maintaining a local school could help to instill an outward-looking orientation and one that would foster civic values. School choice could impede such civic impulses among parents. The dynamics of charter schools could legitimize self-interest so that feelings of responsibility toward the community as a whole would be supplanted by each parent's drive to find the best school for his or her children. In the minds of some, charter schools pose the same threat that school voucher policy does: "Vouchers transform what ought to be a public question ('What is a good system of public education for *our* children?') into a personal question ('What kind of school do I want for *my* children?'). It permits citizens to think of education as a matter of private preference" (Barber 1984: 296). Stated more bluntly, "[Choice] will fragmentize ambition, so that the individual parent will be forced to claw and scramble for the good of her kid and her kid only, at whatever cost to everybody else" (Kozol 1992: 92). School choice does not have the language and the concepts for delivering a message about civic values and the public interest. The messages communicated by this education reform assure parents that it is permissible to focus on one's own interests to the exclusion of the community's interests. The intended targets of information about charter schools could lose sight of government's overall responsibility to promote the public good or could overlook their own role in the community and the neighborhood school. In short, the consumer mind-set might suppress civic impulses.

Notably, this possibility is countered by an empirical study of public school choice. This study found that choice could "increase the capacity of the citizen/consumer to act as a responsible, involved citizen" (Schneider et al. 1997: 91). Parents who are empowered to make decisions about their child's schooling seemed more inclined to feel connected to their community. Giving parents the right to choose might foster a new-found

self-confidence and greater satisfaction with life in that particular community, enhancing parents' civic impulses or at least tempering inclina-
tions toward privatism.

Another concern is that the consumer mind-set discourages the use of
"political voice," a range of activities that includes listening, talking, delib-
erating, negotiating, obtaining information, writing, and analyzing. In contrast to traditional public schooling, there would be neither the need nor
the inclination to use political mechanisms in a market-based education
system. Making exit from a school convenient and acceptable, as in Arizona, removes incentives to exercise one's voice as a citizen (Hirschman
1970). For those parents whose children attend charter schools, voice
would be practiced within the boundaries of a customer feedback system,
and voice as a political mechanism would atrophy. The parent-as-consumer
might prefer customer service mechanisms to political voice, using surveys, complaint forms, and other devices or procedures borrowed from the
market to interact with government (Smith and Huntsman 1997), but voice
exercised in the polity well may be superior to the market version of voice
that relies on customer service mechanisms.

The special relationship between voice and exit suggests another possible implication of the consumer mentality. Those most concerned about
an organization's quality are also most likely to use voice and to leave
when given the option to exit (Hirschman 1970). Consequently, the function or organization that could benefit from citizen involvement—from
political voice—could be deprived of this resource as individuals pack up
and leave. Applying this idea to education, the existence of the consumer
mind-set could result in the so-called transfer of an important resource—
parents who are interested and active in their child's school—from conventional public schools to charter schools. The effects of such a transfer
would not be felt until there is a large-scale exodus of students (and their
parents) from a school district or a group of schools.

Some Thoughts on Education as a Private Good

In discussions of the problems plaguing public education, the usual topics include school violence, dropout rates, inequities in funding, and low
test scores. These problems warrant sustained and thoughtful efforts. A
different concern is raised here—the attitude that treats primary and secondary education as a private good. This perspective finds expression in
Chubb and Moe's (1990: 30) comments on the purpose of education:

> Almost everyone's first impulse is to think that the purpose of schools is to
> provide children with academic training, with essential information about
> society and the world, with an understanding of citizenship in a democracy,

or something of the sort. On reflection, however, it should be apparent that schools have no immutable or transcendent purpose. What they are supposed to be doing depends on who controls them and what those controllers want them to do.

If a significant number of citizens supported this view, they could affect the institutional arrangements of public education. Transforming public education into a private good could result in democratic society losing control of its means of reproduction. Configuring education as a private good could exclude most of society from participating in the governance of education because the group of legitimate stakeholders would consist only of parents of school-age children.[6] The rest of society could lose their right to influence education, a loss that would deny them part of their citizenship. Not only would this signal that society had lost control of education, it would undermine democracy itself. "A society is undemocratic—it cannot engage in conscious social reproduction—if it restricts rational deliberation or excludes some educable citizens from an adequate education" (Gutmann 1987: 95). Treating education as a private good would restrict rational deliberation by denying non-parents access to the governing processes for education.

School choice could balkanize the education system and, in a sense, the community as well. Because the group of legitimate stakeholders would be reduced to parents only, schools would no longer have the moderating influence of the entire community. Precisely because education would be presented and treated as a private good, parents would be free to choose the type of schooling they want for their children rather than having to develop a common vision of education. Unable to participate in the local decisionmaking process and aware that parents are sending their children to a variety of different schools, non-parents might not see any value in trying to devise and promote societal goals of education or in continuing to support local schools, financially or otherwise.

Transforming education into a private good might also intensify a problem noted above by Gutmann: Some children—educable citizens—could be excluded from receiving an adequate education. Like voucher supporters, charter school advocates fail to acknowledge that market principles and values could undermine government efforts to achieve and maintain equity (Henig 1994). A system that treats education as a private good emphasizes market values, such as efficiency, competition, and choice. In the absence of government intervention, equitable treatment is neither a priority nor a concern of the marketplace. Hence, some children might not receive the education they deserve if inequitable practices are allowed to persist. And not all parents are inclined or capable of performing as savvy consumers in the education marketplace. Communication, problem-solving, and analytical skills are necessary to assess a child's educational needs and interests, to survey the range of options available, and to identify the school or program that best suits the child. Some parents possess the requisite skills and some do not. Children of parents in the latter group might be denied the education they should receive.

In addition to the concerns about inclusion and equity, education as a private good might impair those democratic institutions associated with public education. Jeffrey Henig suggests that the real danger of school vouchers—and possibly of charter schools as well—is that "they will erode the public forums in which decisions with societal consequences can democratically be resolved" (1994: 220). For some, the market is now "perceived as a primary means of democratic participation or popular control" (Johanek 1992: 145). This perception could help to legitimize the use of market mechanisms in political society generally and education in particular.

Although school choice can be touted on the grounds that it would empower parents, it also might represent a delegation of parental authority. One of the attractive features of configuring education as a private good is that it gives parents an opportunity to select a school consonant with the family's beliefs and principles, thus enhancing the private benefits of schooling. Charter schools might reinforce the values taught by parents; indeed it could be more convenient for the family to rely on schooling for instilling values and beliefs in children rather than doing it at home or in church.

Conclusion

Are we expecting too much from parents by implying that they should view education primarily as a public good? Understandably, concern for their children and a desire for them to succeed in life has much to do with how parents view schooling. Various societal forces help make the idea of education as a private good attractive. It is no wonder that parents favor private associations for their children in the face of numerous dangers such as violence, drug use, and lax discipline lurking in and around schools. Concern for a child's future social and economic status may prompt parents to seek a school or program that will help their children attain "social mobility through educational credentialing" (Hogan 1992: 182). As stated above, the relationship between the two conceptions of education is not necessarily an either-or proposition; certainly in the case of social purposes and private goals there is room for both. But democratic society continues to rely on public education to prepare future citizens, and the conception of education as a public good is a valid one essential for the continuation of democratic society.

A comment offered in the mid-1980s is still relevant today: "[T]he choice debate reflects a 'crisis of faith' in the 'unofficially established national church'—the public school" (Wagoner 1986). Improving public education would help secure its status as a public good, as would a concerted, thoughtful, and sustained effort aimed at informing the public about the role of education in democratic society. What citizens need to see is a government committed to improving the public schools. They also must be able to use their (political) voice effectively, meaning that government must listen to its constituents (Gutmann 1987; Henig 1994; Hirschman 1970). Henig observes that government can be "an attractive partner" in improving the public schools because of "its ability and willingness . . . to mobilize resources, manage them effectively, and engage in a dependable system of cooperation" (Henig 1994: 188). Informing the public about the purpose of public education and its importance for democracy might help citizens to understand why it is—and should remain—a public good. Twenty years ago, R. Freeman Butts noted (1979: 9) that discussion about the societal purposes of education was "all but missing," and he suggested there is a need "to reeducate the public about the civic role of public education." Retaining its purpose and image as a public good might prove to be the major challenge facing public education for the foreseeable future, particularly if charter schools and vouchers continue to grow in popularity.

Notes

1. Other schooling options and circumstances also might play a role in reinforcing or introducing the characterization of education as a private good. School vouchers, public school choice, and housing location decisions include the element of choice. They also could include a private element in the cases where parents are seeking to increase or change the private benefits of schooling for their children (Levin 1987; 1991). These parents see education as a private good or prefer that it be configured in this manner. The point is that parents whose children are not in a charter school also could experience, through their child's schooling, the idea that education is or can become a private good.

2. The rest of the community also might be influenced by the presence of charter schools. As the benefits of the program are touted using language from the market—choice, competition, increased efficiency—and as a portion of the student population is dispersed among independently operated schools, some of which focus on or attract a particular culture, other members of the community might begin to think of education as a private good as well. In Phoenix (and later Tempe) Arizona, the ATOP Academy advertises itself as a school whose mission is to develop African-American leadership, and Gan Yeladeem of Scottsdale, Arizona, has a strong Hebrew language program.

3. Whether parents who enroll their children in a charter school already view education as a private good or make this determination based upon their

experience with the program is not readily apparent. Ideally, a longitudinal study that uses a pre-test/post-test design with a control group and that includes a sufficiently large number of families new to the program at the time of the pre-test would help determine whether and how parents are affected by their participation in a choice program.

4. This is not intended to be a criticism of parents who emphasize the private benefits of schooling. The distinction made here is important in helping to understand that, for some families, the social goals of education are of little concern.

5. See Loudon and Bitta (1984: 43) for a description of the consumer decision process.

6. In a way, this already has happened in Milwaukee. Households that do not participate in the Milwaukee Parental Choice Program (MPCP), the longest-running school voucher program in the nation, have lost their status as stakeholders in the MPCP schools. They still can be involved in the Milwaukee public schools and can contact their state representatives about the choice program. The crux of this issue, though, is that parents who believe in limiting stakeholdership are expressing a willingness to exclude other citizens from local governance of schools. For example, parents might question whether non-parents have the right to speak up at school board meetings.

References

Barber, Benjamin. 1984. *Strong Democracy: Participatory Politics for a New Age.* Los Angeles: University of California Press.

Battistoni, Richard M. 1985. *Public Schooling and the Education of Democratic Citizens.* Jackson: University Press of Mississippi.

Becker, G. S. 1964. *Human Capital.* New York: Columbia University Press. Quoted in Henry M. Levin, "Education as Public and Private Good," *Journal of Policy Analysis and Management* 6 (4):629.

Blinderman, Abraham. 1975. *American Writers on Education Before 1865.* Twayne's World Leaders Series, edited by S. Smith. Boston: G. K. Hall and Co.

Buchholz, Rogene A. 1986. "Conceptual Foundations of Public Policy." In *Business Environment and Public Policy: Implications for Management and Strategy Formulation.* Englewood Cliffs, N.J.: Prentice-Hall.

Butts, R. Freeman. 1979. "Educational Vouchers: The Private Pursuit of the Public Purse." *Phi Delta Kappan* 61 (1):7–9.

Butts, R. Freeman, and Lawrence A. Cremin. 1953. *A History of American Culture.* New York: Holt, Rinehart, and Winston.

Carnegie Foundation for the Advancement of Teaching. 1992. *A Special Report: School Choice.* Princeton, N.J.: Carnegie Foundation for the Advancement of Teaching.

Chubb, John E., and Terry M. Moe. 1990. *Politics, Markets, and America's Schools.* Washington, D.C.: Brookings Institution.

Cookson, Peter W. 1991. "Private Schooling and Equity." *Education and Urban Society* 23 (2):185–199.

Curti, Merle. 1935. *The Social Ideas of American Educators.* New York: Charles Scribner's Sons.

Fuller, Bruce, Richard F. Elmore, and Gary Orfield. 1996. "Policy-Making in the Dark: Illuminating the School Choice Debate." In *Who Chooses? Who Loses? Culture, Institutions, and the Unequal Effects of School Choice,* edited by B. Fuller, R. F. Elmore and G. Orfield. New York: Teachers College Press.

Godwin, R. Kenneth. 1993. "Using Market-Based Incentives to Empower the Poor." In *Public Policy for Democracy,* edited by H. Ingram and S. R. Smith. Washington, D.C.: Brookings Institution.

Gutmann, Amy. 1987. *Democratic Education.* Princeton: Princeton University Press.

Haveman, R. H., and B. L. Wolfe. 1984. "Schooling and Economic Well-Being: The Role of Nonmarket Effects." *The Journal of Human Resources* 19:377-407. Quoted in Henry M. Levin, "Education as Public and Private Good," *Journal of Policy Analysis and Management* 6 (4):629.

Henig, Jeffrey R. 1994. *Rethinking School Choice: Limits of the Market Metaphor.* Princeton: Princeton University Press.

Hirschman, Albert O. 1970. *Exit, Voice, and Loyalty: Responses to Decline in Firms, Organizations, and States.* Cambridge, Mass.: Harvard University Press.

Hogan, David. 1992. ". . . the Silent Compulsion of Economic Relations." *Educational Policy* 6 (2):180–205.

Holmes, B. 1986. "Soviet Education: Travellers' Tales." In *Western Perspectives on Soviet Education in the 1980s,* ed. J. J. Tomiak, 30-56. New York: St. Martin's. Quoted in Peter W. Cookson, "Private Schooling and Equity," *Education and Urban Society* 23 (2):185 (1991).

Hyman, David N. 1993. *Modern Microeconomics: Analysis and Applications.* 3d ed. Boston: Irwin.

Ingram, Helen, and Anne Schneider. 1993. "Constructing Citizenship: The Subtle Messages of Policy Design." In *Public Policy for Democracy,* edited by H. Ingram and S. R. Smith. Washington, D.C.: Brookings Institution.

Johanek, Michael. 1992. "Private Citizenship and School Choice." *Educational Policy* 6 (2):139–159.

Kozol, Jonathan. 1992. "I Dislike the Idea of Choice, and I Want to Tell You Why . . . " *Educational Leadership* 50 (3):90–92.

Labaree, David F. 1997. "Are Students 'Consumers'?" September, 17, 1997, URL: http://*www.edweek.org/ew/vol-17/03labare.h17.*

Lamdin, Douglas J. and Michael Mintrom. 1997. "School Choice in Theory and Practice: Taking Stock and Looking Ahead." *Education Economics* 5 (3):211–244.

Landy, Marc. 1993. "Public Policy and Citizenship." In *Public Policy for Democracy,* edited by H. Ingram and S. R. Smith. Washington, D.C.: Brookings Institution.

Levin, Henry M. 1987. "Education as Public and Private Good." *Journal of Policy Analysis and Management* 6 (4):628–641.

_____. 1991. "The Economics of Educational Choice." *Economics of Education Review* 10 (2):137–158.

Loudon, David L. and Albert J. Della Bitta. 1984. *Consumer Behavior: Concepts and Applications.* 2d ed. McGraw-Hill Series in Marketing, edited by C. D. Schewe. New York: McGraw-Hill.

Meyer, Adolphe E. 1967. *An Educational History of the American People.* 2d ed. McGraw-Hill Series in Education, edited by H. Benjamin. New York: McGraw-Hill.

Pangle, Lorraine Smith, and Thomas L. Pangle. 1993. *The Learning of Liberty: The Educational Ideas of the American Founders*. American Political Thought, edited by W. C. McWilliams and L. Banning. Lawrence: University Press of Kansas.

Reich, Robert B. 1988. "Policy Making in a Democracy. In *The Power of Public Ideas*, edited by R. B. Reich. Cambridge, Mass.: Ballinger.

Schneider, Mark, Paul Teske, Melissa Marschall, Michael Mintrom, and Christine Roch. 1997. "Institutional Arrangements and the Creation of Social Capital: The Effects of Public School Choice." *American Political Science Review* 91 (1):82–93.

Smith, Gerald E., and Carole A. Huntsman. 1997. "Reframing the Metaphor of the Citizen-Government Relationship: A Value-Centered Perspective." *Public Administration Review* 57 (4):309–318.

Stone, Deborah A. 1988. *Policy Paradox and Political Reason*. New York: Harper Collins.

Tyack, David B. 1967. *Turning Points in American Educational History*. Waltham, Mass.: Ginn.

Wagoner, Jennings L., Jr. 1986. "Choice: The Historical Perspective." Paper presented at the Conference on Choice in Education, Charlottesville, Virginia, April 29. Quoted in Michael Johanek, "Private Citizenship and School Choice," *Educational Policy* 6 (2):153 (1992).

Wise, Arthur E., and Linda Darling-Hammond. 1984. "Education by Vouchers: Private Choice and the Public Interest." *Educational Theory* 34 (1):29–47.

3

The Death of One Best Way: Charter Schools as Reinventing Government

ROBERT MARANTO

Reinventing Government is a social movement that, arguably, has had more impact on the public sector than anything since the scientific management movement of the Progressive era. This essay briefly outlines the origins and prescriptions of Reinventing Government. I also describe two sets of criteria for judging public administration outputs: the politics-based governance model of Karen Hult and Charles Walcott (1990) and the economics-based model of E. S. Savas (1987). Finally, I use these criteria to judge school reform in general and Arizona charter schools in particular, employing interviews conducted by phone and in person from November 1997 to December 1998 with twenty-nine Arizona policy makers, Department of Education officials, charter school operators, district school officials, and teachers' union officials. The bureaucratic production of public services, including education, was developed as scientific managers of the Progressive era sought the "one best way" of providing uniform public services (Schultz and Maranto 1998). Hult and Walcott's governance model suggests that such traditional bureaucratic approaches are ill-suited to provide public service when both the social goals and the technologies used to achieve those goals are highly controversial, as in education. Savas points out that education can be provided effectively by markets through vouchers or public school choice. Indeed, markets have advantages over traditional bureaucratic approaches.

Reinventing Government in Two Waves

Reinventing Government occurred in two broad waves. The first came during the Reagan administration, though it had precursors in partial management reforms under President Nixon and in a changing marketplace of ideas in the 1970s. The second wave, which reflects the confluence of the information age economy and the ideas of New Democrats, is ongoing and has produced widespread and significant improvements in public service.

The Reagan Reinvention

Presidents reflect their times, so it is not surprising that the Reagan administration's approach to the civil service was influenced by 1970s writings depicting bureaucracies as inherently inefficient because they were rule-bound, not subject to market discipline, had unclear and immeasurable goals, and had tenured staffs who could not be fired or disciplined. Some of these writers, such as Niskanen (1971) and Savas and Ginsburg (1973) were conservative or libertarian, but others, such as Peters (1978), were liberal or neoliberal. Once in office, President Reagan's reinventing of government was manifested in "supply-side management," which sought to make public administration more like business administration, in part by focusing on individual incentives and measurable outputs rather than democratic processes, and in part by contracting out government work to the private sector where possible (Carroll et al. 1985; Savas 1987).

New Democrats Reinvent Government

The highlight of President Clinton's New Democratic agenda was a reinventing effort, the National Performance Review (NPR) led by Vice President Gore (1993). The NPR copied reinventions in numerous states and localities (Schultz and Maranto 1998: 205–213). On all levels of government, the reinvention movement of the 1990s has been driven by four forces. First, fiscal pressures pushed innovative managers to find new and better ways to provide services more efficiently (Barzelay and Armajani 1992; Osborne and Gaebler 1992; Marshall 1997). Second, international examples from Britain, Canada, Australia, and New Zealand encouraged American reinventors (Campbell and Wilson 1995; Schwartz 1992, 1997). Third, examples and ideas from business encouraged reinventing. Such writers as Tom Peters and Robert Waterman (1982) argued that greater efficiency and innovation were achieved by cutting layers of middle management and red tape, thus freeing employees to do their jobs, and by focusing on core missions.

Finally and most importantly, Reinventing Government was driven by changing ideas, particularly those of neoliberal, "New" Democrats. For two decades, neoliberals such as Charles Peters, editor of the *Washington Monthly* and the mentor to a number of influential journalists, argued that Americans would never again support an activist government until they were convinced that government could work. Unlike Republican conservatives, many of whom wanted to dismantle government programs, neoliberals wanted to improve government so that it could play a positive, appreciated role (e.g., Peters 1992; Kaus 1992; Marshall 1997). At the same time, New Democrats believed in capitalism and felt that government had much to learn from the business sector. Naturally, the bible of the "Rego" movement was *Reinventing Government*, by journalist David Osborne and former city manager Ted Gaebler (1992). The authors argued that the fall of communism and the seeming incapacity of traditional government bureaucracies to solve basic social problems de-legitimized the hierarchical, bureaucratic, civil service paradigm imposed by the Progressives. To determine what should come next, the authors explored more than a dozen state, local, and federal government success stories in search of lessons. Osborne and Peter Plastrick (1997) extended the search for success to foreign lands. The journalistic work of Osborne and his coauthors combines with more scholarly treatments by Savas (1987), Barzelay and Armajani (1992), Garvey (1993), Durant (1992), Horner (1994), Kelman (1990), and others to present a new paradigm in government management. Rego proposes that:

(1) Free markets innovate rapidly and provide services efficiently, but government is needed to solve collective problems and assure justice and social equity. By using market structures, public administration can take on the favorable attributes of markets in pursuing public aims.

(2) Accordingly, public services need not always be provided by government bureaucracies. A variety of alternative arrangements can be employed, including:

Contracting with private companies, other governments, or non-profits.

Vouchers to individuals that enable citizens to choose their own services, as in the case of the GI Bill, which enables veterans to choose either a public or private education at any of hundreds of colleges.[1]

Competition in which units of government compete with other government agencies or the private sector. For example, charter schools are public schools that compete with both public and private schools for students.[2]

(3) When government provides services, it can do so more efficiently and effectively by changing organization culture and structure by:

Cutting procedures and red tape, particularly in contracting and personnel systems.

Cutting middle management and headquarters, since empowered workers need fewer managers to tell them what to do.

Changing organization structure by having fewer hierarchical relationships and more teams bringing together those with different skills (e.g., bringing together lawyers, policy analysts, and scientists to write environmental regulations).

Emphasizing variety in service provision, rather than "one-size-fits-all" monopolies. One implication is that different subunits have more discretion and can compete with each other.

Using information technology to reengineer work.

Focusing on measurable results (such outputs as student test scores or crime reduction) rather than budget inputs or adherence to procedure.

Holding bureaucrats accountable by using financial (and other) rewards and (occasionally) punishments. At the same time, managers should not punish reasonable failures, for to do so would discourage innovation.

In short, the Reinventing Government paradigm argues for letting a thousand flowers bloom. Though borrowing from some of the Reagan reformers, particularly E. S. Savas (1987), Reinventing Government does not disparage government workers. Rather, it sees them as good people trapped in bad, bureaucratic systems.

A Systematic Look at Reinvention:
Criteria for a Movement

Reinvention argues against procedure and permanence and for greater flexibility. But are all public services in need of reinvention? Should some in fact be provided by bureaucratic structures imposing a single service output? Here I outline two sets of criteria to address this question: the fit between policy and organizational design and the divisibility of costs and benefits.

Policy Setting and Organization Design

The most elegant framework for typing organizations by their work is the governance model developed by Hult and Walcott (1990). They argue that an organization's goals and technologies can be characterized by consensus, by uncertainty (under which actors are not sure), and/or by controversy (under which different actors *disagree* on desired goals or appropriate techniques). Technical and, particularly, goal controversy make public management more difficult.

Different organizational governance structures are suited to different policy settings. When goals and techniques are certain, conventional bureaucracies are suitable and politics can be separated from administration, with politicians making policy and career bureaucrats carrying out policy. For example, as a liberal, high-level career bureaucrat serving in the Office of the Secretary of Defense said in a 1987 interview, "Making war is a highly technical function," so "the person promoted before [the Reagan administration] is not from the previous administration, but he's an expert in nuclear engineering, targeting, law, personnel, whatever. . . . Party doesn't carry a great deal of weight here. Concern for defense does" (Maranto 1993: 121).

But that all public policies were so simple. When goals and technologies are uncertain, Hult and Walcott suggest allowing decisions to emerge from the decentralized, unguided interplay of actors—in effect, a competition between government organizations free to experiment by emphasizing different goals and employing different technologies. As controversy (either goal or technical) rises and becomes polarizing, confrontational or quasi-judicial governance structures are needed for closure. Of course, such structures can delay implementation, particularly if courts and legislatures take those roles. When goals or technologies are uncertain, Hult and Walcott advocate diverse teams to develop and explore alternatives. The teams should be dominated by career technical experts if technologies are uncertain, politicians or group representatives if goals are uncertain. In this regard, it is notable that political appointees in government increase in number as missions become more controversial (Maranto 1993).

The U.S. Environmental Protection Agency (EPA) is the polar opposite of the Defense Department. In EPA, both goals and technologies are highly controversial. Competing interest groups and their supporters in the bureaucracy cannot agree on how to reconcile the agency's competing goals: preserving human health, protecting endangered ecosystems, researching environmental hazards, remediating those environmental hazards, litigating to recover the costs of remediation, and not harming the economy. Similarly, controversies rage over the methods used to reduce pollution and clean up waste sites. Controversy plays out in the broader polity, and within the EPA, in battles between lawyers (favoring lawsuits), engineers (backing quick remediation of toxic sites before liability is set), scientists (wanting research before action), and economists (who oppose remediation on cost-benefit grounds) (Landy et al. 1994; McGarity 1991). Vague and contradictory legislative mandates (reduce CO_2 emissions through the best available technology without sacrificing economic growth) make success elusive, particularly since methods of measuring compliance to mandates are highly uncertain (Allison 1984). Conflict produces a free-wheeling agency culture (Maranto 1993).

As will be detailed below, the policy setting for education is today more akin to that of the EPA than the Pentagon. The goals of education (curricula) and technologies (teaching methods) are each very controversial.

Size and Excludability of Costs and Benefits

Modifying (thought not citing) Mancur Olson (1965), E. S. Savas (1987) builds a framework based on the divisibility of costs and benefits to determine which goods must be provided by monopolistic government bureaus and which are better provided by market or market-like arrangements (see Table 3.1).

As Savas (1987: 35–57) explains, private goods are relatively cheap so they can be purchased by individual consumers, who can exclude others from their use. In contrast, toll goods (such as utilities, National Parks, or limited access roads) are too big to be provided by individuals—in economics jargon, they have a "lumpy" supply curve. Non-payers can be excluded from them, however, so individual consumers can be charged, and the goods can thus be provided by market arrangements (such as regulated utilities) as well as by government. Common pool goods such as clean air are consumed by individuals who cannot be excluded from their use. They are also too large to be provided by individuals and must be provided by governments. Finally, collective (or "public") goods such as national defense and a criminal justice system are too large to be provided by individuals and are consumed by whole societies rather than individuals; hence they also must be provided by governments.

Savas adds a dimension to the Hult and Walcott framework. Increasingly, *society is divided over the nature of services that should be supplied by government, in part because of the breakdown of common cultural norms and experiences* (Hunter 1991; Kaus 1992; Gerzon 1996); thus the goals of public bureaucracies are more controversial. For collective goods such as national defense, society must come to agreements on the nature and extent of goods provided, since they cannot be provided in varying dimensions. After all, the United States cannot have both liberal and conservative levels of nuclear deterrence. On the other hand, for Savas's private goods (such as education) and toll goods (such as libraries and theaters), gov-

TABLE 3.1   Typology of Private and Collective Goods

Consumption Type	Exclusive	Not Exclusive
Consumed by individuals	Private goods	Common pool goods
Consumed jointly	Toll goods	Collective goods

SOURCE: Adapted from Savas 1987: 40–41.

ernment bureaucracies can sidestep debates over basic values by letting individuals choose their services, often via vouchers. For example, the National Endowment for the Arts could avoid conflicts over the merits of subsidizing particular artists by allowing the public to make decisions through arts vouchers.

As Hult and Walcott show, policies with controversial goals and controversial technologies to achieve those goals are prone to stalemate. Where markets can be used to decentralize controversy and provide different types of goods to different consumers, as in the case of education, markets may move beyond stalemate for both providers and consumers of services.

Lessons for Education Reform:
Markets as a Way Out

Controversial Goals: Curriculum Wars

In their outstanding history of reform in American public education, David Tyack and Larry Cuban (1995) show that talk about school reform has been more or less constant since the 1890s. Many reforms have actually been implemented, from the development of the high school and the tracking of students into different programs to school building heating and lavatory systems. Yet most reforms involving curricula and teaching methods have been implemented only partly or not at all. Constant reform activity and partial reform implementation is "an inevitable result of conflicts of values and interests built into a democratic system of school governance and reflecting changing climates of public opinion" (Tyack and Cuban 1995: 41)—a point also made by Chubb and Moe (1990). There is no consensus on the core purpose of public education. Tyack and Cuban note:

> Some degree of conflict over goals has been a constant, just as some degree of change in institutional practices has been a constant. Americans have wanted schools to serve different and often contradictory purposes for their own children: to socialize them to be obedient, yet to teach them to be critical thinkers; to pass on the best academic knowledge that the past has to offer, yet also to teach marketable and practical skills; to cultivate cooperation, yet to teach students to compete with one another in school and later in life; to stress basic skills but also to encourage creativity and higher order thinking; to focus on the academic "basics" yet to permit a wide range of choice of courses. (42–43)

Although parents have conflicting expectations, school systems do little in the way of civic education to clarify tradeoffs, much less seek input from parents regarding curricular choices. Curricula are determined without significant parental input. School systems typically discourage parents from taking a meaningful role inside schools, though they welcome parental support so long as it is limited and controlled (Tyack and Cuban 1995). In part this is because parents and teachers often disagree about what schools should do. Parents emphasize discipline and memorization of basic information, whereas teachers are more likely to emphasize creativity and self-discovery. This parallels a conflict among academics, for whereas education schools stress teaching methods, other academicians emphasize mastery of subject matter. Even the business community is divided. Some companies want schools to produce technically proficient graduates, whereas others want workers who are honest, punctual, and follow directions (Doherty 1998; Hirsch 1996).

Conflicts over education have become even more pronounced since the 1960s, reflecting broader social conflicts. Trust in all American institutions and in expert authority generally have declined since the 1960s, so it would be odd if schools were exempt (Uslaner 1993; Nye et al. 1997). In part, however, citizens do not trust schools to teach their values because there is no longer a consensus on what values to teach. As James Davison Hunter (1991: 174) writes, schools are ground zero of the culture wars:

> Education is strategic in the culture war because this is the central institution of modern life through which the larger social order is reproduced. Together, the curriculum, the textbook literature, and even the social activities of the school convey powerful symbols about the meaning of American life—the character of its past, the challenges of the present, and its future agenda. In this way the institutions of mass education become decisive in socializing the young into the nation's public culture. Public education is especially significant territory in this regard, primarily because it reflects the will and power of the state vis-à-vis the nation's public culture.

Curriculum wars rage about the presentation and non-presentation of the nation's founders, religion, sex education, multiculturalism, capitalism, and homosexuality. Conflicts have engaged interest groups ranging from the Christian Coalition to the Green Party (Spring 1997; Ravitch 1983). Hunter (1991: 197) finds "all but a formal declaration of war over the public schools."

Controversial Technologies: Warring Methods

Not only are the basic goals of education highly controversial, so too are the technologies to achieve those goals: teaching methods. In this century, heated debates have lasted for decades over the Dalton Plan, High Schools of Tomorrow, teaching by machine, and, most famously, Progressive Education (Ravitch 1983; Tyack and Cuban 1995). On both college and K–12 levels, scholars still disagree about the utility of lectures (Hirsch 1996), as opposed to active learning (Glasser 1992). Reforms of teaching methods tend to fail in part because they typically seek to change whole systems without first gaining support from teachers and parents. As street level bureaucrats with considerable control over the classroom "core" of school policy, teachers tend not to implement new methods they dislike. Similarly, parents often organize to oppose methods not in keeping with their expectations of how a "real school" should work. Schools have faced wave after wave of half implemented reforms, increasing cynicism among teachers (Hess 1999; Tyack and Cuban 1995). As Tyack and Cuban (1995: 83) write, "Reforms have rarely replaced what there is; more commonly, they have added complexity. When reforms have come in staccato succession, they often have brought incoherence or uncomfortable tensions."

Lessons from Savas: Markets as a Way Out

Reforms tend to fail because reformers attempt to find and impose a single best curriculum and method. As Tyack and Cuban (1995) detail, reformers have typically assumed that the same practices work for all teachers in all schools. The scientific management, "one best way" approach means that, as the Hult and Walcott framework suggests, controversial educational reforms are unlikely to be approved by public authorities, and even less likely to be implemented by independent street level bureaucrats (teachers). Opting for uniformity over diversity dooms to failure approaches that, if tried voluntarily by small groups of teachers and parents, might work *for those groups*. Regarding the failures of urban school systems, Savas writes:

> What should you do when you do not know what to do? *Answer*: Do many different things. . . . A variety of educational approaches should be encouraged to see which ones can prove themselves fit and able to educate the city's children. Today's monolithic public school system is inadequate, yet it cannot effectively facilitate broad experimentation or tolerate alternative pedagogical approaches. Diversity has never been the strong suit of government. (1987: 252–253)

In contrast, markets provide diversity and allow teachers and parents to sort themselves into like-minded groups. As Chubb and Moe (1990) find, market-based private schools are more likely to have coherent, agreed upon missions than their larger and relatively monopolistic public sector counterparts. Notably, Savas's sniping at monopolistic government was more accurate when he wrote it in the 1980s than in the age of Rego.

Most importantly, *choice-based education has the potential to bring peace to the culture wars and teaching methods wars that wrack many school systems.* Parents, teachers, and administrators often have deeply held and deeply contrasting beliefs about curricula and teaching methods. Diane Divoky (1989) describes a school district serving farmers and ranchers who wanted a back-to-basics education, counterculture parents who wanted a school without walls, and more conventional suburban parents who wanted a "regular" track. Eventually, the district provided three tracks for the three groups. This ended years of culture wars, and diverse parents and teachers learned to work together to support funding for *each others'* programs and for common capital projects. Indeed, in some cases after sending a child to their preferred option, parents found that in fact a different program worked better for that child. Similarly, when Oregon introduced a new math curriculum using active learning techniques developed by the National Council of Teachers of Mathematics (NCTM), parents complained that the new methods were not challenging. Many of the state's school districts responded by allowing parents to opt for either the new or old curricula. As with many education practices, research suggests that the NCTM curriculum works better than traditional curricula for some students but worse for others. Choice allowed parents to judge what worked best for their children (PBS 1998).

I learned respect for diversity in education in 1990 when I protested a local middle school that replaced tracking with a common school model. The program was supported by a friend, who taught at the school. Tracking was eventually reinstated, but I became convinced that the common school approach could have worked. For her part, my friend realized that the common school could have worked as a program *chosen* by like-minded parents and teachers. As a top-down reform *forced* on reluctant teachers and parents, it had divided the school and community.

Reinventing Public Education in Arizona

Arizona enables the organization structure of school systems to match the inherent policy setting (Hult and Walcott) of education; that is, by allowing parents and teachers to embrace the reform plans they want for their schools, the charter school system allows innovation to take place even though the goals and technologies of education are highly controversial. Rather than being all things to all students and parents, charter schools can specialize to do a few things well. This removes power from education experts, district school officials, and unions, and it empowers teachers and parents, who are able to embrace the education visions they believe in within small school communities. It is axiomatic that if teachers and parents believe in their school's goals and methods, the school is more likely to succeed.

The Variability of Charter Schools

As Bryan Hassel reports in Chapter 5, charter schools provide the potential for education innovation, though this does not mean that innovation will necessarily occur. Indeed, as Robert Stout and Gregg Garn report in Chapter 10, there is little true innovation taking place in Arizona charter schools. Yet there is considerable *variation* among Arizona charter schools. The charter universe includes Montessori schools, Waldorf schools, Core Knowledge schools, multiple intelligence schools, back-to-basics schools, trade schools, arts schools, schools for at-risk students, and schools with ethnic based themes. Although nearly everything taking place in the charter school universe also occurs somewhere and in some form in the district school universe, as a matter of course such options are seldom available to parents. After all, it does a parent little good to know that a district school in a distant district has an option they find attractive; indeed they are unlikely to find out about it. Charter schools develop, present, and advertise their offerings to parents in order to gain enough adherents for adequate funding. As Chapter 8 suggests, this competition might push district schools to inform parents about existing curriculum options, and indeed to expand such options. For example, a number of interviews suggest that the success of Ben Franklin charter schools may have forced the Mesa district to expand its own Ben Franklin magnet program. Similarly, in Chapter 14 Lee Hager, an official of the Flagstaff Unified District, suggests that competition from charters has encouraged such reforms in his district.

Some charters offer a back-to-basics education and thus appeal to politically and culturally conservative parents. As one such parent put it, "You can't find [district] school textbooks that talk about the founding fathers as good men. They were all drunken slobs and so on, . . . while Malcolm X is a great hero. . . . It's amazing to me that teachers are not even exposed to phonics."[3] In contrast, charter schools such as Flagstaff Arts and Leadership Academy and the Pine Forest School emphasize the arts and environmental preservation and are more attractive to liberals. By allowing groups of like-minded parents and teachers to have the educational curricula and methods they want, the charter school system increases the legitimacy of public education by making public administration more responsive to public demands. It may also decrease the demand for private education and for home schooling (Hunter 1991: 208–209).

Previously, groups wanting unusual curricula would be blocked when their proposals came before public bodies. Indeed, in the curricular culture wars, such groups would often block each other's programs (Divoky 1989; Spring 1997: 12–13; Hunter 1991). Under the charter regime, each group can get what it wants, and this is likely to defuse the culture wars. For example, for several years Flagstaff parents lobbied their local school board to provide a Waldorf option but were consistently blocked by opposition from Christian conservatives and from teachers. As a Flagstaff district official recalled, "Teachers objected. Some thought it was some sort of a religious thing because of the focus on nature. [Waldorf teachers] would start in the morning with the kids singing a song about the sun touching their faces. So they went out on their own when the charter school legislation came." A Waldorf teacher complained that "if we were waiting to be chartered through our local district it would be a long time." After the charter school law passed the proposal could no longer be blocked, and Pine Forest School was born. The charter school law gave previously disaffected communities a stake in public policy by increasing the responsiveness of the political system in providing services they wanted.

Indeed, by uniting diverse groups of parents who have a common stake in the health of the charter movement in the face of attempts to regulate charter school curricula and practices, the charter school movement may have produced new alliances crossing political chasms. After the 1998 election of Attorney General Janet Napolitano, both liberal and conservative charter operators expressed like concerns that charters (but not other public schools) would come under increased scrutiny, and they pondered working together to safeguard their schools. Alliances do not end with politics. In interviews, it was common to hear charter school operators with very different philosophies describe working together to face common concerns about grounds and facilities, special education, and accounting procedures.

Small Is Beautiful

The Hult and Walcott and Savas frameworks suggest that in education, small is beautiful. A large number of small schools will be better able to match the diverse demands of teachers and parents than will a small number of large schools. Each charter school has its own goals, which it communicates to likely parents and teachers. Thus all of those in the school building are likely to agree on its goals, unlike in many district schools (Chubb and Moe 1990). This may explain why, as Chapter 6 shows, Arizona charter school teachers report better and closer relations with colleagues and with parents than do their district school counterparts.

Charter schools are small enough that they need not have a diffuse mission. They can serve a niche market. As Chapter 6 details, Arizona charter elementary schools had a mean of 161 students in fall 1997, less than a third the size of district elementaries. Probably since most charter secondary schools are for at-risk students, secondary charters had a mean size *less than one tenth* that of district high schools. Small size means not only that charters can serve a niche market and survive, but also that the principal knows all the teachers and parents. In small schools, individual parents can have a substantial impact on school affairs. Small organizations can overcome the free rider problem, in which individuals are tempted to free-ride off the efforts of others (Olson 1965). Small size means that social pressure can enforce norms, and that the effort of a single individual is felt. The size and relative focus of charter schools thus encourages charter parents, students, and teachers to take seriously their responsibilities as *citizens of a community*. This is particularly important for at-risk students, who, numerous respondents suggested, were often advised by their district schools to attend nearby charters. As a career Arizona Department of Education official said, this means that district schools "can avoid a drop-out, which is a stat the districts do not want." By providing small learning communities, charter secondary schools may help district schools by taking the students that districts function better without.

Extending State Capacity

As Marc Landy and his colleagues (1994: 6–9) suggest, policy also must be judged by its effect on the institutions of government. Do charter schools threaten the existence of district schools? Or do they extend public resources to provide better service? Only a long-term test can provide answers, but initial results suggest the latter. As Chapters 6 and 14 suggest, the movement to charters already may be slowing, in part since, as Chapters 8 and 14 suggest, competition from charters pushes districts to do a better job pleasing parents. Further, the practitioner account in Chapter 15 and interviews with two former district teachers who started charter schools indicate that the charter system enables teachers to become entrepreneurs starting their own schools. The most acclaimed charter schools in the state, such as Edupreneurship in Scottsdale and Flagstaff Arts and Leadership Academy (FALA), were started by teachers. Districts often have refused teachers such options. For example, a Flagstaff informant said the FALA operator "had already applied for a couple a years within the district to do the exact same thing she's doing and, guess what? They turned her down! Teacher of the Year, they turned her down! Said: 'We don't want to risk that!'" (This account was confirmed by a district official.) The charter system allows such teachers to make full use of their talents and, as Chapter 8 suggests, may push districts to take the ideas of teachers more seriously in order to keep them in the fold.

Because charters are schools of choice that reflect the goals of their teachers and parents, they are able to solicit considerable volunteer and material contributions from their members and from businesses, houses of worship, civic organizations, and other parts of civil society. Like other Arizona public schools, charter schools get a per-pupil subsidy from the state. Unlike district schools, charters (as of 1998) lacked bonding authority and thus are thought to spend somewhat less public money than district schools, though officials could not provide reliable statistics.[4] If in fact charter schools spend less public money, then this means charters extend public resources. By allowing teacher-entrepreneurs to try new things, they also increase public value by perfecting methods that can then be adopted by district schools: Some district schools have copied practices at nearby charter schools, including extended school hours and calendars, home visits, inservice customer service training of staff, and more traditional curricula.

By giving parents choices over their children's education, the charter school system is likely to improve the civic education of Arizona parents, who now have more incentive to learn about the schools in their area and perhaps to discover new options. Further, as Chapter 8 suggests, the charter school regime may be pushing school districts to do a better job informing all parents about curriculum options and school performance. In part, such information depends on the accuracy of another reform measure—the Arizona Department of Education school report cards, which report disciplinary figures, calendars, standardized test scores, and school mission statements for all public school in the state. As Chapter 9 finds, by the fall of 1998 the state had not yet provided sufficient resources to assure accurate report cards. Even if imperfect, however, report cards and school choice seem likely to improve the level of civic education by increasing public knowledge about schools.

Two Caveats: Technical Merits and Segregation

The freedom of market-based education is enticing, but not without costs. What if some parents and teachers make very poor choices about education? What if some charter schools do not meet very basic technical merits? As Arizona state senator Mary Hartley reports in Chapter 13, for at least a few charter schools the technical merits are in fact highly suspect. Indeed, the Arizona State Board of Education initially approved (but quickly rescinded) a Scientology-based school. Still, charter supporters argue that district schools that fail gain less attention. Whereas nineteen charter campuses have been closed (and thus held accountable) by either market (enrollment) or administrative forces (the sponsoring boards), district schools do not close for poor performance.[5] Indeed, there are no good mechanisms for determining when districts fail. Charter schools at least have market mechanisms (parents deserting failing schools). In theory, charters also have institutional accountability since chartering authorities can revoke charters, though the State Board for Charter Schools is very pro-charter and unlikely to revoke. (Some future board could have different biases.)

A more potent criticism by Hartley and others is the threat of disunity. Market-based education could increase ethnic and social segregation, a point also made by Halchin in the prior chapter. Interviews suggest that although some charter operators have attempted to develop ethnically integrated schools, for others this is not a priority. Indeed, some schools teach Hispanic, Native American, African-American, Mormon, or, in one case, Jewish culture. Although charters cannot discriminate in admissions and must use a lottery if too many parents apply, recruiting networks may promote ethnic segregation. Still, the charter sector as a whole has demographics similar to those of district schools. The tendency for charter high schools to educate at-risk students is reflected in student demographics. The state enrollment database provided by the Arizona Department of Education indicates that in 1997 charter secondary students were 43.7 percent Caucasian (Anglo), 44 percent Hispanic, 7.2 percent Native American, and 4.2 percent African-American; district secondaries were 55.8 percent Caucasian, 28.8 percent Hispanic, 10.6 percent Native American, and 3.3 percent African-American. In contrast, charter elementary schools are somewhat whiter than their district counterparts. Charter elementary schools serve a population that is 69.8 percent Anglo, 11 percent Hispanic, 10.3 percent Native American, and 7.6 percent African-American. District elementaries are 54 percent Anglo, 31.9 percent Hispanic, 8.6 percent Native American, and 4.1 percent African-American.

Although the charter sector as a whole is integrated, the choice process may segregate individual schools. To test this hypothesis, I used an index of racial exposure developed by Massey and Denton (1993). In 1997 the modal white student in a charter elementary school was in a 75.2 percent white school, whereas the modal white district student was in a 64.5 percent white school. For secondary schools the comparable figures are 56 percent for charters and 59.5 percent for district schools. Depending on the fineness of one's criteria, charter elementary schools are either somewhat or substantially more segregated than district schools. Notably, Casey Cobb and Gene Glass (1999), using time series data, find that the charter sector is growing more segregated over time—a disturbing trend that bears watching.

Yet this is not the whole story. The small size of charter schools makes it likely that students of different races will know each other, take a common curriculum, and be involved in the same extracurricular activities. In contrast, students of different ethnic groups within large public schools tend to be academically and socially segregated. Thus charter schools may do more than district schools to foster inter-racial relationships (Powell et al. 1985; Greene 1998). Still, even if significant racial segregation does not occur, choice makes some cultural segregation inevitable; indeed this is key to defusing the culture wars. In the long run, this may prove a telling weakness of market-based education.

Conclusion: (Mostly) Praising Arizona

In short, though there are legitimate concerns regarding segregation, overall the public administration criteria I have used in this essay portray the Arizona experiment in market-based education as a successful example of Reinventing Government. Education is a policy area with highly controversial goals and methods. Accordingly, past education reforms often failed because they sought to impose a single vision of education on often reluctant and occasionally hostile teachers and parents. In today's multicultural democracy, education cannot be provided effectively by Progressive style bureaucracies imposing a single vision. The Reinventing paradigm suggests that education can be provided by an active market of teacher entrepreneurs and parent consumers. Arizona's market has freed teachers and parents to move beyond the traditional stalemates of culture and curriculum wars. By allowing parents and teachers to pursue their own education dreams, Arizona has given them incentives to learn more about their options, improving civic education. The charter system may also strengthen communal values, since charter schools are small, self-governed communities rather than large institutions ruled by external boards and bureaus.

Charter schools have increased the capacity of the state education system as a whole. The charter system has brought new resources into Arizona public education and has made a wide range of education options available to a large number of students who for whatever reason did not fit in conventional schools. The charter system has proven responsive to the desires of citizens, potentially increasing the legitimacy of public education among formerly marginalized groups such as ethnic minorities, Waldorf supporters, and even cultural conservatives. Perhaps most importantly, charter schools have defused conflicts over curricula and teaching methods by allowing more than one group to win. The fact that Arizona charter schools have superseded the culture wars that are wracking education may be their most significant contribution.

Notes

1. Many people also propose granting vouchers to the parents of children unhappy with their local public schools. Indeed this became an issue in the 1996 election, with Republican Robert Dole supporting vouchers that low income parents could use at either public or private schools. President Clinton instead supported public school choice, though his former domestic policy adviser, William Galston, now supports private school choice for low income children (Chubb and Moe 1990; Ravitch and Galston 1996).

2. There are numerous other examples. Osborne and Gaebler (1992: 332–348) list thirty-six separate means of service provision, though many are some variation of these three.

3. A liberal policy maker who visited that parent's school complained about a "heroes' list" taught to elementary school students: "Every female on the list was either a martyr or a wife."

4. Though it has not yet taken effect as this book goes to press, the Arizona legislature passed legislation during its 1999 session that grants charters bonding authority. See Chapter 13.

5. In addition to the nineteen charters that have been closed, three charters that had been Bureau of Indian Affairs schools returned to their previous status.

References

Allison, G. T. 1984. "Public and Private Management: Are They Fundamentally Alike in all Unimportant Respects?" In *Public Administration: Concepts and Cases,* ed. Richard J. Stillman. Boston: Houghton Mifflin.

Barzelay, M., with B. J. Armajani. 1992. *Breaking Through Bureaucracy.* Berkeley: University of California Press.

Campbell, Colin, and Graham K. Wilson. 1995. *The End of Whitehall: Death of a Paradigm.* Oxford: Blackwell.

Carroll, James D., A. Lee Fritschler, and Bruce L. R. Smith. 1985. "Supply-Side Management in the Reagan Administration." *Public Administration Review* 45 (6): 805–814.

Chubb, John E., and Terry M. Moe. 1990. *Politics, Markets, and America's Schools.* Washington D.C.: Brookings Institution.

Cobb, Casey D., and Gene V. Glass. 1999. "Ethnic Segregation in Arizona Charter Schools," *Education Policy Analysis Archives* 7 (1):URL: http://epaa.asu.edu/epaa/v7nl/.

Divoky, Diane. 1989. "Reflections on Twenty Years of Alternatives, Options, and Now . . . Choice." In *Public Schools by Choice,* ed. Joe Nathan. St. Paul, Minn.: Institute for Teaching and Learning.

Doherty, Kathryn N. 1998. "Changing Urban Education: Defining the Issues." In *Changing Urban Education,* ed. Clarence N. Stone. Lawrence: University of Kansas Press.

Durant, Robert. 1992. *The Administrative Presidency Revisited.* Albany: State University of New York Press.

Garvey, Gerald. 1993. *Facing the Bureaucracy: Living and Dying in a Public Agency.* San Francisco: Jossey-Bass.

Gerzon, Mark. 1996. *A House Divided: Six Belief Systems Struggling for America's Soul.* New York: G. P. Putnam's Sons.

Glasser, William. 1992. *The Quality School: Managing Students Without Coercion.* New York: HarperCollins.

Gore, Al. 1993. *Creating a Government That Works Better and Costs Less: Report of the National Performance Review.* New York: Times Books.

Greene, Jay P. 1998. "Civic Values in Public and Private Schools." In *Learning from School Choice,* ed. Paul E. Peterson and Bryan C. Hassel. Washington, D.C.: Brookings Institution.

Hess, Frederick M. 1999. *Spinning Wheels: The Politics of Urban School Reform.* Washington, D.C.: Brookings Institution.

Hirsch, E. D. 1996. *The Schools We Need and Why We Don't Have Them.* New York: Doubleday.

Horner, Constance. 1994. "Deregulating the Federal Service: Is the Time Right?" In *Deregulating the Public Service: Can Government Be Improved?* ed. John J. Di-Iulio Jr. Washington, D.C.: Brookings Institution.

Hult, Karen M., and Charles Walcott. 1990. *Governing Public Organizations: Politics, Structures, and Institutional Design.* Pacific Grove, Calif.: Brooks/Cole.

Hunter, James Davison. 1991. *Culture Wars: The Struggle to Define America.* New York: Basic Books.

Kaus, Mickey. 1992. *The End of Equality.* New York: Basic Books.

Kelman, Stephen. 1990. *Procurement and Public Management: The Fear of Discretion and the Quality of Government Performance.* Washington, D.C.: AEI Press.

Landy, Marc, Craig Thomas, and Steven Roberts. 1994. *The EPA: Asking the Wrong Questions from Nixon to Clinton.* Rev. ed. New York: Oxford University Press.

Maranto, Robert. 1993. *Politics and Bureaucracy in the Modern Presidency: Careerists and Appointees in the Reagan Administration.* Westport, Conn.: Greenwood Press.

Marshall, Will., ed. 1997. *Building the Bridge: Ten Big Ideas to Transform America.* Lanham, Md.: Rowman & Littlefield.

Massey, Douglas S., and Nancy A. Denton. 1993. *American Apartheid: Segregation and the Making of the Underclass.* Cambridge, Mass.: Harvard University Press.

McGarity, Thomas. 1991. *Reinventing Rationality: The Role of Regulatory Analysis in the Federal Bureaucracy.* New York: Cambridge University Press.

Niskanen, William A., Jr. 1971. *Bureaucracy and Representative Government.* Chicago: Aldine-Atherton.

Nye, Joseph S., Jr., Philip D. Zelikow, and David C. King, eds. 1997. *Why People Don't Trust Government.* Cambridge: Harvard University Press.

Olson, Mancur. 1965. *The Logic of Collective Action.* Cambridge: Harvard University Press.

Osborne, David, and Ted Gaebler. 1992. *Reinventing Government: How the Entrepreneurial Spirit Is Transforming the Public Sector.* Reading, Pa.: Addison-Wesley.

Osborne, David, and Peter Plastrick. 1997. *Banishing Bureaucracy: The Five Strategies for Reinventing Government.* Reading, Pa.: Addison-Wesley.

PBS. 1998. *The News Hour with Jim Lehrer,* May 11.

Peters, Charles. 1978. "A Kind Word for the Spoils System." In *The Culture of Bu-*

reaucracy, ed. Charles Peters and Michael Nelson. New York: Holt, Rhinehart, and Winston.

_____. 1992. *How Washington Really Works.* Reading, Pa.: Addison-Wesley.

Peters, Tom J., and Robert H. Waterman Jr. 1982. *In Search of Excellence.* New York: Warner Books.

Powell, Arthur G., Eleanor Farrar, and David K. Cohen. 1985. *The Shopping Mall High School.* Boston: Houghton Mifflin.

Ravitch, Diane. 1983. *The Troubled Crusade: American Education 1945–1980.* New York: Basic Books.

Ravitch, Diane, and William Galston. 1996. "Scholarships for Inner-City School Kids." *Washington Post,* December 17, A23.

Savas, E. S. 1987. *Privatization: The Key to Better Government.* Chatham, N.J.: Chatham House.

Savas, E. S., and Sigmund G. Ginsburg. 1973. "The Civil Service: A Meritless System?" *The Public Interest,* no. 32: 70–85.

Schultz, David, and Robert Maranto. 1998. *The Politics of Civil Service Reform.* New York: Peter Lang.

Schwartz, Herman. 1992. "Privatizing and Reorganizing the State in Australia, Denmark, New Zealand, and Sweden." Paper presented at the annual meeting of the American Political Science Association, Chicago, Illinois, August 31.

_____. 1997. "Reinvention and Retrenchment: Lessons from Applications of the New Zealand Model to Alberta, Canada." *Journal of Policy Analysis and Management* 16 (3): 405–422.

Spring, Joel. 1997. *Political Agendas for Education.* Mahwah, N.J.: Lawrence Erlbaum.

Tyack, David, and Larry Cuban. 1995. *Tinkering Toward Utopia: A Century of Public School Reform.* Cambridge: Harvard University Press.

Uslaner, Eric M. 1993. *The Decline of Comity in Congress.* Ann Arbor: University of Michigan Press.

4

Congress and Charter Schools

DAVID L. LEAL

Although all eyes are on charter school legislation in state capitals, the federal government has recently taken significant steps in the area. In order to understand the Arizona experience and the charter school movement in context, it is useful to understand the politics of charters in the nation's capital during the 1991–1998 period. This chapter discusses the inaugural federal charter school law of 1994 and the political context of education reform that year. Subsequent charter efforts in the next two congresses also will be discussed. Much has changed since 1994: Not only has funding appropriation increased from $6 million to $100 million, but in a classic trade-off, the requirements imposed on states in exchange for federal dollars are growing more extensive. Federal education laws are also becoming more "charter-friendly" over time.

This chapter is based on both printed and electronic sources and interviews with House and Senate staff members who have worked with the charter school issue.[1] The interviews were conducted during October 1998.

Getting Started: The 1994 ESEA Reauthorization

Charter schools were first funded by Congress through a small provision in the $12.7 billion 1994 reauthorization of the 1965 Elementary and Secondary Education Act (ESEA).[2] The measure passed on October 5, in the final days of the 103rd Congress.

The charter school provision was included under Title X, Part C—"Programs of National Significance." It authorized $15 million (or .001 percent of the total reauthorization and 3.5 percent of Title X spending) for the start-up of public charter schools. The federal money was to be sent to the states, which would distribute it to school districts to help fund the start-up expenses of charter schools. Allowable expenses included professional development, educational materials and supplies, curriculum development, publicizing the school in the community, and other costs not covered by state or local dollars. The money also was to be used to examine student achievement in these schools (Wells 1994a). Ten percent of the $15 million was to be used for "'national activities'—research, dissemination of information, and other activities designed to assist the overall charter school movement" (Schroeder 1997: 1).[3]

A federal role in charter schooling had been proposed first in 1991. The primary original sponsor was Senator Dave Durenberger (R–MN). In 1991, Durenberger's Minnesota had been the first state to pass a charter school experiment program. Joining him was Senator Joseph Lieberman (D–CT), one of the leading congressional advocates of school choice. The bill went nowhere in 1991 or 1992, was reintroduced in 1993 with the support of House members David McCurdy (D–OK) and Tom Petri (R–WI), and then was incorporated in the 1994 ESEA (Schroeder 1997).

The small-scale, uncontroversial, and bipartisan cast of the legislation helps to explain the lack of media attention it received. An examination of the public record suggests the charter initiative was an uncontroversial element of the reauthorization. The charter measure was barely mentioned in *Congressional Quarterly Weekly Reports* (CQ) and was ignored by the *Washington Post* and the *New York Times*. This lack of attention and controversy established a pattern that would remain in subsequent years.

Although the initial program was relatively small, it is important to keep in mind that Congress was one of the very first political institutions to support charter schools. In fact, "the ink was hardly dry on Minnesota's pioneering charter school law in the fall of 1991 when David Durenberger (R–MN) introduced the 'Public School Redefinition Act,' the forerunner of the federal charter grant program" (Schroeder 1997: 2).

At the beginning of 1994, there were only a few state-sponsored experiments across the county. So why did Congress promote charters? Although Democrats and Republicans often have very different ideas for school reform, charters did not arouse the ire of either side. "Choice" is an appealing idea that enjoys bipartisan support and that becomes controversial only when it means that students and dollars are leaving the public school system for private schools. Since the choice measure was coupled with increased financial support, more liberal Democrats were comfortable. Finally, Congress wants to influence how the money is spent. The compromise promised to increase choice and spending, while permitting congressional influence and maintaining the integrity of the public schools.

Charter schools also are viewed as serving a number of possible goals. As the Congressional Research Service (CRS 1998: 24) has noted, "The charter school concept has attracted support from a wide range of individuals and groups who frequently do not agree on education policies or strategies." Some conservatives believe that charter schools could fracture the traditional public school monopoly and serve as a stalking horse for school vouchers.

Meanwhile, some public school supporters see charters as a reasonable compromise that maintains public schooling. Others see charter schools as a stratagem with which to fend off vouchers. By supporting charters, voucher opponents can claim that they are planning increased parental choice. The hope is that this will satisfy the demand for reform and reduce interest in more direct attacks on traditional public schooling.

The 1994 Legislative Context

When reauthorization of the ESEA began in Congress in 1994, charter schools were almost invisible next to a host of more prominent educational issues. One issue that attracted a great deal of attention in the 1994 debates was that of school vouchers. In recent years when federal funding for schools has been considered, conservatives often have used the opportunity to push for vouchers. In 1994, again, all these efforts were unsuccessful. One amendment by John Boehner (R–OH), for example, was rejected by the House education subcommittee even though it would have limited choice to public schools. In the Senate, an amendment by Daniel Coats (R–IN) to fund a $30 million voucher demonstration project was rejected 41–52.

Another controversial issue in the 104th Congress was home schooling. At issue was an amendment to the ESEA authored by Democratic Representative Dan Miller (CA) that would have required school districts to use only teachers certified in their subject areas. Home schooling advocates feared this would be interpreted to require home schooling parents to earn credentials, so in February they "besieged members with phone calls, letters and faxes for over a week, brow-beating them into killing a mandate actually aimed only at public school teachers" (Kuntz 1994a). The House rushed to kill the Miller amendment on a vote of 424 to 1. As Dale Kildee (D–MI) said, "The goal is to spare every member of Congress another weekend of phone calls" (Kuntz 1994a).

A third controversial issue attracting attention was school prayer. The House passed an amendment by Sam Johnson (R–TX) that would have denied federal funds to schools preventing students from engaging in "constitutionally protected" school prayer. The language was replaced in the House-Senate conference by a weaker requirement that the ESEA could take funds from a district only if a judge found the district guilty of violating a court order allowing prayer (Wells 1994b). Senator Jesse Helms (R–NC) was so unhappy with this change that he filibustered the bill for two days before a motion to shut off debate was approved 75–24.

A fourth major issue was the distribution of Title I money to the states. Title I has enjoyed bipartisan support over the years, in part because it spreads money across the country; more than 90 percent of school districts received at least some funds in 1994. President Clinton proposed dramatically increasing the share of money targeted to the poorest districts and barring the wealthiest districts from receiving any money (Kuntz 1994b). In the end, this plan proved virtually impossible to sell in either chamber, and a compromise bill was passed that directed slightly more Title I money to children in poor districts (Wells 1994b).

In short, many controversial issues crowded out a more complete public examination of charter schools, issues unlikely to disappear in future considerations of education reform.

The 1998 Charter School Law

The first authorization for Fiscal Year (FY) 1995 was for $15 million, even though Congress eventually appropriated only $6 million.[4] Since then, the amount appropriated by Congress on charter schools has increased rapidly. It grew to $18 million in FY 1996, $51 million in FY 1997, $80 million in FY 1998, and the latest legislation (Charter School Expansion Act of 1998) increased spending to $100 million for FY 1999 (CRS 1998).[5] Congressional staffers who work on charter schools expect the appropriation will continue to rise in future years, especially since charters have not been funded at the expense of any particular program.

Only fifty members of the House opposed the 1998 charter school law, HR 2616. Supporters therefore outnumbered opponents almost eight to one. Although many more Democrats than Republicans opposed the bill, the overall figures still showed strong bipartisan support for the measure. The Senate never conducted a recorded vote on charters.

The Republican opponents were somewhat more conservative than their party average. The ten Republicans had an average American Conservative Union (ACU) score in 1997 of 94, compared to the House Republican average of about 87.[6] The forty Democratic opponents were also slightly more conservative than the membership as a whole. The Democratic opponents had an average ACU score of 21, compared to the average score of 19 for House Democrats.

The Senate never conducted a roll-call vote. After the House vote the relevant minority and majority staffers from the House and Senate met in an informal "pre-conference" committee to work out differences between the House version and the likely Senate version. Usually this process of compromise does not occur until after both chambers have voted. The resulting bill was approved by a voice vote in the Senate and sent on to the House, where it passed easily.

Charter School Provisions in 1998

How does the federal government determine what constitutes a charter school? The CRS (1998: i) noted that charter schools must be created under an enabling statute, exempt from a significant number of restricting state and local regulations, nonsectarian, and created from existing public school districts or from private schools. Charter schools can not charge tuition, must use a lottery to determine admissions if there are more applicants than spots, and must meet basic health and safety requirements. In addition, the CRS (1998: 12) noted that charters must meet several other criteria relating to federal nondiscrimination and equal opportunity legislation.

Initially, Congress did not settle on a formula to direct the allocation of money to the states. Instead, the Department of Education was allowed to develop its own criteria. In the 1998 legislation, however, Congress decided to include language that would prioritize funding. This new provision, passed by a Republican Congress, tied funding to the strength of a state's charter school law. After wrestling with the question of how to do this without micromanaging state programs, Congress decided to prioritize funding according to four criteria (in addition to the basic selection criteria).[7] In fiscal years 1999–2001, $51 million will be subject to this formula, as will all subsequent appropriations.

The first criteria is that priority generally will be given to states with charter laws requiring the review and evaluation of each school at least every five years. Congress was concerned that many charter schools never underwent any sort of evaluation. States now will be required to test charters with whatever instrument they test all public schools. Funding will then be prioritized to states meeting at least one of three additional criteria.

The first additional criteria is that a state show progress in requiring more of its charter schools to set measurable objectives in the charter. The second criteria is whether authority over charters has been transferred from local school districts to a special "alternative chartering authority" such as a local university or a state board. This condition also can be met by the creation of an appeals process within the state education authority in case a local district rejects a charter application. The reasoning was that local districts are far less likely to wield the chartering authority aggressively than are other chartering agencies. The third criteria is a vague requirement that each charter school have a high degree of authority over its expenditures and budget. According to one staffer, the goal is not to rank every state and distribute money accordingly, but to encourage states with weak laws to strengthen them.

The 1998 legislation specified that in order for state charter schools to qualify for federal money, the state must have a specific charter school statute. In some cases, like Oregon, charter-like schools existed but there was no charter law. The definition of what counts as a charter school was also tightened. The Charter Friends National Network (1998) termed this "a major victory over efforts by some states and Members who had sought to allow alternative or magnet schools in non-charter states to qualify for grants." The secretary of education also must consider the number of charter schools in each state when determining the size of the grant. This congressional stipulation addresses the concern that some states were trying to restrict charter growth by capping the number of schools.

Charter schools are often plagued by uncertainty regarding their resources and needs. When a new charter school opens, it is not clear how many children will attend it, how many will be from low-income families, and whether there will be any special education children. A new charter school may not receive its first-year authorization from programs like Title I or IDEA (Individuals with Disabilities Education Act) until the following year. Also, charters that expand quickly can have problems with quickly getting the funding to which they are entitled.[8] To address these issues, the 1998 law requires charters to receive all eligible funds no later than five months after they start or expand.

Some of the new federal requirements are informational. A state must tell its charter schools what federal funds might be available to them and is to disseminate the most promising charter practices to all charter schools in the state. States must specify in their grant applications how charters will comply with IDEA.[9]

Congress also has begun to reexamine education programs when they come up for reauthorization in order to see how they impact charter schools. For example, some charter schools are legally classified by their states to be their own Local Education Agency (LEA), whereas others are incorporated within a traditional school district LEA. Charter schools designated as LEAs are eligible to apply for almost all federal education programs, but charters not so designated are unable to qualify for these funds. Congress is therefore making adjustments to allow even charters that are not their own LEAs to be eligible for these programs.

Many charter advocates wanted to extend federal funding from the first three years of a school's life to the first five years, but the Senate was opposed. The Senate version was retained, ensuring that the federal role will continue to focus on launching, rather than maintaining, charter schools. However, states now will be allowed to set aside 10 percent of their federal grants to allow existing charter schools to engage in activities like assisting new schools, working with traditional public schools, or pursuing studies of charter school performance. Another notable change in the law is that the percentage of funding the U.S. secretary of education can use for national activities was cut to 5 percent from the 10 percent figure in 1994.[10]

Finally, the 1994 law allocated money to evaluate the success of charter schools. Although the Department of Education is conducting the required studies, one House staffer reported that there is no sense on the Hill that future appropriations are contingent upon demonstrated positive outcomes. A Senate staffer, however, argued that support for charters will hinge on public confidence in the idea, and test data could impact that confidence.

The initial reports are encouraging to charter advocates. The ED released a study in May 1998 finding that charter schools enroll at least as many minority students and as many low-income students as do traditional public schools.[11] The Hudson Institute reported in 1997 that large percentages of charter school students and parents compared their charter school favorably to their former public school.[12]

Conclusions

Most accounts of how laws are enacted examine controversial issues with strong proponents and determined opponents who clash in dramatic battles (Cohen 1995; Waldman 1995). The passage of charter school legislation was not a battle. Instead it was a slow, unremarkable march towards significant policy change. Education reform is a central topic in American political discourse, yet a new approach to schooling was launched and has grown into a $100 million program with no fanfare. In many ways, therefore, this chapter echoes Martin's (1994) *Lessons from the Hill*, which detailed the story of a small and little-noticed education program with a significant potential impact.

Why does charter schooling, which has the potential to dramatically alter public education, receive so little notice in Washington? First, there is little to attract media interest because charters are not politically controversial.[13] Second, the program is small by government standards. Third, the unusual alliance of conservative and liberal members on both the pro and con side reflected differing priorities for the future of public education that could not be summarized by a simple and familiar partisan or ideological split.

More generally, this lack of media coverage on issues like charters may help to explain low public approval of Congress. When members "do something" and do so without unseemly "partisan bickering," the public may never hear of it. When the parties engage in a pitched battle, the public is led to think this is the norm. The problem is that the media experience great difficulty covering an institution with dozens of committees and subcommittees, multiple leaders, and 535 voting members. Controversy makes the media's job easy, but the result does not provide an accurate view of Congress at work. As Martin (1994: 153) concluded about her education bill, "The situation is typical of much of the work of Congress: it is done with little, in any, notice by the press."

Limited media coverage does not mean that charter legislation is unimportant. In fact, although the noise generated by other education issues distracted attention from charter provisions, charters ultimately may prove more significant than many more carefully scrutinized policy proposals. In the words of Senator Lieberman:

> It would not be too difficult to overlook this legislation. Compared to some of the high-profile education bills we have considered recently, this is a modest and largely anonymous proposal. . . . Nevertheless, I believe that this may turn out to be one of the most important and constructive bills that we enact into law during this season. What we have agreed to do today will help take the charter school model from novelty to the norm in this country, and thereby bolster the most promising engine of education reform at work in America today.[14]

What is the future of the federal role in charter schools? One congressional staffer said there is "no political will" to cut charter schools, and very few people or organizations are outspoken in their opposition to them. Although some members of Congress have "concerns" or "questions" about charters, few desire to lead the charge against them. Some members might prefer different spending priorities for education dollars, but that does not translate into actively opposing charters.

One possibility is that Congress will change the program from a discretionary/competitive grant-making process to one with an allocation formula. Other suggestions for change include targeting federal money to the acquisition of new charter school physical facilities and to developing and testing new types of achievement tests in order to better ensure accountability (CRS 1998: 27–30).

Notes

1. The electronic sources are World Wide Web sites and were recommended by either the congressional staffers or education policy scholars interviewed.

2. Also known as the "Improving America's Schools Act of 1994." The ESEA was one of the key pieces of legislation from the Johnson administration's War on Poverty. For a legislative history of the original act see Eidenberg and Morey (1969).

3. According to education officials, "the Department of Education (ED) has organized its national activities into three broad areas: (1) engaging the public, (2) research and development, and (3) outreach" (General Accounting Office 1998: 24–25). In addition, the Goals 2000: Educate America Act allowed states to "use federal funds to promote charter schools" (GAO 1998: 5). Up to 10 percent of state Goals 2000 funds can be used for "various reform activities including promoting public charter schools (Congressional Research Service 1998: 9).

4. The information for this section was obtained through interviews with congressional staff members who work with charter school legislation, as well as through the "Update on Passage of Changes in the Federal Charter School Grant Program Legislation," Charter Friends National Network, October 12, 1998.

5. The first grants in 1995 were made to 10 states (AZ, CA, CO, GA, LA, MA, MI, MN, OR, TX, plus two schools in NM); then nine states were added the following year (AK, CT, DE, FL, IL, KS, NJ, NC, and WI, plus Washington D.C., Puerto Rico, and an additional school in NM); then followed the addition of PA, SC, and two schools in HI.

6. Scored 0 to 100, based on a member's position on a number of votes chosen by the ACU. In this case, 0 means perfectly liberal and 100 means perfectly conservative. Other groups have their own rating systems.

7. According to CRS (1998: 9–10), selection includes seven basic criteria: "(1) the contribution the funds will make to helping educationally disadvantaged and other students meet state education standards; (2) the degree of flexibility provided by the state education agency (SEA) to charter schools; (3) the ambitiousness of the objectives of the state's charter school program; (4) the quality of the strategy for assessing the achievement outcomes of charter schools; (5) the likelihood that a state's grant program supported with these federal funds will meet its objectives and improve education; (6) the number of charter schools that are operating, or are approved to operate, in the states; and (7) if the state proposes to use any funds for dissemination/technical assistance grants, the quality of those proposed activities." It goes on to note that "for LEAs [Local Education Agency] that apply directly to ED for PCS [Public Charter School] funds (in states that do not participate in the program), there are also 7 *selection criteria*, [emphasis in original] although these differ slightly from those for SEAs [State Education Agency]. Five of these criteria are essentially the same as (2)-(5) and (7) above. The 6th LEA grant criteria is 'the quality of the proposed curriculum and instructional practices'; and the 7th is 'the extent of community support for the application.'"

8. Although the GAO (1998: 11) noted these and other barriers to funding, it also found that "our survey revealed that most charter school operators who applied for Title I and IDEA funds received them. Moreover, most charter school operators who expressed an opinion told us that they believed that these federal funds are fairly allocated to charter schools."

9. This is largely a restatement of the 1994 law, which already defined charters as being in compliance with IDEA.

10. This will not actually change the amount of money available, however, because expenditures were doubled in the 1998 legislation.

11. See U.S. Department of Education (1998).

12. Hudson Institute (1997). The results in this paragraph were reported in the *Congressional Record*, "Findings from Key Studies on Charter Schools," October 9,

1998. A congressional staffer, however, pointed out that one problem with the kind of study released by the Hudson Institute is that it relies on student and parent satisfaction surveys. Hard data, such as whether individual students increase their test scores when they move to a charter school, are not available. The new testing provision, however, should address this problem over the next few years.

13. Coverage of charters seems to have increased somewhat recently, however. Stories have appeared in national forums such as the *New York Times Sunday Magazine.*

14. *Congressional Record,* October 9, 1998.

References

Charter Friends National Network. 1998. "Update on Passage of Changes in the Federal Charter School Grant Program Legislation." October 12, URL: http://www.charterfriends.org/federal.html.

Cohen, Richard E. 1995. *Washington at Work: Back Rooms and Clean Air.* Boston: Allyn and Bacon.

Congressional Research Service. 1998. *Public Charter Schools: State Developments and Federal Policy Options* (97-519 EPW). November 4. Washington, D.C.: Congressional Research Service.

Eidenberg, Eugene, and Roy Morey. 1969. *An Act of Congress: The Legislative Process and the Making of Education Policy.* New York: W. W. Norton and Company.

General Accounting Office. 1998. *Charter Schools: Federal Funding Available but Barriers Exist* (GAO/HEHS-98-84). Washington, D.C.: General Accounting Office.

Hudson Institute. 1997. *Charter Schools in Action.* Washington, D.C.: Hudson Institute.

Kuntz, Phil. 1994a. "Home-Schooling Movement Gives House a Lesson." *Congressional Quarterly Weekly Reports,* February 26.

_____. 1994b. "House Panel Rejects Shifting Money to Poor Schools." *Congressional Quarterly Weekly Reports,* February 5.

Martin, Janet M. 1994. *Lessons from the Hill: The Legislative Journey of an Education Program.* New York: St. Martin's Press.

Schroeder, Jon. 1997. "Defining a Proper Federal Role in Support of Charter Schools." Washington, D.C.: Progressive Policy Institute.

U.S. Department of Education. 1998. *A National Study of Charter Schools: Second Year Report.* Washington, D.C.: U.S. Department of Education.

U.S. Department of Education, Office of Educational Research and Improvement. 1997. *A Study of Charter Schools.* Washington, D.C.: U.S. Department of Education.

Waldman, Steven. 1995. *The Bill: How the Adventures of Clinton's National Service Bill Reveal What Is Corrupt, Comic, Cynical–and Noble–About Washington.* New York: Viking Books.

Wells, Robert Marshall. 1994a. "Education Bill Provisions." *Congressional Quarterly Weekly Reports,* December 17.

_____. 1994b. "Senate Ends Prayer Filibuster, Clears $12.7 Billion Bill." *Congressional Quarterly Weekly Reports,* October 8.

_____. 1994c. "Elementary-Secondary Aid Bill Passes House, 289–128." *Congressional Quarterly Weekly Reports,* March 26.

5

Charter Schools: A National Innovation, an Arizona Revolution

BRYAN C. HASSEL

When Minnesota passed the first charter school law in 1991, even the reform's staunchest advocates could scarcely have predicted the charter idea's rapid spread across the United States. The next year, California joined Minnesota, enacting the nation's second charter statute. Six more states signed on in 1993. By the end of 1998, fully 34 states and the District of Columbia had charter school laws on the books, and state legislatures in several more states were gearing up to consider charter proposals in 1999. As the 1998–1999 school year opened, more than 1,000 charter schools educated over 200,000 students (Center for Education Reform 1998). Though Arizona was not among the first states to enact charter legislation, its charter school program has grown rapidly since the passage of a charter law in 1994. In 1998–1999, nearly a quarter of all the nation's charter schools were in Arizona, which accounts for only 2 percent of the country's overall public school enrollment. Almost 34,000 students attended charter schools in Arizona when school opened for the 1998–1999 school year (Todd and Mitchell 1998: A6; National Center for Educational Statistics 1998: Table 10).

It is quite common for everyone from politicians to journalists to talk about "charter schools" and "innovation" in the same breath. The association of charter schools with innovation has two sources. First, charter school programs are themselves regarded as an innovative *policy*. Though they bear a family resemblance to many other proposed reforms of public education, they are undoubtedly "something new" in American education. Less than a decade ago, there were no charter school laws and no charter schools.

Second, one of the core purposes of charter school programs is to produce innovations in the *practice* of schooling. With the burden of regulation lifted, the argument goes, charter schools have the opportunity to experiment with new curricula, new instructional methods, new ways of organizing and governing themselves, new ways of allocating resources. Students who attend the pathbreaking institutions will reap the benefits of this experimentation, but charter advocates envision innovations spreading beyond the walls of charter schools. Charters are intended to serve as "laboratories" or "lighthouses" for conventional public schools, showing the way toward new approaches to educating children. And since they compete with school districts for funds, charter schools create incentives for conventional schools to innovate as well, sparking new thinking system-wide. The legislative intent sections of charter laws typically include some reference to innovation as part of the rationale for the legislation.

So in theory, at least, charter school programs are both an innovative policy and an innovation-producing policy. But do *actual* charter school programs live up to this potential for innovation? Do real-world charter school policies depart as substantially as they might from the status quo of public education? And are charter schools themselves producing innovations in practice, both within their walls and without?

Origins and Diffusion of the Charter School Idea

Many observers credit Ray Budde with coining the term "charter" in the educational context. In his book, *Education by Charter: Restructuring School Districts* (1988), he proposes to empower teams of teachers to develop "educational charters": comprehensive plans for educational ventures that they would present to local school boards for endorsement. Others point to the school district in Philadelphia, the site of experimentation with significant school restructuring known as "chartering" (Fine 1994). Still others look abroad to Great Britain's 1988 Education Reform Act, which gave local schools the opportunity to "opt out" of local school authorities and become part of a sort of national school district (Wohlstetter and Anderson 1994).

Although these early ideas contained some important elements of what we now think of as charter schools—teams of people starting from scratch in the design of new schools, site-level control over key decisions, evaluation of the venture's results—the full-blown charter concept grew out of numerous different movements for education reform. Five among these proved important: (1) the push for more *choice* for students and families; (2) the related idea of *competition*, breaking school districts' monopoly over educational provision; (3) the general concept of *school-based management*, delegating key decisions to the front lines; (4) the related push for *deregulation*, lessening the burden of law and regulation on schools; (5) calls for greater *accountability for results*, for schools to set concrete goals and then face consequences for meeting them.[1] Many observers would argue that is was Ted Kolderie (1990) who brought all of these ideas together into what we now think of as the charter school concept. Kolderie's "nine essentials" (1993) form the core of the charter idea.

State legislatures from all regions of the country have adopted charter laws in the last five years. As Figures 5.1 and 5.2 display, the number of states with charter statutes has grown dramatically since the first law passed in 1991.

How has this policy spread so rapidly across the country? Certainly a central factor has been charter schools' bipartisan appeal. Republicans have gravitated to charter schools as at least a first step toward the broader systems of school choice they espouse. So-called "New Democrats" find the idea appealing not as a step toward something else but as an ideal way to bring elements of choice and competition into the public school system without compromising some of the fundamental values of public education, like open, tuition-free enrollment and the separation of church and state. More traditional Democrats may find charter schools unpalatable on principle but, nonetheless, an acceptable compromise that appears to take the wind from the sails of more radical choice reforms. Because of these sorts of calculations, unlikely coalitions have passed charter school laws in many states, though states with Republican governors and legislators have been most eager to press charter schools.[2]

FIGURE 5.1   Increasing Prevalence of State Charter Laws

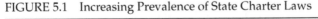

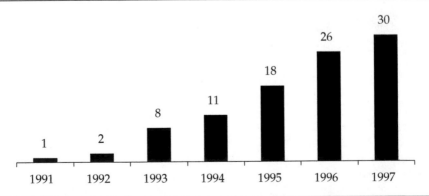

SOURCE: RPP International (1998).

FIGURE 5.2   Spread of State Charter School Laws Over Time

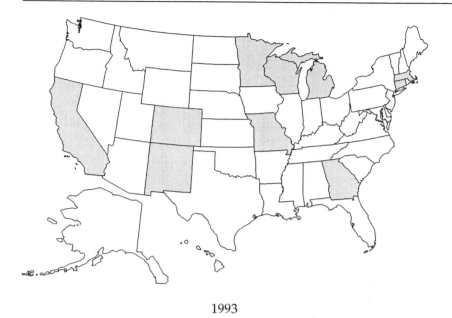

1993

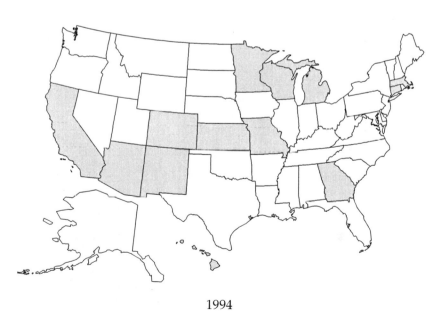

1994

(continues)

FIGURE 5.2 (continued)

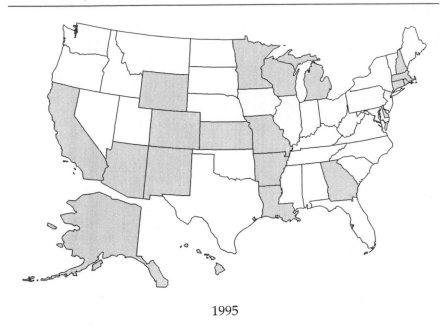

1995

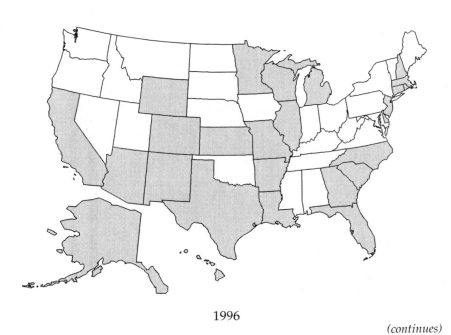

1996

(continues)

FIGURE 5.2   (continued)

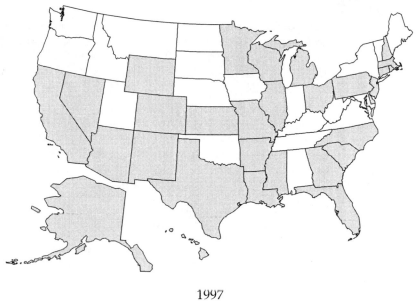

1997

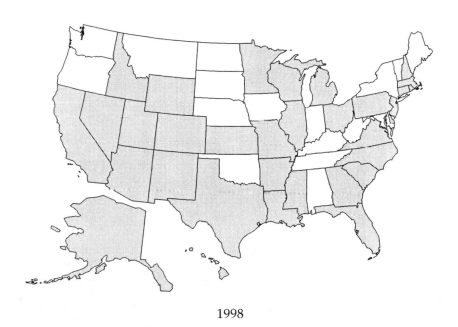

1998

According to research by Michael Mintrom and Sandra Vergari (1997), the spread of charter schools has been hastened also by the existence and development of dense "policy networks" through which ideas flow among "policy entrepreneurs." Surveying individuals involved in charter school policymaking nationwide and applying a sophisticated quantitative analysis to the diffusion of charter laws, Mintrom and Vergari found considerable evidence that individuals (like Ted Kolderie) and organizations (like the National Conference of State Legislatures) played pivotal roles in spreading the charter idea from state to state. Drawing on such actors, policy makers collected print information, personally conversed with counterparts elsewhere, visited other states, and invited experts from states with charter laws to testify in their states about charter schools. The authors found these sorts of information-transfer activities vital determinants of the consideration and adoption of charter laws in the states.

What's Innovative About the Charter School Idea?

When people say charter schools are an "innovation," one of two ideas may lie behind their statements. First, they may mean that charter school programs themselves are an innovative policy, a new way of structuring the governance of public education. Second, they may mean that charter school programs are designed to *produce* innovations in practice at the school level. This section explores each of these two ideas in turn.

Charter School Programs as an Innovative Policy

Beyond the trivial observation that charter school programs are a *new* policy, in existence for less than a decade, what is innovative about them? Charter school programs represent a new way of regulating schools and school systems, in three critical respects:

1. Schools gain significant autonomy with regard to what they teach, how they teach it, how they organize themselves, whom they hire (and fire), and how they allocate resources.
2. Schools' overseers gain the ability to hold schools accountable for results, closing schools that fail to achieve agreed upon levels of student performance.
3. Choice and competition become pervasive elements of the educational system as new providers are invited to "supply" public education, families gain the ability to choose their children's public schools, and families' choices have real financial consequences for the schools.

At first glance, perhaps these three elements do not look terribly innovative. After all, both the education policy literature and actual education policymaking are laced with calls for and attempts to enact various forms of site-based management, accountability for results, and family choice in education. If the core elements of charter school policy are this commonplace, what makes charter school programs innovative? Part of the answer is that charter school programs bring the three elements together into a coherent policy in a way that previous reform has not, combining autonomy, accountability, and choice into a system of school regulation with its own logic. But even within each of the elements, a closer look at the history of reform makes clear that charter school policies are distinct from past experience.

Begin with autonomy. One comprehensive review of efforts to institute school-based management found that "proposals to delegate decision-making authority to subunits of school districts or to individual sites . . . have been enacted, rescinded and reenacted for decades." (Malen, Ogawa, and Kranz 1990: 296). But in the form envisioned by their proponents, charter schools differ from past efforts at school-based management in two respects: breadth and depth. First, the autonomy charter school programs grant to schools is *broader* than the control granted in most site-based management initiatives; that is, it applies to a wider range of decisions that schools make. Charter schools gain, in theory, decisionmaking authority over most of the core elements of school management, from curriculum and instruction to budgeting. By contrast, traditional site-based management plans tend to empower site-based actors to make only a small range of decisions. Betty Malen and her colleagues (1990: 303–310) found that school-based actors reported influence over only a small fraction of school decisions, and that these decisions tended to be "'routine,' 'blasé,' 'trivial,' 'peripheral.'" Where plans have offered schools authority over important domains, they generally have limited the breadth of that authority (e.g., authority over educational programs, but not budget or personnel). A more recent study of prominent decentralization reforms in four large school districts found that even in these relatively aggressive efforts, schools gained little if any control over budgets or personnel (Bryk, Hill, Shipps et al. 1998).

The second dimension of autonomy on which charter schools differ is the *depth* of the control they gain, the degree to which school-level actors are actually able to make decisions rather than just provide input or make suggestions. Charter schools, in theory, gain the authority to decide critical school matters without asking for approval from any higher body, a very "deep" form of autonomy relative to traditional school-based management. Malen and associates (1990: 305) concluded that site-based actors "typically characterize their involvement as 'listening,' 'advising,' 'endorsing the decisions others have already made,' taking 'rubber stamp' or 'token' action." The Bryk, Hill, and Shipps study came to similar conclusions, reporting that school-level educators rarely knew even in which areas they were empowered to make decisions. In short, though attempts at "school-based management" have been commonplace in recent years, actual programs have fallen fall short of the charter school idea in both the breadth and depth of autonomy granted to school-level actors.

The story with accountability is much the same. Charter school programs envision a very meaningful form of accountability in which charter schools sign binding contracts obligating them to meet certain standards for student performance. The contracts carry a fixed duration (typically three to five years), at the end of which schools must show evidence that they have met their targets or face revocation of their charters. Outside the charter realm, "holding schools accountable for results" is clearly one of the most talked about ideas in American education today (Ladd 1996). But actual accountability plans typically lack the "teeth" that charter school programs promise.

Initiatives to impose accountability for results are most common at two levels: the state and the district. At the state level, the state board of education typically establishes standards for schools to meet, requires assessments, collects and disseminates results, and attaches some rewards and sanctions to performance. But recent studies of the implementation of these accountability programs suggest that they fall short in at least two respects. First, the standards states are setting are not always clear and rigorous. *Education Week*'s 1998 "Quality Counts" report assigns letter grades to each state on both the rigor and the clarity of its standards in math and English/language arts, creating a four-part assessment of states' standards. Of the forty-seven states that had standards, only two received an A or an A- on at least two of the four measures. All but five received a C or lower on at least one of the four (*Education Week* 1998: 80).

In addition to questions about rigor and clarity, recent studies have cast doubt on what actions states are willing to take when school performance falls short. In a typical state accountability program, low-performing schools first go on some kind of probationary status under which they are urged to improve and because of which they are provided with some assistance. After some number of years, if performance fails to improve, the state may intervene in various ways, from ordering the school's management replaced to taking over the school entirely. Some state programs—nineteen of the fifty, according to *Education Week* (1998)—stop short of imposing these ultimate "sanctions" on low-performing schools. And even where sanctions are in place, states often find it difficult to impose the consequences made possible under the accountability law. An analysis of accountability programs in fifteen southeastern and mid-Atlantic states found that in no state were more than 5 percent of schools on the state's version of "probation"; the analysis also reported no instances of school takeovers or staff replacements through 1996 (Southeastern Regional Education Board 1997).

Some districts also have created accountability plans of their own. In the most aggressive plans, school boards retain the power to order the "reconstitution" of schools that under-perform chronically, replacing a large proportion of the schools' staff with new personnel. In practice, due largely to political difficulties, districts have invoked reconstitution in only the rarest of cases (e.g., Reinhard 1997).

On the third element of charter school policy—family choice—the picture is somewhat less clear. Charter schools are schools of choice; no student is required to attend them. And the per-pupil funding attached to the student follows the child from his or her home district to the charter school. These arrangements are not particularly new to public education. Like autonomy and accountability, choice has been much talked about in education literally for centuries, with Thomas Paine and John Stuart Mill only two of the famous minds that have weighed in on the side of the family's right to choose. Currently, a wide variety of choice plans are in force throughout the country, including magnet schools, inter-district choice transfer programs, and "voucher" or "scholarship" programs.

To see what sets charter schools apart, it helps to array these different types of choice programs along three dimensions. The first two dimensions are displayed in Figure 5.3. One is "competitive impact": the degree to which families' choices result in the movement of dollars. This dimension is important because in addition to providing options to families, one of the fundamental purposes of a school choice initiative is to create competitive dynamics under which all schools have strong financial incentives

FIGURE 5.3   Differences Between Forms of School Choice

		Adherence to public school values	
		Low	*High*
	Low	Magnet programs	
Competitive Impact			
	High	Voucher programs	Charter programs
			Inter-district choice

to improve. This dimension sets magnet schools apart from the other three forms of choice. Since magnets are part of existing school districts, families' choices to attend them do not necessarily result in a loss of funds by other schools. A second dimension is "adherence to public school values": the degree to which schools involved in the choice program are required to follow certain core public school values, like not charging tuition, not engaging in selective admissions, and not teaching religion. This dimension sets charter and inter-district choice programs apart from most voucher and magnet programs. At least in theory, schools involved in voucher programs may charge tuition, admit students selectively, and teach religion. Though magnet schools are tuition-free and non-religious, they often impose admissions standards on students. Charter school and inter-district choice programs score "high" on both dimensions, since money follows children to schools that are "public" in all the respects noted.

The third dimension, not pictured in Figure 5.3, is "sources of school supply": Who can step forward and offer "public" education to families? This dimension sets charter school programs and voucher plans, which allow private individuals and organizations to supply schooling, apart from magnet and inter-district choice programs, under which school districts remain the only providers of public education. Together, the three dimensions make it clear that charter school programs are an innovation in "choice" as well as in autonomy and accountability. Alone among choice initiatives, charter school programs allow a range of eligible suppliers (public and private) to compete for students and dollars while adhering to basic public school values regarding access and church-state separation.

Charter School Programs as Producers of Innovative Practice

In addition to being an innovative way of regulating schools and school systems, charter school programs also are said to be "innovative" in a second respect: They are supposed to foster innovative practices at the school level. The nation's first charter school law, enacted by Minnesota, listed encouraging the use of "innovative teaching methods" among the six purposes of the statute, and most other charter laws have followed suit. But it is also possible to imagine other kinds of school-level innovations charter schools might undertake as they search for new ways to involve parents, govern themselves, find staff, contract for services, assess students' work, and so on.

But will they do so? In thinking about this question, it is helpful to realize that "innovative" is a special case of "different." First and foremost, charter policies provide charter schools with the authority and the incentive to be different. Doing something differently is what allows charter schools to convince families to give up the schools they know well in favor of an upstart school. Whether this something "different" is "innovative" depends on the circumstances in which a school finds itself. Three factors would appear most important. First, do charter schools have the *authority* to be innovative? Second, do charter school operators have the *means* to be innovative?[3] Third, do the *dynamics of the marketplace* support innovative practice? More precisely, is there a demand in the community for innovative practice?

In short, charter school programs have the *potential* to produce innovative practices, but only the potential. By their very nature, charter policies leave decisions about practice up to charter operators, and these decisions ultimately determine how innovative any one charter school or the charter sector as a whole will be. Whether charter school programs are innovation-producing, then, is an empirical question.

In fact, whether charter school programs are innovative policies, in the sense discussed earlier, is also an empirical question. The discussion of the charter school idea's distinctiveness so far has centered on an "ideal" charter program, of the sort envisioned by charter proponents. But before a charter program can begin, it must be enacted by a state legislature. And that state legislature may well modify this "ideal" charter program, perhaps beyond recognition (Hassel 1999). For this reason, any assessment of the innovativeness of charter school programs must not stop with the theory of charter schools. An analysis of actual charter school laws is in order.

How Innovative Are Real Charter School Policies?

An analysis of the thirty charter laws on the books at the end of 1997 (twenty-nine states and the District of Columbia) suggests a very mixed picture in each of the three dimensions of innovativeness described in the previous section: autonomy, accountability, and choice/competition. Table 5.1 displays an overview of autonomy-related provisions in these thirty charter laws. One aspect of autonomy concerns whether charter schools can be legally independent entities. Seventeen of the thirty laws allow charter schools to be legally independent of their local school districts. A second dimension of autonomy is the degree to which charter schools gain exemptions from state and district laws and policies. In only fourteen of the thirty states do charter schools receive broad, automatic waivers of laws and regulations. In the remaining sixteen, the exemptions they receive are either severely limited, or they must request waivers on a case-by-case basis. A final dimension of autonomy relates less to the formal independence of charter schools than to what we might call their "political independence." If local school boards can veto any charter application arising in their districts without appeal, they are in a position to exert control over charter schools in their jurisdictions, *even if the schools have legal independence and broad automatic waivers.* The fourth column of Table 5.1 illustrates that sixteen of the thirty laws deny local boards the power to veto charter applications, but fourteen grant them this power.

If one examines these three provisions together, the mixed nature of charter laws becomes clear: Seven of the laws contain none of the autonomy-enhancing provisions; seven contain all three; seventeen contain two or more; thirteen two or less. Charter schools in different states are operating under significantly different conditions, with some enjoying the sort of autonomy envisioned in the charter ideal and others experiencing far less latitude.

In the simple framework of Table 5.1, Arizona receives high marks on all three dimensions of autonomy. But even among the high-autonomy states, Arizona stands apart, in three respects. First, charter schools in Arizona not only are legally independent entities but also enjoy a great deal of financial independence because they are directly funded by the state. In some other states where charter schools are legally independent, their reliance on local school districts for funding creates a financial dependence that can compromise their autonomy.

Second, charter applicants in Arizona have many more potential authorizers to choose from than other states. Charter schools in Arizona can approach not only the state board of education, as in many other states, but also a specially created charter school board and, interestingly, the local school board of any other school district in the state, no matter how far away.

Third, almost all state charter laws limit schools' initial charters to three to five years; Arizona allows fifteen-year terms, a distinction shared only by the District of Columbia. With the need for charter renewal that far in the future, charter schools enjoy a measure of autonomy unusual elsewhere.

Statutory analysis is less enlightening when it comes to provisions related to the accountability of charter schools, the second issue on which charter school programs appear innovative on paper. All charter school laws say charter schools will be held accountable for results, that their overseers have the authority to shut them down if they fail to meet agreed upon criteria for performance. But as in the case of conventional public school accountability, the real question surrounding charter school accountability is the degree to which actual charter school authorizers will invoke this authority, and under what circumstances. As of this writing, it is too early to tell. The vast number of charter schools have not reached the end of their three-to-five year charter periods, and thus most have not faced the "moment of truth" implied by their charters. As of

TABLE 5.1   Autonomy-Related Provisions of Charter Laws in Twenty-Nine States and the District of Columbia

	Legal Independence Possible	Broad, Automatic Waivers of Laws and Regulations	No Veto Possible by Local School Board	Number of Provisions Included
Alaska				0
Arizona	◆	◆	◆	3
Arkansas				0
California	◆		◆	2
Colorado	◆		◆	2
Connecticut	◆		◆	2
Delaware	◆	◆	◆	3
District of Columbia	◆	◆	◆	3
Florida	◆	◆		2
Georgia				0
Hawaii		◆		1
Illinois	◆	◆		2
Kansas				0
Louisiana		◆		1
Massachusetts	◆		◆	2
Michigan	◆		◆	2
Minnesota	◆	◆	◆	3
Mississippi				0
Nevada		◆		1
New Hampshire	◆	◆		2
New Jersey	◆		◆	2
New Mexico			◆	1
North Carolina	◆	◆	◆	3
Ohio	◆	◆	◆	3
Pennsylvania	◆			1
Rhode Island			◆	1
South Carolina		◆	◆	2
Texas	◆	◆	◆	3
Wisconsin[a]				0
Wyoming				0
Number of laws with provision	17 of 30	14 of 30	16 of 30	

[a] Amendments to Wisconsin's law in 1997 create alternate charter authorizers, but only in the city of Milwaukee. Because of the limited geographic area covered by this provision, this table still codes Wisconsin's law as allowing local veto.

September 1997, four charters had been revoked prematurely, two because of financial mismanagement and two because of violations of provisions of their charters. According to a national survey, at least twenty-nine schools had come up for renewal by September 1997; all twenty-nine charters had been renewed (RPP International 1998: 11–13).

Because of the limited track record in this area, it is possible to look only at the systems that charter authorizers have put into place so far to hold charter schools accountable. In general, analysts of these systems have found them wanting. Though some states have made progress in defining target outcomes, devising means of measuring schools' performance relative to these targets, and establishing procedures for reviewing data and making decisions, most have not. The Hudson Institute's nationwide study of charter schools concluded that "today's charter school accountability systems remain underdeveloped, often clumsy and ill-fitting, and are themselves beset by dilemmas" (Manno et al. 1997). Authorizers are struggling with how charter schools should fit into existing state and district standards and testing regimes; with how to handle accountability for charter schools with unconventional goals, learning processes, or student populations; with how precisely to implement the "meet your goals or lose your charter" requirement; with the basic question: How good is good enough? As authorizers begin to make decisions about how to address these issues, it will be possible to assess whether charter school programs in practice are innovative in the realm of accountability, but at this point the jury is still out.

Arizona again stands apart when it comes to accountability. With fifteen-year charters in hand, charter schools come up for renewal in Arizona less frequently than they do in other states. And with so many separate charter authorizers in the state, there is no one central point of oversight of charter schools. Controversy rages in Arizona (and nationally) about whether these aspects of Arizona's charter law will undermine accountability (Todd 1998). Charter authorizers there, however, have proven willing to step in and close schools in advance of their renewal dates, usually because of financial mismanagement (Matthews 1998: A7–8).

Finally, how innovative are actual charter school programs when it comes to introducing choice and competition into the public education system? Table 5.2, displaying information about three choice- and competition-related aspects of charter school laws, presents a mixed picture similar to that in Table 5.1. The first aspect, identical to the third in Table 5.1, is whether local school boards can veto local charter applications. If they can, the prospects for choice and competition are obviously limited, since control over the very opening of a charter school rests in the hands of the charter school's would-be competitor. Only sixteen of the thirty charter school laws deny local school boards this power.

A second aspect of choice and competition concerns restrictions on the supply of charter schools. Some state laws allow a relatively wide range of individuals and organizations to start charter schools and enable a relatively large number of charter schools to start. Those that do both receive a mark in the third column of Table 5.2. Other states either limit the range of possible starter-schools (typically to existing public schools that

TABLE 5.2 Choice- and Competition-Related Provisions of Charter Laws in Twenty-Nine States and the District of Columbia

	No Veto Possible by Local School Board	Limited Restrictions on Source/ Number of Schools	Full Per-Pupil Operating Funds Follow Children	Number of Provisions Included
Alaska				0
Arizona	◆	◆	◆	3
Arkansas				0
California	◆	◆		2
Colorado	◆	◆		2
Connecticut	◆		◆	2
Delaware	◆		◆	2
District of Columbia	◆	◆	◆	3
Florida		◆		1
Georgia				0
Hawaii			◆	1
Illinois			◆	1
Kansas				0
Louisiana			◆	1
Massachusetts	◆			1
Michigan	◆	◆	◆	3
Minnesota	◆	◆	◆	3
Mississippi				0
Nevada			◆	1
New Hampshire		◆		1
New Jersey	◆	◆		2
New Mexico	◆			1
North Carolina	◆	◆	◆	3
Ohio	◆		◆	2
Pennsylvania		◆		1
Rhode Island	◆		◆	2
South Carolina	◆	◆	◆	3
Texas	◆	◆	◆	3
Wisconsin[a]				0
Wyoming		◆		1
Number of laws with provision	16 of 30	12 of 30	17 of 30	

[a] Amendments to Wisconsin's law in 1997 create alternate charter authorizers, but only in the city of Milwaukee. Because of the limited geographic area covered by this provision, this table still codes Wisconsin's law as allowing local veto.

want to convert) or place caps on the number of charter schools that can open within a state or district. As Table 5.2 shows, only twelve of the thirty laws allow a relatively open supply of charter schools along these lines.

The final aspect is whether full per-pupil funding follows children from traditional public schools to the charter schools they choose. Table 5.2 illustrates that seventeen of the thirty charter laws require full per-pupil operating dollars to follow children. The other thirteen either leave funding amounts up to local school districts, provide for less than 100 percent of full operating funding, or reimburse school districts for lost funds.

Taking all three choice and competition provisions together, seven charter laws include all three provisions, whereas six laws have none; fourteen have two or more; sixteen have two or less. As with autonomy, the picture is quite mixed. In some states, charter schools represent an innovative introduction of choice and competition; in other states they do not.

Once again, Arizona's charter law is among the most robust in the amount of choice and competition it introduces. First, as noted above, Arizona's law not only denies veto power to local boards but also gives applicants access to multiple potential authorizers. For local boards in Arizona, saying "no" to a charter application does little to deter the applicants from receiving a charter. Second, Arizona's law is among the nation's most open on the supply side. Though the two statewide charter authorizers face annual limits on the number of charter schools they may authorize, these limits are high; and there is no limit on the number of charter schools local boards may authorize. In addition, virtually anyone may apply for a charter in Arizona. Unlike every other charter law, the state's law even allows for-profit companies to apply for charters without the intermediation of nonprofit community-based organizations. As evidenced by the fact that Arizona now hosts a quarter of the nation's charter schools, Arizona's law indeed fosters the kind of competitive-sector charter advocates envision.

In summary, although charter school policies are a significant innovation on paper, the degree to which actual charter school laws depart from the status quo varies greatly from state to state. In some jurisdictions, like Arizona and the District of Columbia, charter school laws look like a dramatic departure from business as usual. In other states, like Alaska and Kansas, charter school laws contain little that is innovative. And in virtually all states, the degree to which charter school programs will represent innovations in the area of accountability for performance remains to be seen.

How Innovative Are Real Charter Schools?

Ideally, a study of the innovativeness of actual charter schools would rest on an empirical assessment of practice in charter schools, comparing it to prevailing norms in conventional institutions. At this point, we have only fragmentary information on this topic, mostly from comprehensive state-mandated evaluations of charter school programs. Five of these studies—in California, Colorado, Massachusetts, Minnesota, and Texas—examine the extent of innovation in charter schools, with some interesting findings. Most of the "innovation" reported by charter schools appears to represent not path-breaking new ideas, but implementation of well-known if not widely implemented ideas, such as thematic instruction, team teaching, unconventional ways of grouping students, the use of individualized learning plans for all students, year-round calendars, and interesting uses of technology (Center for Applied Research and Educational Improvement 1996; SRI International 1997; Clayton Foundation 1997; Taebel et al. 1997). In a few respects, though, charter schools did appear to be significantly different from most traditional public schools. Almost 30 percent of California charter schools reported an emphasis on home-based learning, with parents serving as students' primary instructors. Fifteen of the sixteen schools in the Texas study were using curricular materials other than those approved for use in conventional Texas public schools. And charter schools everywhere are distinguished primarily by their small size. Around six in ten charter schools in 1995–1996 enrolled fewer than 200 students, compared to one in six conventional public schools (RPP International and University of Minnesota 1997: 3–4).

The Massachusetts study is unique in that it focuses explicitly on the question: What is innovative about charter schools in Massachusetts? Accordingly, this study bears closer attention. Several interesting findings emerge. First, the authors find many examples of what they call "retrovations": practices that are quite distinct from today's prevailing educational approaches, but that may have been very common at some time in the past. Charter schools in Massachusetts are proving themselves *different* from other public schools, but not necessarily because they are adopting radically new practices. Second, what set charter schools most clearly apart from conventional public schools was not so much the specific classroom and management practices they adopted, but the fact that the charter schools' practices appeared linked together in comprehensive "innovation systems" focused on a coherent mission. Members of charter staffs and their broader constituencies seemed highly committed to these missions, creating a strong sense of community at schools. By contrast, the study's authors found that innovative practices were common in district schools as well, but that these practices appeared to be added on to existing programs rather than part of comprehensive overhauls of school operations. Finally, the last point not withstanding, the Massachusetts study did find a number of specific innovations to be more prevalent in charter than in district schools. These included: extended day programs, performance-based compensation, parent contracts, and individual learning plans for all students (Rosenblum Brigham Associates 1998).

Even without more detailed national information in hand, it is still possible to investigate the presence or absence of the three conditions sketched in a previous section: the *authority* charter schools have to innovate, the *means* or resources available to support innovation, and the *demand* for innovation in the marketplace. Evidence on these factors comes from the author's study of charter school programs across the United States; the study drew upon more than fifty interviews with knowledgeable individuals in four case-study states, as well as upon a review of relevant documents and media reports (Hassel 1999).

Authority to Innovate

Do charter schools in the United States have the authority to pursue innovative practices? As the previous section indicates, the answer varies from state to state. Many state charter school laws have severely restricted the authority of charter schools to innovate, or at least to do so without the approval of higher political bodies such as local or state boards of education. But what about the states in which charter school laws appear to grant the schools a great deal of authority to do things differently?

The author's study of three such states (Colorado, Massachusetts, and Michigan) led to two conclusions about charter schools' actual authority to innovate in these states. First, all charter schools interviewed for the study report wide latitude on almost all critical areas of school management, and especially on matters of curriculum and instruction. School officials say that they are free to follow their own courses when it comes to setting most school policies, and that they do not have to seek higher approval. The one exception is Colorado, where schools do have to request exemptions on a case-by-case basis from state law and regulation from the state board of education. But Colorado schools interviewed reported no instances in which they sought and were denied exemptions.

Second, however, the study found that the latitude reported by charter schools was highly dependent on the political orientation of the agencies charged with overseeing charter schools. Because officials heading these agencies favored autonomy for charter schools, the schools indeed enjoyed autonomy. For example, most of Michigan's charter schools are overseen by Central Michigan University, whose board is appointed by the governor, who in turn is one of charter schools' strongest advocates in the state. Massachusetts's charter schools were overseen (during the time of the study) by an appointee of that state's governor, also a staunch supporter of wide latitude for charter schools. And Colorado's elected school board happened to include a majority favoring autonomy for charter schools, greasing the skids for requests for exemptions. If the political stars had not been lined up in these ways, charter schools in these states might have reported a much different experience (and might do so in the future as circumstances change). For a more extensive discussion of this issue, see Hassel (1999: chapter 5).

Arizona's charter school law empowers two statewide entities to issue charters: the Arizona State Board of Education and the State Board for Charter Schools. Since these boards provide a non-local route for prospective charter schools, they make it possible for charter schools to depart markedly from district-based practices. But as in the other states examined above, these boards' openness to such departures depends upon their political orientations. The Arizona State Board of Education includes eight members appointed by the governor and a ninth ex officio member, the elected state superintendent of schools. The State Board for Charter Schools includes twelve members: the state superintendent, three members of the legislature jointly appointed by the president of the senate and the speaker of the house, and eight members appointed by the governor. With a Republican governor, a Republican superintendent of schools, a 38–22 Republican majority in the state house and an 18–12 Republican majority in the state senate in 1998, both boards are thus fully appointed by Republican political leaders. Since Republicans have generally supported more autonomy for charter schools, the current political situation in Arizona provides schools with quite a bit of authority to innovate. As this section shows, charter schools in at least some states have won the authority to innovate. But that victory is fragile, subject to the whims of politics.

Means or Resources to Innovate

Having the authority to innovate is the first prerequisite for innovation. But because doing things in a novel way is hard work and requires the dedication of substantial time and other resources, possessing the authority to innovate is not enough. As countless studies have documented, doing things in thoroughly novel ways is difficult, time-consuming, and often expensive (see, for example, essays in Altshuler and Behn 1997).

The author's study suggests that charter schools face some serious challenges in this regard: the funding challenge and the leadership challenge. The funding challenge arises because, by and large, charter schools are receiving a less-than-per-pupil share of resources in their states. This predicament arises from three factors:

1. *Start-up costs:* As a general rule, states do not provide funding for the start-up of charter schools. Per-pupil operating dollars begin to flow only upon the opening of the school (and, in some cases, after the opening of the school). Though a U.S. Department of

Education grant program has helped close the gap, most charter schools do not receive the $1,000 or so per pupil experts estimate they need to cover the costs of opening.

2. *Facilities costs:* Most states do not provide charter schools with any special funding for facilities (or, for that matter, with facilities). As a result, charter schools find themselves making lease or mortgage payments out of their regular operating funds.

3. *Disadvantageous funding formulas:* Even for ongoing operating costs, charter schools often receive something less than the per-pupil expenditures in their districts. In Colorado, for example, charter schools must negotiate funding levels with their local school districts. Although districts may not offer less than 80 percent of per-pupil operating revenues (PPOR), PPOR amounts to just a fraction of the total expenses of local school districts. In fact, a Colorado Department of Education document indicates that 80 percent of PPOR equals just 52 percent of overall per-pupil spending (Pendley 1995).

Financial records of charter schools confirm that they face a constrained fiscal situation. In Michigan, where the most complete financial information is available, per-pupil state revenues fell short of per-pupil costs by more than $500 during the 1995–1996 school year. By raising non-state funds, most charter schools were able to cover their costs. But without access to those alternative sources, fully fifteen of the twenty-four schools upon which complete data is available would have been insolvent in that school year (Michigan Department of Education 1996).

In a larger-scale survey, in which almost all charter schools in the country were polled, RPP International and the University of Minnesota (1997: 7) found that resource issues topped charter schools' list of concerns. When asked to rate the importance of a list of potential barriers to developing and implementing their schools, charter operators listed "lack of start-up funds" first (59 percent), "inadequate operating funds" third (37 percent), and "inadequate facilities" fourth (35 percent).

In addition to these financial challenges, charter schools also face a leadership challenge that impinges on their ability to innovate. It is by now a cliché in discussions of charter schools to note that charter schools are "like small businesses": that it is not enough for operators to have a compelling educational vision, they must also have a degree of business and financial acumen in order to succeed (e.g., Nathan 1996; Finn et al. 1996). Typically, discussions of the importance of the "business side" of charter schools focus on the threats these issues pose to charter schools' very survival. Indeed, as noted above, the few charter schools that have been forced to close have done so not because of educational failure, but because of financial mismanagement or malfeasance.

But the importance of business management in charter schools also has implications for their ability to innovate. In interviews with charter schools for the author's study, charter officials uniformly reported that an inordinate amount of school leaders' attention was focused on administrative matters—meeting payroll, making sure buses ran on time, fulfilling reporting requirements, managing contracts, overseeing the hiring of employees, maintaining facilities, and the like. In the flurry of activity surrounding the start-up and early life of a new enterprise, charter operators reported little time to think about the educational direction the school was taking. This small-sample result received some confirmation in the larger RPP International and the University of Minnesota study (1997: 7), in which charter school operators ranked "lack of planning time" second (after only "lack of start-up funds") among barriers to developing and implementing their schools. With the demands placed upon them to pilot a small enterprise through the early stages of life, charter leaders are likely to have trouble devoting attention to innovation.

In Arizona, four factors have mitigated some of these resource-based problems for charter schools. First, in passing its initial charter legislation, Arizona's legislature established a "stimulus fund" to provide start-up dollars for charter schools. In conjunction with federal grant funding for charter start-up, Arizona's stimulus fund creates one of the most advantageous start-up environments in the country for charter schools. Second, charter schools in Arizona receive one third of their annual operating funds up front, further smoothing the early days of operation (Flake 1998). Third, charter schools receive per-pupil facilities funding that is generous by national standards, amounting to around $1,000 per student per year. In many states, by contrast, charter schools receive none. Finally, Arizona has hosted the explosive growth of a company called Arizona Benefit Solutions (now ABS Services). This organization provides a variety of back-office services to some 50 percent of Arizona charter schools, helping them achieve economies of scale and freeing up school leaders to focus on curriculum and instruction. Working against these factors, though, is the fact that Arizona's per-pupil funding is among the lowest in the nation, amounting to just 79 percent of the national average in 1995–1996 (National Center for Education Statistics 1998: Table 35).

Demand for Innovation

Since charter schools receive their funding on a per-pupil basis, they must attract families in order to prosper. Attracting families means shaping the school's offerings, at least to some degree, to the wishes of parents or other family members who make educational decisions. The programs offered by charter schools, then, will reflect the preferences of the "market" the schools are seeking to attract. Only if enough parents are looking for schools engaging in innovation will charter schools be sites of significant path-breaking activity.

Recent public opinion surveys have made clear that, in general, parents of American students are wary of many of the innovations currently promoted for use in schools. Public Agenda's *First Things First* report, for example, found overwhelming majorities uncomfortable with even relatively mild innovations currently popular in reform circles (Public Agenda 1994). Results like this suggest that charter school operators offering even more radical innovations than the ones discussed will not find many takers in the American marketplace.

Of course, even if the great majority of parents favor a relatively traditional approach to education, a charter school does not need to attract the great majority of parents to make its operation a success. The school can appeal to a market "niche," a group of parents favoring more innovative approaches than the mass of parents would tolerate. If the school can attract enough such parents, the fact that few others would even consider the school is not a problem.

Although appropriate for individual schools, this "niche" approach pervasively applied would undermine the ability of the charter school movement to achieve its hoped-for impact. For one thing, the overall potential for growth in charter schools would be limited to the small proportion of families seeking educational boutiques. In addition, school districts might well view the exodus of innovation-seeking parents as a positive development. Rather than work harder to retain them, districts might breathe a sigh of relief as perennial troublemakers exited (Hirschman 1970: 59–60). The potential for charter schools to serve as meaningful competitors with the mainstream educational system would be lost. It seems more likely to expect many charter schools, though not all, to engage in fairly uninnovative practices. In doing so, they enhance their financial viability by appealing to a larger swathe of the market.

One possibility worth considering is that market dynamics may encourage most charter schools to be innovative in selected ways while remaining more traditional in others. Parents may care deeply about what their students are learning, how they are being taught, and how they are being tested. If parents as a whole are the traditionalists they appear to be in public opinion research, market-driven schools may well respond by offering fairly traditional curricula, instructional techniques, and assessment practices. But parents may care less deeply, or have less traditional views, about other aspects of schooling, such as practices of management and governance. If so, we might expect charter schools to do most of their innovating in these domains rather than in the classroom.

Conclusion: Directions for Research

Further research on charter school programs is needed to probe the reform's innovative potential. On the question of charter school programs' innovativeness as a *policy*, several questions appear paramount. First, to explore how much autonomy charter schools enjoy under various state charter laws, scholars need to look beyond broad statutory language to examine the precise areas in which charter schools do and do not enjoy autonomy over their affairs. Although this chapter has taken that step for three states, this analysis is far from the representative sample that would be needed to draw firm conclusions about the autonomy charter schools enjoy. Second, much more research is needed to understand the ways in which charter schools are (or are not) being held accountable for results by their overseers. Most of the information available on this subject is anecdotal rather than systematic. Finally, further research could illuminate the degree to which charter schools are serving as meaningful competitors to existing school districts. Rofes's (1998) pioneering report and the research reported in this volume on charter schools' competitive effects have begun this process, but more work will be needed to determine how districts are or are not responding to the presence of charter schools and charter school laws.

On the question of the innovativeness of charter schools in *practice*, a useful line of research would be one that probed school-level practice for evidence of innovativeness, asking: How are charter schools using the autonomy they have? What are they doing that they otherwise would not be able to do? Are certain types of innovation (like changes in governance and management structures) more common than others (like changes in educational practice)? Only a detailed examination of actual school practice could answer these questions.

The charter school experience to date highlights many of the difficulties involved with innovating in government: the politics that threaten to water down innovations as they move toward approval in legislatures; the continuation of politics beyond the legislative phase as programs are put into place; the challenges of conducting path-breaking experiments when financial and human resources are limited; the complications introduced when an organization's "customers" may not favor innovative practice. Although the course charter school programs take in the face of these issues remains to be seen, this reform promises to provide interesting new information about innovation as it moves ahead.

Notes

The author wishes to thank Alan Altshuler, Bill Parent, Eric Rofes, and the editors of this volume for their helpful comments on this paper. Several funders made possible the research reported here: Harvard's Program of Innovations in American Government, the Taubman Center on State and Local Government and Program Education Policy and Governance, and the Aspen Institute's Nonprofit Sector Research Fund.

1. Here are a few key references for each of these policy areas: (1) Choice: Early treatments from a variety of ideological perspectives include Friedman (1962: chapter 6); Levin (1968); Fantini (1973); Coons and Sugarman (1978). More recently book-length arguments for (Chubb and Moe 1990) and against (Henig 1994; Cookson 1994) wide-reaching school choice have emerged along with several edited volumes or articles from differing viewpoints (Clune and Witte 1990a, 1990b; Rasell and Rothstein 1993; Cookson 1992; Fuller, Elmore, and Orfield 1996; Peterson and Hassel 1998). (2) Monopoly: Most writing about the school-system monopoly appears in this choice literature. See also Peterson (1990) and Hill (1995). (3) School-based management: For an overview of the research, see Malen, Ogawa, and Kranz (1990). (4) Deregulation: See Fuhrman and Elmore 1995. (5) Accountability for results: see Ladd (1996).

2. For a detailed discussion of partisan alignment regarding charter schools, see Hassel (1999: chapter 2).

3. Some would argue that the precise opposite is true: that innovation is more likely to come about when resources are scarce and innovation is necessary for survival. An extensive literature on the subject is summarized in Kanter (1988: 181–183).

References

Altshuler, Alan A., and Robert D. Behn. 1997. *Innovation in American Government: Challenges, Opportunities, and Dilemmas.* Washington, D.C.: Brookings Institution.

Archer, Jeff. 1997. "States Struggle to Ensure Data Make the Grade." *Education Week,* 15 January.

Bryk, Anthony S., Paul Hill, Dorothy Shipps et al. 1998. *Decentralization in Practice: Toward a System of Schools.* Chicago: The Consortium on Chicago School Research and The Institute for Public Policy and Management.

Budde, Ray. 1988. *Education by Charter: Restructuring School Districts.* Andover, Mass.: Regional Laboratory for Educational Improvement of the Northeast and the Islands.

Center for Applied Research and Educational Improvement. 1996. *Minnesota Charter Schools Evaluation: Interim Report.* Minneapolis, Minn.: CAREI.

Center for Education Reform. 1998. "Charter School Highlights and Statistics." September 1, URL: http://www.edreform.com/pubs/chglance.htm.

Chubb, John E., and Terry M. Moe. 1990. *Politics, Markets, and America's Schools.* Washington, D.C.: Brookings Institution.

Clayton Foundation. 1997. *1997 Colorado Charter Schools Evaluation Study: The Characteristics, Status, and Student Achievement Data of Colorado Charter Schools.* Denver: Colorado Department of Education.

Clune, William H., and John F. Witte. 1990a. *The Theory of Choice and Control in Education.* Vol. 1 of *Choice and Control in American Education.* London: Falmer.

_____. 1990b. *The Practice of Choice, Decentralization and School Restructuring.* Vol. 2 of *Choice and Control in American Education.* London: Falmer.

Cookson, Peter W., Jr. 1994. *School Choice: The Struggle for the Soul of American Education.* New Haven: Yale.

_____, ed. 1992. *The Choice Controversy.* Newbury Park, Calif.: Corwin.

Coons, John E., and Stephen D. Sugarman. 1978. *Education by Choice: The Case for Family Control.* Berkeley: University of California Press.

Education Week. 1998. *Quality Counts: The Urban Challenge. Public Education in the 50 States.* Washington, D.C.: Editorial Projects in Education.

Fantini, Mario D. 1973. *Public Schools of Choice.* New York: Simon and Schuster.

Fine, Michelle, ed. 1994. *Chartering Urban School Reform: Reflections on Public High Schools in the Midst of Change.* New York: Teachers College Press.

Finn, Chester E., Jr., Bruno V. Manno, and Louann Bierlein. 1996. *Charter Schools in Action: What Have We Learned?* Washington, D.C.: Hudson Institute.

Flake, Jeff. 1998. "Reform, Yes. Regulate, No." *The Tribune Newspaper* (Mesa, Ariz.), 30 August.

Friedman, Milton. 1962. *Capitalism and Freedom.* Chicago: University of Chicago Press.

Fuhrman, Susan H., and Richard F. Elmore. 1995. *Ruling Out Rules: The Evolution of Deregulation in State Education Policy.* New Brunswick, N.J.: Consortium for Policy Research in Education.

Fuller, Bruce, Richard Elmore, and Gary Orfield, eds. 1996. *Who Chooses? Who Loses? Culture, Institutions, and the Unequal Effects of School Choice.* New York: Teachers College Press.

Hassel, Bryan C. 1999. *The Charter School Challenge: Avoiding the Pitfalls, Fulfilling the Promise.* Washington, D.C.: Brookings Institution.

Henig, Jeffrey R. 1994. *Rethinking School Choice: Limits of the Market Metaphor.* Princeton: Princeton University Press.

Hill, Paul. 1995. *Reinventing Education.* Santa Monica, Calif.: The RAND Corporation.

Hirschman, Albert O. 1970. *Exit, Voice, and Loyalty: Responses to Decline in Firms, Organizations, and States.* Cambridge, Mass.: Harvard University Press.

Kanter, Rosabeth Moss. 1988. "When a Thousand Flowers Bloom: Structural, Collective, and Social Conditions for Innovation in Organizations." *Organizational Behavior* 10: 169–211.

Kolderie, Ted. 1990. *Beyond Choice to New Public Schools: Withdrawing the Exclusive Franchise in Public Education.* Washington, D.C.: Progressive Policy Institute.

_____. 1993. "The States Begin to Withdraw the Exclusive." Saint Paul, Minn.: Center for Policy Studies, Public Services Redesign Project.

Ladd, Helen F., ed. 1996. *Holding Schools Accountable: Performance-Based Reform in Education.* Washington, D.C.: Brookings Institution.

Levin, Henry M. 1968. "The Failure of the Public School and the Free Market Remedy." *Urban Review* 2 (7): 32–37.

Malen, Betty, Rodney T. Ogawa, and Jennifer Kranz. 1990. "What Do We Know About School-Based Management? A Case Study of the Literature—A Call for Research." In *The Practice of Choice, Decentralization and School Restructuring.* Vol. 2 of *Choice and Control in American Education,* eds. William H. Clune and John F. Witte. London: Falmer.

Manno, Bruno, Chester E. Finn Jr., Louann Bierlein, and Gregg Vanourek. 1997. *Charter School Accountability: Problems and Prospects.* Washington, D.C.: The Hudson Institute.

Matthews, Paul. 1998. "Spotlight on 6 Schools That Went Dark." *Tribune Newspaper* (Mesa, Ariz.), 23 August.

Michigan Department of Education. 1996. *A Description of Michigan Public School Academies. 1995–96 Report to the House and Senate Committees in Education.* Lansing, Mich.: Department of Education.

Mintrom, Michael, and Sandra Vergari. 1997. "Why Policy Innovations Change As They Diffuse: Analyzing Recent Charter School Laws." Paper read at Annual Meeting of the Midwest Political Science Association, Chicago, Ill., 10 April.

Nathan, Joe. 1996. *Charter Schools: Creating Hope and Opportunity for American Education.* San Francisco: Jossey-Bass.

National Center for Educational Statistics. 1998. *State Comparisons of Education Statistics: 1969–70 to 1996–97.* Washington, D.C.: National Center for Educational Statistics.

Pendley, Byron. 1995. "State Average Per-Pupil Spending." Memorandum to Bill Windler, 22 August.

Peterson, Paul. 1990. "Monopoly and Competition in American Education." In *The Theory of Choice and Control in Education.* Vol. 1 of *Choice and Control in American Education,* eds. William C. Clune and John F. Witte. London: Falmer.

Peterson, Paul, and Bryan Hassel, eds. 1998. *Learning from School Choice.* Washington, D.C.: Brookings Institution.

Public Agenda. 1994. "Education Reform Movement in Jeopardy, Public's Priorities Not in Sync with Leadership's." May 20, 1999, URL: http://www.publicagenda.com/aboutpa/aboutpa3e.htm.

Rasell, Edith, and Richard Rothstein, eds. 1993. *School Choice: Examining the Evidence.* Washington, D.C.: Economic Policy Institute.

Reinhard, Beth. 1997. "S.F. Mulls Retreat from 'Reconstituting' Schools." *Education Week on the Web,* May 28. May 20, 1999, URL: http://www.edweek.org/ew/vol-16/35sf.h16.

Rofes, Eric. 1998. *How Are School Districts Responding to Charter Laws and Charter Schools?* Berkeley: Policy Analysis for California Education, University of California at Berkeley.

Rosenblum Brigham Associates. 1998. *Innovation and Massachusetts Charter Schools.* Boston: Massachusetts Department of Education.

RPP International. 1998. *A National Study of Charter Schools: Second Year Report.* Washington, D.C.: U.S. Department of Education.

RPP International and the University of Minnesota. 1997. *A Study of Charter Schools.* Washington, D.C.: U.S. Department of Education.

Southern Regional Education Board. 1997. *Accountability in the 1990's: Holding Schools Responsible for Student Achievement*. Atlanta: SREB.

SRI International. 1997. *Evaluation of Charter School Effectiveness*. Sacramento, Calif.: Office of the Legislative Analyst.

Taebel, Delbert, Edith J. Barret, Christine T. Brenner, et al. 1997. *Texas Open-Enrollment Charter Schools: Year One Evaluation*. Austin: Texas State Board of Education.

Todd, Cece. 1998. "Guinea Kids: Arizona's Charter School Experiment." *Tribune Newspaper* (Mesa, Ariz.), 23 August.

Todd, Cece, and Kirk Mitchell. 1998. "High Price for Haste: State's Rush for Charters Invites Abuse." *Tribune Newspaper* (Mesa, Ariz.), 23 August.

Wohlstetter, Priscilla, and Lesley Anderson. 1994. "What Can U.S. Charter Schools Learn from England's Grant-Maintained Schools?" *Phi Delta Kappan*, February.

PART TWO

Social Scientists Look at Arizona Charter Schools

6

The Wild West of Education Reform: Arizona Charter Schools

ROBERT MARANTO AND APRIL GRESHAM

Since the passage of Arizona's charter school law in 1994, the state has developed by far the largest charter school sector in the nation, providing the closest existing approximation to comprehensive school choice. What follows is a brief overview of the Arizona charter school phenomenon based on data provided by the Arizona Department of Education and interviews with twenty-nine Arizona policy makers, Department of Education officials, charter school operators, district school officials, and teachers' union officials, conducted by phone and in person from November 1997 to December 1998. We also draw upon the teacher survey described in Chapter 8. We will examine the provisions in the Arizona law that led to the rapid proliferation of charter schools; where Arizona charters appear; some ways in which Arizona charter schools differ from district schools; and how charter school teachers view their schools.

As Chapters 4 and 7 detail, both nationally and in Arizona proposals to provide low-income parents with school vouchers to use at private schools have drawn most of the political fire in the school-choice debate. Yet charter schools have the potential to provide far more comprehensive choice since voucher programs are always limited to those with low income, and are usually restricted in scope as well. Nationwide, fewer than 20,000 students, all low income, took part in public and private voucher programs in 1996–1997 (Peterson 1998), about the same as the number of students in Arizona charter schools. Arizona charters operate as "stealth vouchers," providing more comprehensive school choice than would any voucher plan that has ever come near passage anywhere. At the start of

TABLE 6.1   Charters Granted in Arizona, by Year and by Board

Board	Year			
	1995	*1996*	*1997*	*1998*
State Board for Charter Schools	25	20	25	25
State Board of Education	20	24	10	6
Districts	5	20	10	29
Total granted	50	64	45	60
Total campuses	55	119	222	272
Number of students	7,500	16,000	26,000	34,000
As percent of Arizona public school students	1	2	3.3	4.4

SOURCE: Policy and Planning Staff, Arizona Dept. of Education, and the Arizona Education Association.

the 1998–1999 school year, its fourth year, Arizona's charter school law had spawned over 150 operators with 272 campuses across the state, serving 4.4 percent of Arizona's public school children, about 34,000 students (see Table 6.1). Charter schools exist in fourteen of Arizona's fifteen counties. Virtually every district school in the state is within commuting distance of a charter school. Some school districts have lost more than 10 percent of their potential enrollment to charter schools. A review of charter enrollments within district boundaries suggests that two small districts, Mayer and Queen Creek, lost over 30 percent of their students to charter competition (though Queen Creek later won some of these students back after increasing its use of phonics). The small Sedona/Oak Creek district lost more than 20 percent of enrollment to charters and subsequently had to close down one middle school.

Why So Many Charters?

The Charter Law

Both charter school supporters and opponents agree that Arizona has over 270 charter schools because the state has the nation's least restrictive charter law. As Bryan Hassel notes in Chapter 5, usually charters are granted only by district school boards, or by a single state-level charter board. In Arizona, charters can be granted by local school boards, by the Arizona State Board of Education, or by the State Board for Charter Schools. The latter is made up of gubernatorial appointees serving for staggered terms, to assure that the board would remain pro-charter even were an anti-charter governor elected. Charter applicants apply to whichever authority they think most likely to approve. If turned down they can reapply the next year. Although the two state-level chartering authorities are formally limited to twenty-five new charters annually, a member of the State Board for Charter Schools boasts that the board "is not a fuddy-duddy, do-nothing group. . . . We've done a lot of analysis looking for loopholes" to foster rapid expansion of charters. "Loopholes" in the law and its implementation include:

(1) *Allowing a charter operator to open multiple campuses under a single charter.* In the 1997–1998 school year, thirty-two operators ran multiple campuses. The three largest ran twenty, fourteen, and six campuses respectively. Four operators ran four campuses; ten had three; fifteen had two; and 106 had a single campus.

(2) *Allowing private schools, including for-profits, to open as or convert to charter status.* Eight of the seventeen operators with three or more campuses are for-profit providers. In addition, a few charter schools formerly had a religious affiliation. Many have informal ties (such as recruiting networks) with religious groups, and some rent facilities from houses of worship.

(3) *Allowing school districts to grant charters to operators outside district lines.* As of July 1997, twenty-three of the thirty-five district-sponsored charter campuses did not actually operate in the school district that granted their charters. Two low-income, mainly Native American districts, Window Rock and Ganado, helped fund their district schools by chartering and charging "administrative fees" to schools located in *other* districts. Informants believe that the districts did not oversee these schools. Under criticism, Ganado and Window Rock ceased this practice, prompting another district in need of funds, Higley, to announce that it would charter schools in other districts. Losing their original charters, most of the former Ganado and Window Rock charter holders won charters from one of the two state chartering authorities or from Higley. The Higley superintendent plans to monitor these schools and impose uniform financial reporting, but he admits that his district's main goal is earning money to prepare for rapid growth.

A Changing Movement

As Table 6.1 shows, together the various chartering authorities approved fifty charters in 1995, sixty-four in 1996, forty-five in 1997, and sixty as of December 1998, though not all of these schools opened and a few switched from district to state charter status.[1]

Observers agree that the character of new applications changed over time. The first wave of charter applications came from teachers, parents, and social workers who wanted to start their own schools. Many of them had attempted to start or expand magnet programs, without success. Informants described such operators as "missionaries" because of their dedication, or "mom and pop" operators because of their size. In some cases they went without salaries to keep their schools afloat during the difficult first year. In contrast, business operators "hung back," as one policy maker put it, to see whether charters could succeed. The policy maker suggested that, in the future, businesses might come to run most charter schools, just as HMOs came to dominate the health care industry. (The policy maker was delighted at the prospect, just as others might be horrified.) However, the relatively low per-pupil subsidies that are provided to all Arizona public schools, both charter and district, make this less likely than in states spending more on education.

Whereas district schools can pad the state per-pupil subsidy with local tax levies, as of December 1998 charter schools must rely on the per-pupil subsidy, a small state capital subsidy, and whatever additional revenue sources they can find. No one could supply uncontested statistics, but most state officials we interviewed believe that the modal charter school receives 5–15 percent less money per pupil than the modal district school, though charter schools receive more than district schools in some poor districts. Due to start-up costs (e.g., buying/renting a school building and supplies), most charters are at a financial disadvantage. District schools can offer better facilities, extra-curricular activities, and special education programs. However, as Mary Hartley notes in Chapter 13, Arizona charter operators are allowed to keep their assets (such as a school building) after five years even if the school closes–a potential boon for operators. Charter operators counter that they often have to mortgage their personal property to secure loans for their schools.

Most informants expect corporate charters to rise in importance. Most notably, by the 1997–1998 school year the Sun-Ray preschool and elementary system ran twenty campuses, with plans for many more. Both supporters of district schools and of some charter schools see Sun-Ray's rapid growth as threatening. One policy maker allied with district schools did not fear the much publicized Edison Project, but had this to say about Sun-Ray:

> More troublesome to me is the Sun-Ray Charter School from Sunrise Pre-School, where they hope to keep the kids from six weeks to sixth grade and they hope to make their money from their programs. . . . I really have a problem with funding a for-profit corporation in that manner. They are not offering any innovation, and yet there are twenty of them in the state.

Despite the increased participation of businesses, the growth of the charter school sector has slowed. As Table 6.1 shows, the number of charter school campuses roughly doubled in each of the first two years of the charter law, but increased by only 22.5 percent from fall 1997 to fall 1998. The number of students attending charters increased by 113 percent from 1995 to 1996, 63 percent from 1996 to 1997, but only 31 percent from 1997 to 1998. State-level chartering authorities report fewer applications in 1998 than in the first three years of the charter school law, and both charter supporters and opponents talk openly of the possibility of market saturation in some localities. Still, the charter sector has won consistently an additional 1 percent of the district school market share each year and now has about 4.4 percent of Arizona's total public school enrollment.

As Lisa Keegan mentions in Chapter 12, the rapid growth of charter schools took everyone by surprise. The slowing of growth is less surprising. The teachers and social workers who dreamed of opening their own schools probably have already done so. Further, as is noted above, Arizona spends less on education than most states and thus has not attracted as many for-profit operators as some policy makers had hoped (and others had feared). Demand-side forces may be even more important. Parents who desperately wanted a different option for their children have already gone to charters. The 95 percent who remain in district schools are probably happy there. Further, as Chapter 8 suggests, districts losing large numbers of children to charter schools try to win those children back. Sometimes those efforts pay off, so over the long term we should not expect the movement from districts to charters to always go in one direction. Additionally, lawsuits and organizational age may make charter schools as unchanging as district schools, prompting reformers to seek still more reforms. As one teachers' union official predicted, charters might become "part of the establishment, . . . one more part of the public school monopoly that everyone rails against."

In addition to supply- and demand-side changes, some districts take steps to discourage charter schools. These steps also may contribute to a slowing of charter growth. One charter operator claimed that districts near his campuses had spread rumors to the effect that his school was about to go bankrupt, discouraging parents from enrolling their children and causing venders to demand payment up front—a serious obstacle for a new business. Many charter operators and even a few district officials complain that some school district and union officials have spread rumors accusing individual charters of insolvency, racism, or academic weakness, in order to discourage parents from sending their children to charters. Some charter operators told us that they personally encounter hostility, such as stares and name-calling from district school administrators, teachers, and even parents. In 1998, Tucson changed zoning rules to require hearings before schools of small size (meaning charters) can open.

Such reactions are understandable. Charters cause trouble. They have been known to hire away talented district school teachers. Unpredictable charter enrollments make for unpredictable district enrollments, making it difficult to staff schools adequately. In particular, district officials worry about transfer of students to and from charters. When charters close, as has happened nineteen times as of spring 1999, district schools are required to accept all displaced students within their geographic boundaries, even when those students may have had a very different (and some would claim inferior) education. As one district official lamented, "One operator sent a letter to parents one day telling the parents not to come back; his school was closed. So the next day we [the district] have thirty new kids to deal with!" Other officials tell horror stories of having to accept students from a failed charter in the spring of their senior year—and graduate them even when they are not sure the students have been adequately educated. On the other side of the coin, charter operators complain that district high schools often arbitrarily refuse to accept their graduating elementary students' credits, making it risky for parents to enroll their children. Yet as will be noted below and in Chapter 14, not all interactions between the sectors are hostile.

A Supportive Political Climate

Despite such opposition, a supportive Republican state legislature, governor, and superintendent of public instruction have protected charter schools, and specific state administrative actions have bolstered charters. As Chapter 9 details, state regulators seldom have closed schools for inadequate compliance with special education regulations and untimely paperwork, choosing instead to work with operators. Arizona schools receive state funding based on enrollment. Since parents often apply to several charter schools, operators find it difficult to predict true enrollments in early fall. However, state funding comes at the start of the school year, before schools can be sure of their actual enrollments. Although the money is necessary for charters operating on shoestring budgets, it requires an early and often inaccurate assessment of enrollment. (The state now funds district schools at this time as well.) Charter operators sometimes overestimate their enrollments—supporters believe these are honest mistakes; opponents are less sure. When some charters overestimated fall enrollments and received overpayments, the Arizona Department of Education agreed to generous repayment plans to avoid forcing schools into bankruptcy.

Another example, mentioned in Chapter 15, of administrative actions that have helped charters concerns transportation funding. One operator reimbursed parents for driving their children to school with a fraction of the state transportation subsidy, using the rest to purchase a school building. The operator boasted: "That generated $270,000 in transportation revenue, at which some of these people in Phoenix started to wake up to, 'Oh, my God, those people are entrepreneurs!' They wanted to change the law so [the] parents wrote letters and that legislature chose not to deal with it, so they changed the law the following year."

Another consequence of the clout charter schools have in the state legislature is the Arizona Education Association's minimization of open conflict with the Arizona Charter School Association. The two organizations even work together on some issues, particularly on support for increased state capital funding for all forms of public education.

Where Do Charters Appear?

In theory, charters locate where district schools fail to adequately serve all or part of the local population, or where affordable sites exist. Calculating which districts have lost the most students to charter schools is difficult, since a single charter may draw from many districts, as discussed in Chapter 8. Interviews suggest that five areas have particularly active charter school movements. In the rural Prescott Valley/Sedona region, an influx of parents and educators from outside the state—as one informant put it, "counterculture types from California"—increased the demand and supply for new education options. One Montessori school that located in Prescott after the charter law passed now has five campuses in the area. Indeed, a Prescott middle school became the only district school in rapidly growing Arizona to close because of competition from charters. In the Yuma area, the first charter schools served "at-risk" students and had good relations with the local districts. In 1997 Yuma charters began to serve mainstream populations and began to experience friction with local districts. In 1997, half of new charter applications came from Tucson, where growth was seen as demand driven. Hispanics and Native Americans who felt ill-served by district schools applied to open more than a dozen charter schools focusing on educating children from their groups.

Flagstaff Unified is thought to be the most impacted medium-sized school district in the state. The eleven charters within district limits in 1998 accounted for 7 percent of district public enrollment (with another 3 percent thought to attend charters just outside district limits). Flagstaff hosts charter schools for at-risk children, a Waldorf-based elementary school, a performing arts school located in the Museum of Northern Arizona, an International Baccalaureate school, and several Montessoris (described in Chapter 15). Some think the Flagstaff district has reached market saturation, with additional movement to charters unlikely. One charter closed abruptly in 1996, and two approved charters failed to open in fall 1997. The Flagstaff concentration is thought to reflect both supply and demand. The home of Northern Arizona University and a noted resort, Flagstaff is seen as a place where many parents demand alternative education and where many teachers want to live. In addition, some fault the district for unchallenging curricula.

Perhaps the most hotly contested education market in the state is in the southeast Phoenix suburbs, particularly in the Mesa, Gilbert, and Chandler school districts. (There is thought to be little charter penetration elsewhere in Phoenix, save in the inner city.) Though charter schools operating inside the Mesa district boundaries enroll only 3.2 percent of Mesa's total public enrollment, some observers believe that Mesa has lost from 5 to 8 percent of enrollment because many Mesa students attend charters located in nearby cities. As one charter operator boasted, "We've actually wiped out their [Mesa's] growth. They're now a flat-rate system."

Respondents, including those opposed to charter schools, reported that the growth of charters in Mesa reflected a lack of responsiveness on the part of the Mesa Unified District, the largest in the state. Two Mesa officials deny this, and insist that charter success is due to advertising: The district now advertises its schools in response. Others note that having opened a back-to-basics Ben Franklin magnet school popular in Mesa's large Mormon community, the district then failed to expand the program. This led a number of charter operators to offer similar curricula in or near Mesa. (Supposedly, the district retaliated by opening a new Ben Franklin magnet campus near the site of a Ben Franklin charter school.) In addition, some charter supporters perceive Mesa as weaker than suburban districts elsewhere in Phoenix, particularly in Peoria and Deer Valley. Charter opponents contend that Mesa schools are no weaker but are less traditional. Finally, inexpensive commercial property is more common in and near Mesa than elsewhere in the Phoenix metropolitan area, leading more charter operators to locate there.

Anecdotal evidence suggests that charter schools draw well where parents are unhappy with their local school districts. Still, they have not drawn as many students as might be expected from districts with low test scores in and around inner city Phoenix and Tucson. In part this reflects the decisions of many charter operators to locate elsewhere. Yet one suburban charter operator who chose to open a second campus in the inner city faced low enrollments at the second campus, mainly since many low-income parents did not know that charters are free public schools. Possibly, growth in inner city areas will be led by school district officials themselves. In fall 1998 the mainly minority Wilson Elementary District in inner city Phoenix became the first elementary school district to charter its own high school. Unhappy with high drop-out rates at the high school district his schools fed into, the Wilson superintendent decided that he could do a better job educating his students by hanging on to them through twelfth grade.

Charter Schools Differ from District Schools

Smaller and More Variable

Obviously, charters are new, although some led previous lives as private schools. Still, most of them face the typical problems of starting a small business—creating a financial plan, finding consumers for their educational product, hiring staff, and finding a place to operate. In addition, they also have to learn the ways of an educational institution, the requirements for special education students, how to file the proper paperwork, how to ensure that their school building meets the special rules for educational buildings; they even have to guarantee lunches (or at least a refrigerator to store bag lunches) for their students. (In Chapter 15, Jim Spencer, who was already an experienced private school operator, describes the trials and tribulations of starting a charter school.) According to all our interviews, charter operators typically have little money and even less time. They may mortgage their own property to gain collateral for bank loans to buy their school building. They may have trouble finding suppliers who will work with someone on a shoestring budget. They also need to determine their niche—their dream curriculum—and implement it, altering it when reality intervenes. Often a charter operator must be a new principal, a new recruiter for students and staff, a new accountant, and perhaps even a new teacher.

As Table 6.2 shows, charters serve a variety of age groupings, though few Arizona charters are middle schools. The same is true of charters nationwide (RPP International and the University of Minnesota 1997). Of those approved to open in Arizona in the 1997–1998 school year, seventy-two charter schools were essentially high schools (grades 9–12); fifty-five were elementary schools or kindergarten (K–5); only four were middle schools (grades 6–8), and 120 crossed conventional grade boundaries.

Most operators pride themselves on having lean administrative staffs and inexpensive facilities (often storefronts or modular buildings), focusing resources on small class sizes. Charters' attention to small classes is acknowledged by many district officials, one of whom suggested that small class sizes might not be sustainable since charter operators had difficulty with "uniform accounting systems, the transportation services, the services for disabled students. . . . It's a rude awakening for some charter school people who started out with much lower class sizes but now wish they had put more aside for administrative costs. There are

TABLE 6.2   Distribution of Age Groupings of Arizona Charter Schools (Open or Approved to Open) in the 1997–1998 School Year

Grades	Number of Campuses
K	3
K–2	3
K–3	29
K–4	11
K–5	8
K–8	32
K–9	9
K–12	19
1–6	2
1–9	2
4–6	2
4–11	2
6–12	23
7–12	12
9–12	70
Other	24
Not available	4
Total	255

some good people working themselves half to death." In some cases, charters limited their administrative structure by using the expertise of parents as lawyers, counselors, and even construction and maintenance workers.

Most charter schools are small, resulting in both positive and negative consequences. Many charter operators seek to develop small learning communities in which the principal knows all of the parents and students personally. One operator said she had originally intended for her school to grow to 200 students, but after a year of operation decided that "130 was actually about right." According to the Arizona Department of Education enrollment database, in fall 1997, for Arizona charter elementary schools, the mean number of students was 160.9 with a median of 109.5; for district elementaries the comparable figures were 581.5 and 590. For secondary schools the differences were even more pronounced. Secondary charters had a mean of 88.2 students (median = 65), whereas district secondaries had a mean of 1092 (median = 871). On average, then, district secondary schools were more than ten times as large as charter schools in 1997! Similarly, charter schools nationally are significantly smaller than their district counterparts (RPP International and the University of Minnesota 1997). Research suggesting that smaller schools are more orderly implies that lower levels of violence will be found in charters (Finn 1998).

Still, as district officials are quick to point out and as charter operators admit, the small size of charter schools makes it difficult for them to provide a wide range of curricular options and to serve special education students. One charter operator admitted that serving a large number of special education students could drive many charter schools out of business, and that creative charter opponents might in fact attempt to encourage large numbers of special education students to attend a particular charter school. Chapter 13 notes reports that some charter schools discourage special education students from attending. Arizona Department of Education officials report that only 3 percent of charter students are special education, compared to 9 percent in district schools. Those charters that do educate large numbers of special education students often work with districts or with other charters to leverage their resources.

The great variety of charter schools is lauded by charter supporters. As the state charter board member quoted above brags, "You name the methodology or the type and someone out there is doing it. We have Montessori. We have Core Knowledge. We have Multiple Intelligences. We have some rather controversial ones in a few cases. Everything that exists, we have one." However, as Robert Stout and Gregg Garn note in Chapter 10, nearly everything done in Arizona charter schools also occurs in some district. Consistent with Hassel's predictions in Chapter 5, Arizona charter schools are not discovering new education methods, though they are making more options *available* to parents who want them. Of course, the very variety of charter schools has in fact led to some controversial proposals. In one case, the Arizona State Board of Education initially approved and then rescinded an application from a Scientology-based school.

In general, Arizona's charter elementary schools offer relatively "mainstream" academic options. Charter secondaries are very different. Though there are a few performing arts charter schools and academies, thirty-five of the fifty-four charter secondary schools open as of February 1997 were for "at-risk" students, most of whom had failed in conventional district schools. The largest secondary charter franchise in Arizona, PPEP TEC, provides vocational training at fourteen campuses around the state and opens only where welcomed by the local school district. Asked why so few charter secondary schools offered mainstream programs that might compete directly with district schools, one operator responded:

The elementary is an easier system to get into because there are fewer barriers to entry. Academics are more important, but, as kids get older, extracurriculars get even more important and there's a funneling effect. Parents disagree a lot more on what kids should have at high school level and the cost for extracurriculars simply isn't possible for charters, except simple extracurriculars like in the elementary schools. We can't afford swimming pools and football teams. ... High schools only focus on certain themes or at-risk kids. The ones that focus on at-risk kids are very nice for [district schools], who like to tell their problem kids to try the local competing charter school!

Several Arizona Department of Education officials confirmed that district schools often call the department to ask about charters with open space for their at-risk students.

The tendency for charter high schools to educate at-risk high school students is reflected in student demographics. Using the 1997–1998 state enrollment database noted above, we find that, statewide, charter secondary students were 43.7 percent Caucasian (Anglo), 44 percent Hispanic, 7.2 percent Native American, and 4.2 percent African-American; district secondaries were 55.8 percent Caucasian, 28.8 percent Hispanic, 10.6 percent Native American, and 3.3 percent African-American. In contrast, charter elementary schools were somewhat whiter than their district counterparts. Charter elementary schools served a population that is 69.8 percent Caucasian, 11 percent Hispanic, 10.3 percent Native American, and 7.6 percent African-American. District elementaries were 54 percent Anglo, 31.9 percent Hispanic, 8.6 percent Native American, and 4.1 percent African-American.

How School Teachers View Their Schools: A Comparison

Finally, how do charter and district school teachers, respectively, view their schools? As detailed in Chapter 8, in March 1998 we conducted a mail survey of elementary school teachers in Arizona and Nevada. In this section we compare Arizona district and charter elementary school teachers on a number of dimensions, to see how each population views its school working conditions. Only charter schools that had been in operation for at least two years were selected. Respondents were paid $5 for their participation. Among charter school elementary teachers, 63 percent of those sampled returned the surveys (N = 125); for Arizona district teachers, 79 percent returned (N = 1065).

To measure teacher empowerment, teachers were asked to rate the amount of influence they had over the operation of their schools, with responses ranging from 1 (no influence) to 6 (complete influence). On nearly all of the dimensions, charter school teachers felt that they had significantly more power than their district school counterparts. Table 6.3

TABLE 6.3   Comparing the School-Level Influence of Charter and District
School Teachers[a]

	Charter %	District %	Chi-Squares(df)	Statistical Significance
Establishing curricula	62	25	$X^2(5) = 134.5$	.00000
Selecting instructional materials	76	44	$X^2(5) = 26.23$	.00000
Classroom discipline	73	71	$X^2(5) = 13.5$	.01915
Determining class schedules	55	17	$X^2(5) = 74.72$	.00000
Hiring new teachers	22	19	$X^2(5) = 25.20$	.00013

[a] Percentages, tested by chi-squares, with complete or near complete influence (6 or 5).

gives the percentages of charter and district teachers who felt strongly
that they had influence (rating 5 or 6) on various dimensions; the table
also shows the chi-square, testing the overall distribution of differences
between charter and district teachers.

Large majorities of charter school teachers reported having complete or
near compete influence over establishing curricula and determining class
schedules; fewer than half as many district school teachers reported being
so empowered. Similarly, 76 percent of charter teachers, compared to 44
percent of district teachers, reported high influence over choosing instructional materials. By a very small (but statistically significant) margin,
charter school teachers reported more influence over classroom discipline. In short, the data suggest that charter school teachers are more
empowered than their district school peers: They are more likely to be
treated as professionals. This is particularly important since charter teachers lack the security of contracts offered to teachers in district schools.
They are "at-will" employees who can be hired and fired easily by school
operators, and who often are asked to perform duties that go well beyond
classroom teaching. As both charter supporters and teachers' union officials point out, a few charter school teachers have returned to district
schools for these very reasons. Given these drawbacks, it is notable that
most charter school teachers rate their working conditions more highly
than do their district school peers.

Though the differences are less pronounced, indicators of school culture suggest that charter teachers belong to more cohesive organizations
than their district school counterparts. Table 6.4 reports the percentages
of both charter and district teachers who agree strongly (ratings of 5 or
6) that they have a positive school culture; the table also reports the

TABLE 6.4   School Culture Questions: Percentages of Charter and District
Teachers Who Agree or Strongly Agree (5 or 6), and Chi-Squares Testing
Differences Between Teachers

School Culture Items	*Charter %*	*District %*	*Chi-square(df)*	*p-value*
I take an interest in my students' moral development.	95	89	$X^2(5) = 20.7$	.00093
My principal has helped improve my teaching.	56	48	$X^2(5) = 17.54$	.00358
Other teachers have helped improve my teaching.	78	68	$X^2(5) = 9.65$	.08552
Parents have helped improve my teaching.	37	17	$X^2(5) = 45.95$	.00000
My colleagues share my beliefs and values about the mission of the school.	83	75	$X^2(5) = 16.63$	.00526
School goals and priorities are clear.	57	63	$X^2(5) = 4.9$	n.s.
I am treated as a valued employee.	68	62	$X^2(5) = 10.09$	.07271
I look forward to each working day at this school.	77	75	$X^2(5) = 10.72$	.05708
My success/failure teaching is due to factors beyond my control rather than my own efforts.	21	25	$X^2(5) = 6.5$	n.s.

chi-squares, testing the overall distribution of differences between charter
and district teacher ratings on these dimensions. The table shows that
charter teachers, by narrow but statistically significant margins, are more
likely to report that their principal and parents have helped improve their
teaching. Charter teachers are also more likely to report that colleagues
share their values, that they are treated as valued employees, and that
they look forward coming to work each day.

Just as charter school teachers are more likely to report that parents
have improved their teaching, they are also somewhat more likely to report close relationships with parents. Of charter school teachers, 83 percent, compared to 73 percent of district teachers, report meeting with over
80 percent of their student's parents during the school year. 51 percent report phone contact with most of their parents at least once a month, compared to 40 percent of district school teachers. Most notably, 36 percent of
charter teachers report being observed by parents monthly or more often,
compared to 14 percent of district school teachers. Only 9 percent of char-

ter school teachers, but 27 percent of district teachers, report *never* being observed by parents.

In Conclusion: A Viable Choice

By passing and aggressively implementing the nation's strongest charter law, Arizona has created an education market—something that few charter supporters or opponents had predicted would happen. Removing the barriers to entry unleashed energy from parents, teachers, and charter school entrepreneurs, creating a new school system from scratch. It seems likely that other states would have similarly large numbers of schools of choice were they to allow both multiple chartering authorities and single charter holders to open multiple campuses. At the same time, charter schools seem unlikely to replace district schools. Charters still have under 5 percent of total public enrollment, and their growth may be slowing, perhaps since the teachers and parents who most wanted to leave their district schools have now done so, and perhaps since districts are being pushed to do a better job pleasing their clientele. It may be that in a freer public education market schools of choice will not replace traditional schools; rather they will take and hold a 5 to 15 percent market share statewide, with larger percentages in locales where the district schools are unpopular.

The 272 charter schools in Arizona pursue a range of curricula and age groupings, though in general, charter elementary schools serve mainstream students, whereas secondary schools focus on at-risk youth. The latter are less apt to arouse the ire of districts. Charter schools are far smaller than district schools. Finally, charter schools have higher teacher morale. Teachers in charter elementary schools, at least, feel that they have more power over school policy, work in more collegial school cultures, and have more (and more pleasant) interactions with parents.

In short, the Arizona experience suggests that comprehensive school choice is quite viable. Should other states do as Arizona does, the results will not be disastrous. Whether one believes in charters or not, Arizona public education has not collapsed under their influence. However, whether an education free market actually works better than a district-based system, whatever "better" is, remains to be seen.

Notes

1. The great number of district sponsored charters issued in 1998 does not reflect increased district support for charter schools; rather, Ganado and Window

Rock schools about to lose their charters switched to Higley and are counted as new district charters.

References

Finn, Chester E., Jr. 1999. "Comment." In *Brookings Papers on Education Policy 1999*, ed. Diane Ravitch, 315–320. Washington, D.C.: Brookings Institution.

Peterson, Paul E. 1998. "School Choice: A Report Card." In *Learning from School Choice*, ed. Paul E. Peterson and Bryan C. Hassel, 3–32. Washington, D.C.: Brookings Institution.

RPP International and the University of Minnesota. 1997. *A Study of Charter Schools*. Washington, D.C.: U.S. Department of Education.

7

Why Arizona Embarked on School Reform (and Nevada Did Not)

STEPHANIE TIMMONS-BROWN AND FREDERICK HESS

In 1994 the Arizona state legislature passed the nation's most ambitious charter school law. The law's liberal provisions for charter approval, together with aggressive implementation by two activist state boards and by revenue-seeking local districts, created a burgeoning charter school sector. During the same time period, Nevada, a neighboring state with relatively similar educational performance and socioeconomic characteristics, responded differently to concerns about educational performance. Why?

We believe the Arizona-Nevada comparison illustrates factors shaping the adoption and non-adoption of charter schooling. The comparative state analysis suggests that although student performance may have played some role, party and interest group dynamics were key in explaining the different responses of the two states. In Nevada, strong teachers' unions and the close partisan balance in the state legislature kept strong charter laws off the agenda. In contrast, Republican dominance and weak unions in Arizona made a strong charter law possible, and nearly led to the adoption of a voucher scheme.

Student Performance

During the late 1980s and early 1990s, Arizona parents and legislators expressed increasing concern about the mediocre performance of the state's students. The *Arizona Republic* (1994) editorialized on several occasions about the need to improve state schooling, opining, for example: "Many schools in Arizona fail students, parents and teachers. Many creative, in-novative teachers are trapped in a system that refuses to recognize it has lost sight of its primary goal, educating children. Test scores are down. Graduates lack basic job skills. Dropout rates are increasing."

In 1992, scores on the National Assessment of Education Progress (NAEP) tests put Arizona in the bottom third of the forty-one states par-ticipating in the state-level assessments in 1992. Only 27 percent of Ari-zona students took the ACT Assessment, the dominant college-entrance exam in the state. In 1994, only 50 percent of Arizona seniors went on to higher education, eighth lowest nationally (Miller 1997). The state's 14.4 percent dropout rate in 1990 exceeded the national average of 11.2 percent (U.S. Bureau of the Census 1997).

In Arizona, poor performance of conventional public schools spurred interest in radical reform of public education. However, Nevada had equally disappointing student performance. By 1994, Nevada had the highest one-year dropout rate (8.3 percent) among the seventeen states using a uniform federal measure. Only 38 percent of Nevada high school graduates went on to college (Keller 1997). In 1997, a state legislative re-port concluded that Nevada's school systems were failing their students, especially in low-income urban areas (*Las Vegas Review Journal* 1998).

Demographics

Socioeconomic differences do not explain the greater appeal of charter schooling in Arizona since the two states are quite similar demographically, though Arizona's population is somewhat poorer than Nevada's. (For more details on Nevada and Arizona state demographics, refer to Table 8.1 in Chapter 8.) According to the 1990 census, Arizona was 81 percent white, whereas Nevada was 84 percent white. In 1995, the median family income in Nevada was about $5,000 higher than in Arizona. Between 1990 and 1995, Nevada and Arizona were the two fastest growing states in the na-tion, growing by 27 percent and 15 percent, respectively. This rapid popu-lation growth challenged school systems in each state. Nevada's popula-tion growth equated to "more than a classroom of children every day" for several years (Keller 1997: 158). In 1994, Nevada's per-pupil spending ex-ceeded $5,000, whereas Arizona's was approximately $4,611.

Political Context

Contrasting political contexts in the two states proved decisive in explain-ing the fate of charter schooling. In Arizona, Republicans had unified con-trol of the legislature and the governor's office in the mid-1990s. This en-abled Republicans to use the threat of voucher legislation to force the teachers' unions and Democratic opponents to compromise on charter legislation. As illustrated in Table 7.1, Republicans have dominated Arizona state government in recent years, whereas neither party has wielded similar power in Nevada. In Arizona, Republican backers of charter schools could pass a law without Democratic support. In Nevada, partisan balance from 1986 through 1996 meant that reform required bipartisan support.

Conservative Arizona legislators advocated both voucher and charter school bills. The Arizona Education Association (AEA) and Arizona Federation of Teachers (AFT) generally opposed both. Union leaders saw charter legislation as a threat to the professional status, job security, and working conditions of professional educators, in part because charter school teachers were not required to have teaching certification and were "at-will" employees who could be terminated easily. More distasteful to unions than the proposed charter legislation, however, were proposals for school vouchers (Kolbe 1994). Under proposed plans, parents could receive vouchers to pay for the child's education at either a public or an approved private school. Fearing what vouchers would do to the traditional public school system, the AEA, AFT, and their allies opted to compromise and accept the less threatening charter school alternative (Kolbe 1994). Charter proponents lacked such leverage in Nevada, and were therefore unable to win similar victories (Whaley 1997b).

TABLE 7.1   Arizona State Legislature Seats: 1986–1996

	Senate		House	
	Republican	*Democrat*	*Republican*	*Democrat*
1986[a]	19	11	36	24
1988[b]	17	13	34	26
1990[c]	13	17	32	27
1992[d]	18	12	35	25
1994[e]	19	11	38	22
1996[f]	18	12	38	22

SOURCES: [a] Alan Ehrenhalt, ed., *Politics in America* (Washington, D.C.: Congressional Quarterly Press, 1987).
[b] Phil Duncan, ed., *Politics in America* (Washington, D.C.: Congressional Quarterly Press, 1989).
[c] Phil Duncan, ed., *Politics in America* (Washington, D.C.: Congressional Quarterly Press, 1991).
[d] Phil Duncan, ed., *Politics in America* (Washington, D.C.: Congressional Quarterly Press, 1993).
[e] Phil Duncan and Christine C. Lawrence, eds., *Politics in America* (Washington, D.C.: Congressional Quarterly Press, 1995).
[f] Phil Duncan and Christine C. Lawrence, eds., *Politics in America* (Washington, D.C.: Congressional Quarterly Press, 1998).

By conventional measures, teachers' unions may be stronger in Arizona than in Nevada. 79 percent of Arizona teachers are in the AEA, whereas its Nevada counterpart, the Nevada State Education Association (NSEA), includes 65 percent of Nevada's teachers. However, these numbers are deceptive because the AEA suffered a grievous political setback in 1994 when it was forced to settle an illegal campaign financing suit. The result was a weakened AEA, less able to negotiate a hostile legislature and political superstructure.

Arizona's Story

In the early 1990s, there was widespread agreement among legislators, parents, and teachers that Arizona's schools did not adequately educate the state's children. As in many state legislatures since the 1983 *Nation at Risk* report, constituents pressured legislators to improve schooling (U.S. National Commission on Excellence 1983). School vouchers and charter schools, both of which were gaining increasing national attention during the early 1990s, were proposed by conservative state legislators as potential solutions.

Republicans controlled both the state house and the state senate. As Table 7.1 shows, in 1994 they held 19 of the 30 seats in the senate and 38 of the 60 seats in the house. Republican Governor Fife Symington was elected in 1990 and reelected in 1994. (Under indictment, Symington resigned in 1997, to be replaced by Republican Lt. Gov. Jane Hull.)

Senate and House Bills

In 1993, serious negotiations between Republican legislators and the AEA took place. The teachers' unions and their allies elected for political compromise when the passage of statewide voucher legislation seemed likely.

Table 7.2 shows a chronology of events in Arizona related to charter schools. In March 1993, two opposing bills were introduced: Senate Bill 1200 and House Bill 2125. Senator Bev Hermon (R), chairwoman of the senate Education Committee, and state senator Tom Patterson (R) co-sponsored Senate Bill 1200. Representative Lisa Graham Keegan (R), known as a champion of educational issues, sponsored House Bill 2125.

Senate Bill 1200 proposed to funnel state aid directly to individual schools through a charter school system, giving parents a choice of where to send their children. Supporters saw the bill's key measure as the provision that a charter-seeker turned down by the local school district could seek approval from a school district governing board or from the state board of education. This provision meant that local school boards would not be able to control entry into the local educational market. Senate

TABLE 7.2   Chronology of Arizona Charter School Events

	Events in Arizona Related to Charter Schools
1991	School vouchers and charter schools introduced in Arizona
March 1993	Senator Bev Hermon/Senator Tom Patterson introduced Senate Bill 1200 in support of charter schools that would allow state aid, based on student count
March 1993	House Bill 2125 was introduced that would approve: "decentralized training fund," "New Arizona School Fund," and "School Improvement Fund"
February 1994	Lisa Graham Keegan introduced House bill 2505, a $23 million proposal and opposition from Arizona School Boards Association, Arizona School Administrators and, minimally, by AEA
February 1994	Senate Education chairperson, Bev Hermon, introduced Senate Bill 1375, a smaller $10 million proposal; focused on open enrollment and at-risk preschools
April 1994	After the failure of HB 2505, Lisa Graham introduced HB 2002 in special session
June 1994	Arizona sacrificed the voucher initiative and supported charter schools; passage of HB 2002: Schools Improvement Act
July through October 1994	Arizona approved nineteen charter schools only months after new legislation
1995 legislative session	State legislature considered House Bill 2127, which would establish a two-year statewide voucher pilot program for fiscal years 1996/1997 and 1997/1998; would provide a $3,500 voucher to any student in kindergarten through 12th grade; the bill passed the Education Committee on February 15, 1996 and the House Appropriations Committee on February 24, 1996 but died in the House Rules Committee
1996	No further legislative developments were reported on the charter school front
April 7, 1997	Governor Fife Symington signed legislation allowing residents to claim an income tax credit of up to $500 for their donations to any charitable organization that provided scholarships to needy children attending private school. This was the first law of its kind in the country
May 1997	The Arizona Education Association gathered signatures to place a referendum on the ballot opposing the school tax credit

majority leader Tom Patterson (quoted by Shultze 1993: B1) said that he envisioned "charter schools . . . as a little escape valve to the bureaucracy and domination of the public school districts." Although Senate Bill 1200 passed in the senate 16–9, there was no action in the house (S. Wheaton, senate secretary, personal communication, October 28, 1998).

House Bill 2125 did not concentrate solely on charter schools but incorporated a variety of appropriations, funding at-risk, preschool, and all-day kindergarten programs. This bill was more of a means to fund "model" programs, such as those previously attempted in Chicago and Kentucky, than to establish charter schools.

SB 1200 and HB 2125 were both held in committee. The stalemate was broken in February 1994 when house Education Committee chair, Lisa Graham Keegan, elected Arizona's superintendent of public instruction later in 1994, introduced House Bill 2505. HB 2505 was a $23 million education initiative that featured a voucher program. This proposal refocused the debate. By offering an alternative that would permit public education dollars to flow to private schools, Keegan energized traditional public school critics and made charters seem more palatable to their opponents.

HB 2505 included provisions for charter schools, expansion of advanced placement programs, decentralization, school report cards, "Twenty-First Century Schools," vouchers, open enrollment, at-risk preschools, and training dollars for teachers. School report cards would summarize information about each school to help parents choose the best school for their children. Included in the report card would be "the school's educational goals, a summary of student standardized test results, graduation statistics, safety record and a description of the social services available at the school" (Luther 1995: 12). Open enrollment provisions would require district governing boards to allow students to enroll in any school within the district or in another district. Vouchers would grant public funds to low-income residents to use at private schools. The "Twenty-First Century Schools" provision allotted funds for facility improvements.

Almost simultaneously, Senator Bev Hermon introduced Senate Bill 1375, which offered many of the same proposals as Keegan's bill, but at a lower price tag. Hermon's bill included provisions for charter schools, school safety grants, decentralization, "Twenty-First Century Schools," open enrollment, and at-risk preschools. The Hermon bill did not feature vouchers and eliminated the school report card provision and the advanced placement program. The removal of these items helped lower the cost from $23 million to $10 million. Both bills provoked controversy.

Conservatives, including Governor Symington, Keegan, and leading business interests, were adamant about including vouchers in any educational reform package. The *Arizona Republic* observed, "Governor

Symington and other Republicans have declared that, without private-school vouchers, Arizona will just have to wait some more for education-reform legislation" (Greene 1994: B8). The AEA, AFT, Arizona School Boards Association (ASBA), and Arizona School Administrators (ASA), on the other hand, refused to accept any bill containing vouchers. The threat that voucher legislation would indeed pass escalated as HB 2505 made its way to a committee vote. As the *Arizona Republic* reported, "One prominent senator confidently announced: 'I've told the caucus I won't vote for school reform without vouchers. It is like giving aspirin to cancer patients'" (Greene 1994: B8).

In April 1994, the voucher debate still monopolized legislative discussion about education reform. Although a consensus had started to emerge on charter schools, conservative lawmakers wanted legislation to include private schools as well. Heated argument flared. Democratic state senator Stan Furman rejected any voucher provision that would permit public money to flow to private schools. Keegan countered that the money belongs to the public and should be used to educate children of the public most efficiently, not just to maintain a districted public school system. After the house passed HB 2505 on the last day of regular session by a vote of 30–28, the state senate defeated the bill by three votes, leaving the reform-minded Republican majority without a major education package.

During the summer, Governor Symington won legislative approval for a special legislative session to move the charter school issue. House Bill 2002 was a simplified and slimmed-down substitute for Keegan's controversial, $23 million HB 2505. The new bill removed the voucher program, the advanced placement program, and the teacher training funding provision. It retained charter schools, decentralization, school report cards, at-risk preschool dollars, and open enrollment. Fearing resurgence of a school voucher initiative, the key opponents of voucher legislation—the Arizona School Boards Association, the Arizona School Administrators, and the teachers' unions—endorsed charter legislation. Keegan interpreted this change of heart as the decision of these organizations to opt for the lesser of two evils. She explained that she had intended the voucher initiative to serve as a smoke screen that would prevent the teachers' unions from focusing on their opposition to charter schools. According to Keegan, the charter school proposal (HB 2002, introduced April 1994) was introduced at the same time the nebulous voucher bill (HB 2505, introduced February) was announced so that unions would attack vouchers and let the charter bill slip through (*TEA News* 1997). Similarly, an Arizona policy maker recalls that "vouchers was really the top issue that drew all the fire. . . . You had a lot of people who were opposed to vouchers that didn't want to seem like they were totally anti-reform" (personal interview, December 11, 1997). With reluctant support from the teachers' unions, the ASA, and the ASBA, at the end of a three-day special session, on Friday, June 17, 1994, the charter school legislation passed.

Details of the Arizona Legislation

Arizona's legislation is radical. As detailed in Chapter 6, potential applicants include any public body, private organization, or private person. The existence of multiple sponsoring boards means that the chances of getting a given charter application approved are much greater than in other states (*TEA News* 1997). Also, Arizona's funding for charters was relatively generous by national standards. New charter schools can receive grants of up to $100,000 for capital costs for each of their first two years of operation. In 1997, the *Arizona Daily Star* estimated that the state allocated approximately $33 million to charter schools. That amounted to roughly $4,040 per charter school pupil and about $174 per student for transportation (Tapia 1997).

Chapter 6 notes that after the charter legislation passed charter schools proliferated in Arizona, in part because of aggressive implementation of the legislation by the State Board for Charter Schools. On April 7, 1997, Governor Symington signed legislation allowing residents to claim an income tax credit of up to 50 percent for their donations to any charitable organization that provided scholarships for needy children attending private school. The measure was an end run around opposition to spending public money on private schooling and was the first law of its kind in the country. At this writing, court challenges to the law have failed.

Nevada's Story

Nevada's educational policymaking in the 1990s was to prove far less tumultuous than Arizona's. Nevada passed charter school legislation in July 1997, but the limited legislation was relatively uncontroversial. In Nevada, only county school boards may sponsor charter schools. The state requires 75 percent of the teachers in a charter school to be state-licensed; the remaining 25 percent are required to possess certain skills and to work under the direction of a licensed teacher. The legislation authorized no more than twenty-one charter schools in the state, limiting the number per county. Charters must be approved by the state board of education *and* the local school district.

The Nevada charter school legislation reflects the state's different political climate. In Nevada, teachers' unions had little to fear from voucher proponents. Nevada legislators proposed a non-threatening bill with substantial input from the Nevada Education Association. The unions were comfortable with the bill because it advocated only incremental change and posed no threat to collective bargaining or to job security.

Development of Charter School Legislation in Nevada

In 1994–1995, as Table 7.3 shows, Republicans controlled the senate thirteen to eight, whereas the assembly was split evenly between the parties. Although the first charter school bill, Senate Bill 31, won favor in the senate, it died a slow death in the assembly. Because the assembly was split evenly, Republican assemblyman Bill Harrington and Democrat assemblyman Wendell Williams co-chaired the Education Committee. As will be discussed later, Williams ardently opposed charter schools and seemingly acted in concert with the teachers' union in killing SB 31 (Whaley 1997b).

On December 29, 1994, the senate Human Resources and Facilities Committee pre-filed Nevada's first charter school bill, Senate Bill 31 (Ward 1998). Senators heard testimony and discussed SB 31 over a six month period from January 1995 to June 1995. On June 23, 1995, Senator Rawson,

TABLE 7.3 Nevada State Legislature Seats: 1986–1996

	Senate		House	
	Republican	Democrat	Republican	Democrat
1986[a]	9	13	29	13
1988[b]	13	8	12	30
1990[c]	10	11	20	22
1992[d]	10	11	13	29
1994[e]	13	8	21	21
1996[f]	12	9	17	25

SOURCES: [a] Alan Ehrenhalt, ed., *Politics in America* (Washington, D.C.: Congressional Quarterly Press, 1987).

[b] Phil Duncan, ed., *Politics in America* (Washington, D.C.: Congressional Quarterly Press, 1989).

[c] Phil Duncan, ed., *Politics in America* (Washington, D.C.: Congressional Quarterly Press, 1991).

[d] Phil Duncan, ed., *Politics in America* (Washington, D.C.: Congressional Quarterly Press, 1993).

[e] Phil Duncan and Christine C. Lawrence, eds., *Politics in America* (Washington, D.C.: Congressional Quarterly Press, 1995).

[f] Phil Duncan and Christine C. Lawrence, eds., *Politics in America* (Washington, D.C.: Congressional Quarterly Press, 1998).

chair of senate Human Resources and Facilities Committee, spoke in support of the bill on the senate floor, as did other Republican committee
members (Nevada Legislature 1995). Democrats opposed the charter
school legislation for reasons that included no appropriations for transportation and a vague definition of what constituted a charter school. Support and opposition for the bill split along party lines: All but one Republican voted in favor of the bill, and all the Democrats opposed it.

SB 31 would have allowed "a school district's board of trustees to approve a charter school by creating a new school or converting an existing
school, if at least two-thirds of the parents and employees, faculty,
and administrative staff requested the conversion" (Shokraii and Youssef
1998: 95). After receiving approval from the trustees of a school district, a
charter also would need approval from the state board of education. The
bill would have restricted charters to one school per county with a population of 35,000. SB 31 passed in the senate twelve to nine, but was blocked
in the assembly Education Committee. School choice did not reappear
until 1996.

History of Senate Bill 220: Nevada's Charter School Law

In late 1996, state senators Maurice Washington (R–Sparks), Valerie Wiener
(D–Las Vegas), Jon Porter (R–Boulder City) and Ernie Adler (D–Carson
City) sponsored Senate Bill 220. SB 220 enjoyed early support from the
teachers' union, parents, and administrators. Senator Washington boasted
that teachers' union representatives "were involved from the start" (cited in
Olsen 1997: 2). Washington, Wiener, Porter, and Adler accommodated the
union's major concerns: collective bargaining, licensing, and curriculum.
First, the legislation provided for optional collective bargaining. Charter
school teachers could be part of the local district's bargaining unit,
form their own bargaining unit, or negotiate individual contracts with the
school's governing body. Second, the bill specified that 100 percent of
teachers in first through sixth grades in charter schools would be licensed
by the state board of education. The figure would be 50 percent for grades
seven through twelve. Third, the legislation provided charter schools with
a limited course-of-studies exemption. Charter schools would be exempt
from mandated courses except for those that the state required for graduation (such as required math classes, required English classes, etc.). Washington explained the logic behind the accommodations: "We asked the
teachers' union if it would support the bill [because] . . . we knew if they
did not like it, it wasn't going anywhere" (Olsen 1997: 3). Nevada State Education Association lobbyist, Debbie Cahill, told the *Las Vegas Review Journal* that the union was "comfortable with the amended bill approved by the
[Education] Committee. We can support it" (Olsen 1997: 2).

Despite bipartisan support in the Nevada senate, assembly Education Committee chairman Wendell Williams (D–Las Vegas) stopped Senate Bill 220 in his committee from May 8 until the closing days of the session in July (*Las Vegas Review Journal* 1997; see also Whaley 1997c). Williams, who was instrumental in killing similar legislation in the 1996 session, made last minute amendments, including changes to collective bargaining and provisional conditions, with little committee input. Just when the bill's sponsors thought it would die in his committee, Williams took the extraordinary measure of holding a committee meeting on the assembly floor and introduced his own amendments to the bill. Amendments now specified that the legislation's primary purpose was to serve the best interest of at-risk students. Additionally, amendments reduced the potential number of charter schools in Clark County from twelve to four. The amendments also eliminated bargaining between charter teachers and the union regarding working conditions.

Williams said he proposed amendments to the bill, sponsored by a bipartisan group of senators, to make the idea more workable in Nevada (Whaley 1997a). The more likely reasons are that Williams continued to fear that charter schools might threaten the existing public school system and that he was seeking to maintain union support. Interestingly, the first time Williams's committee members saw the amendments was at a press conference right before the assembly floor session, according to assemblywoman Barbara Cegaske (R–Las Vegas), an Education Committee member who complained that "nobody was given the opportunity to work on the bill [in the assembly] except Wendell. . . . I felt it needed to have a legitimate hearing" (Olsen 1997: 2). The changes met with mixed reviews. Senator Adler (cited in Clark 1997: 2), one of the original sponsors of SB 220, saw the new bill as a reasonable compromise, whereas the *Las Vegas Review Journal* editorialized:

> As the bill finally lurched back into view in the closing days of the session it was hardly recognizable. . . . What was once a good-faith effort at reform had been purposely rewritten to make it totally ineffective in offering any alternative path out of the existing bureaucratic swamp, by guaranteeing that new charter schools would be just as deeply mired in that same suffocating ooze from day one. (*Las Vegas Review Journal* 1997; see also Whaley 1997a)

Content of Legislation Deterred Charters

After passage of the legislation, little enthusiasm was evident for actual charter schools. Two days before the April 15, 1998, deadline, only two applications to open publicly-funded charter schools had been submitted (Whaley 1998). Primarily, charters have not opened in Nevada because the legislative restrictions noted above make doing so a relatively unattractive proposition. In particular, Nevada's decision to leave chartering authority in the hands of the school districts drastically limits the prospects of charter applicants. Evidence from other states shows that local school boards have incentives to limit the numbers of charter schools and maintain control over those that do open (Shokraii and Youssef 1998). Indeed, for this reason Nevada's charter legislation is ranked as the nation's ninth weakest by the Center for Education Reform (1997). In addition to the difficulty of gaining approval, at least three parts of Nevada's charter school law deter potential operators.

First, the only applicants allowed to petition for charters are committees "consisting of at least three certified teachers and up to [ten] additional community members" (Center for Education Reform 1996: 59). In Arizona, eligible applicants are broadly defined as any public body, private person, or a private organization. Though Nevada is a right-to-work state, teachers must work under the contract terms of the local bargaining unit (Center for Education Reform 1997); it is thus risky for teachers to offend unions.

Second, Nevada charter schools are expected to serve at-risk students, those most difficult to teach. Of the two schools approved as of spring 1998, one was a community school created by a group in Sandy Valley, Nevada, and the other was a school for teen parents and teens from single-parent homes (Whaley 1998).

Third, Nevada's legislation allows only "new starts" for charter schools: Existing public and private schools are not allowed to convert to charter status. The Nevada Department of Education requires a charter school committee to obtain a copy of a proposed lease or rental agreement for space before it is allowed a charter (Ward 1998). Committees interested in starting a charter school must first secure building funds, legal and business expertise, and formidable start-up costs without the advantage of using the charter to secure loans. Nevada's charter school law provides no funding for start-up costs, typically the greatest hurdle for charter school applicants. In contrast to its neighbor, in the first year of charter schooling Arizona committed $1,000,000 annually in state funding and federal charter school funding for start-up costs (Luther 1995).

Conclusion

For all the attention paid charter schools, relatively little has been devoted to the question of how charter school laws emerge and how state environments influence and shape charter legislation. A brief overview of Arizona and Nevada charter school legislation suggests that, unsurprisingly, the state-level political environment plays a crucial role in determining charter school policy. Particularly significant for the prospect of charter legislation in Arizona was a large pro-voucher coalition and weak teachers' unions. Powerful voucher advocates enabled charter supporters to depict charter legislation as a moderate compromise. In Arizona, even the teachers' unions came to view strong charter legislation as an acceptable compromise. After all, they occupied a weak political position and feared that legislators would enact school vouchers if they did not accept a charter school alternative. In Nevada, teachers' unions were strong and voucher supporters had little clout; thus charter legislation was the most radical alternative on the table. As a result, the NSEA could safely threaten to withhold its support from any education reform if charter advocates did not offer palatable compromises.

The charter school debate often proceeds as a normative argument about what schools should look like, what states should be doing, and how public money should be spent. Each of these issues emerged in the course of policymaking in Nevada and Arizona. Charter advocates, critics, and future policy makers must recognize, however, that the key to charter laws lies largely in the roles that state political environments play in setting the education agenda. Ideas matter, but perhaps not as much as the constellation of political forces.

References

Arizona Department of Education. 1997a. "Charter School Types." November 1997, URL: http://azstarnet.com/public/packages/charterschools/gr061504.gif.

Arizona Republic. 1993. Editorial, 15 March.

Arizona Republic. 1994. Editorial, 23 July.

Arizona Republic. 1997. Editorial, 24 August.

Center for Education Reform. 1996. *School Reform in the United States: State by State Summary*. Washington, D.C.: Center for Education Reform.

_____. 1997. *School Reform in the United States: State by State Summary*. Washington, D.C.: Center for Education Reform.

Clark, Barbara. 1997. "Charter Questions." *Las Vegas Review Journal*, 30 June.

Dale, Angela, and Dave DeSchryver, eds. 1997. *The Charter School Workbook: Your Roadmap to the Charter School Movement*. Washington, D.C.: Center for Education Reform.

Germond, Jack, and Jules Witcover. 1994. "School Voucher Debate Is Taken up in Arizona." *Baltimore Sun*, 12 January.

Greene, Andrea. 1994. "Voucher Debate Again Threatens to Sidetrack Education Reform." *Arizona Republic*, 9 February.

Keller, Bess. 1997. "Up Against Growth." *Education Week: Quality Counts*, 22 January.

Kolbe, John. 1994. "Reforms Gain Despite Union." *Phoenix Gazette*, 1 June.

Las Vegas Review Journal. 1998. Editorial, 1 April. 10 May 1999, URL: http://www.lvrj.com/lvrj_home/April-01-Wed-1998/opinion/7232608.html.

_____. 1997. Editorial, 8 July. 20 May 1999, URL: http://www.lvrj.com/lvrj_home/1997/Jul-08-Tue-1997/opinion/5675195.html.

Luther, Kurt A. 1995. "Legislative Review: The School Improvement Act." *Arizona State Law Journal* (Spring): 389–406.

Mattern, Hal. 1997. "School Tax Credits Get Supreme Court Hearing." *Arizona Republic*, 17 December.

Miller, Julie A. 1997. "Doing More with Less." *Education Week: Quality Counts*, 22 January.

Mitchell, L. A. 1995. "Charter Schools Are Buying; New Institutions Need Many Goods." *Arizona Business Gazette*, 13 July.

Nevada Legislature. 1995. *The Journal of the Senate of the Sixty-Eighth Session of the Legislature of the State of Nevada.* 8 May, 7–14.

Olsen, Erica. 1997. "What Really Happened to the Charter School Bill?" *Nevada Journal*, September. 20 May 1999, URL: http://www.npri.org/nj97/09/cover_story.htm.

Phoenix Gazette. 1994. Editorial, 14 April.

Schultze, Ray. 1993. "Reformers Tout Charter Schools; Establishment Fears Threat to Funds." *Phoenix Gazette*, 13 February.

Shokraii, Nina H., and Sarah E. Youssef. 1998. *School Choice Programs: What's Happening in the States—1998 Edition.* Washington, D.C.: The Heritage Foundation.

Tapia, Sarah Tully. 1997. "Public Schools Alternative: Arizona Leads the Nation in Schools Chartered." *Arizona Daily Star.*[15 June 1997, URL: http://www.azstar-net.com/public/packages/charterschools/2chart1.htm.

TEA News. "Edventurists Hope to Insulate Charter Schools from 'Regulatory Creep.'" 1997. September. 10 May 1999, URL: http://www.nea.org/society/private/creep.html.

U.S. Bureau of the Census. 1997. *Statistical Abstract of the United States: 1997.* 117th ed. Washington, D.C.: Government Printing Office.

U.S. Department of Education, National Center for Education Statistics. 1990. *Digest of Education Statistics: 1990.* NCES 98-015, by Thomas D. Snyder. Production Manager, Charlene M. Hoffman. Program Analyst, Claire M. Geddes. Washington, D.C.: U.S. Department of Education.

_____. 1997. *Digest of Education Statistics: 1997.* NCES 98-015, by Thomas D. Snyder. Production Manager, Charlene M. Hoffman. Program Analyst, Claire M. Geddes. Washington, D.C.: U.S. Department of Education.

U.S. National Commission on Excellence in Education. 1983. *A Nation at Risk: The Imperative for Educational Reform.* Washington, D.C.: U.S. Department of Education.

Ward, Ken. 1998. "Clock Ticking for Charters." *Las Vegas Review Journal,* 21 January.

Whaley, Sean. 1997a. "Lawmaker Says Charter Schools Bill Has Good Chance." *Las Vegas Review Journal,* 2 July.

_____. 1997b. "Charter Schools Hearing Planned." *Las Vegas Review Journal,* 20 June.

_____. 1997c. "School Hearings Planned." *Las Vegas Review Journal,* 25 June.

_____. 1998. "Few Charter School Requests Made." *Las Vegas Review Journal,* 13 April.

8

Do Charter Schools Improve District Schools? Three Approaches to the Question

ROBERT MARANTO, SCOTT MILLIMAN,
FREDERICK HESS, APRIL GRESHAM

Charter schools allow parents and charter operators to select a range of options for individual children and for individual teachers. This may produce useful education programs for a small number of students. However, for some time to come, the vast majority of students will attend traditional public schools. Accordingly, charter schools could have their greatest impact by stimulating improvement in traditional public schools. This chapter will examine whether Arizona charter schools have had such impacts.

The Impact of Competition on Schools

The Market Hypothesis

There are two primary rationales for choice-based efforts to improve schooling. First, for a host of reasons, the children who attend the choice schools may receive a better education. This argument has been offered and contested in a number of empirical works (Chubb and Moe 1990; Greene et al. 1998; Peterson and Noyes 1997; but see Sukstorf et al. 1993; Witte et al. 1994). A second rationale is that children remaining in the traditional public schools will benefit due to competitive pressures generated by choice schools. This argument, often referred to as the *market hypothesis,* assumes that school districts will respond to competition from other schools by becoming more efficient and effective. The market hypothesis presumes that competitive pressures will force schools to shake off limitations imposed by bureaucracy, union influence, democratic conflict, and unclear outcome criteria.

The market hypothesis is fiercely contested. Some choice critics contend that more choice is likely to increase segregation without improving school performance. Other analysts fear that increased competition will only make bad schools worse, without improving good schools (Smith and Meier 1995).

Even if school districts do respond effectively to competition, can they impose change in individual schools? The implementation of organizational reform takes years, and in troubled school systems, superintendents typically have four years or fewer in office. Accordingly, superintendents are likely to announce new reforms without ever having the time to implement them, increasing the cynicism of teachers and parents (Hess 1999; see also Lipsky 1980).

There has been relatively little empirical research making the case that competition will improve the quality of schooling in the traditional public schools. Anecdotal evidence indicates that competition may produce significant—and potentially positive—changes in local school systems. For instance, a Hudson Institute study has noted that districts in Boston; Detroit; Los Angeles; Lansing, Michigan; and Kingsburg, California, have undertaken new measures when pressed by the emergence of local charters (Vanourek et al. 1997). A series of case studies of twenty-five districts with charter schools in eight states and Washington, D.C., found that almost half reported either strong or moderate impact from charter schooling. District reactions included broadening educational offerings by opening magnet schools, creating "add-on" programs such as all-day kindergarten, offering new types of activities, and increasing curricular resources (Rofes 1998: 12–13).

Caroline Hoxby's (1998) innovative econometric research found that school districts facing more competition, either through housing markets or through inter-district transfers, were more effective and efficient. In those metropolitan areas with more competition, Hoxby found that taxpayers paid less, students learned more, and students took more academic courses. Hoxby (1996, 1998) also found that competition from Catholic schools seemed to increase public school efficiency and academic performance. Similarly, David Armour and Brett Peiser (1998) found that school districts losing large numbers of students through inter-district choice programs reacted by changing programs and policies.

Anecdotal evidence also suggests that districts faced with the loss of funds may respond to competition in a more conflictual fashion. Districts have sometimes sought to galvanize support among local parents by announcing that they would cut or reduce popular programs such as art, advanced placement courses, sports, and tutoring. Other observed behaviors have included the harassment of charter personnel, efforts to undermine the ability of charter schools to find suitable facilities, and refusals to provide necessary student records to charter schools (Hassell 1998; Loveless and Jasin 1998; Millott and Lake 1996).

What Is a Good School?

There is dispute as to what constitutes school improvement, with some educators smiling on experimentation and suggesting that educational improvement requires a free-flowing constructivist approach, whereas others suggest that educational improvement requires more discipline and order and that experimentalist teaching can be counterproductive. In general, though, some educational practices are widely accepted as conducive to improved schooling. These practices include increased administrative focus, more participatory decisionmaking in the school, increased efforts to inform parents about school programs, and increased attention to the teachers' professional development (Bryk et al. 1993; Elmore et al. 1996; Fullan 1991; Johnson 1996' Tyack and Cuban 1995). Positive changes in these dimensions should be observable to teachers. These leadership changes must logically precede hoped-for changes in classroom teaching and learning. Therefore we believe that teachers' observations of their schools are more sensitive proxies of institutional change than standard outcome variables.

How Administrators, Policy Makers, and Charter Operators View Competition

Of necessity, most previous studies of the actual or likely impacts of school choice on conventional public schools have been speculative. Authors have often extrapolated from small pilot projects involving magnet schools and private school vouchers. These plans were invariably limited to a single school district, and usually available only to a small number of parents (e.g., Boyer 1992).[1] Further, voucher plans have always been means tested, with support available to only a minority of the parents who sought it.

In short, previous research has been unable to even begin to assess the impacts of comprehensive school choice because a large scale choice regime did not exist in the U.S.—until now. Arizona's extremely expansive charter school law rapidly produced a large number of charter schools. Some areas (e.g., Phoenix) have more charters than others, but all districts are potential charter locations and must recognize the threat of competition from charters. Although districts with many charter schools operating in their boundaries will feel more competitive pressure than districts with few or no charters, all Arizona districts are subject to an unusual degree of market competition.

This statewide potential for competition is the key to Arizona's value as a natural experiment for the market hypothesis. By examining both anecdotal and systematic evidence on how conventional public schools are responding, we are able to examine some preliminary evidence on this question in the only state in the union with an actual educational market.

Interviews

From December 1997 to May 1998 we interviewed thirty Arizona educators and policy makers, asking what accounts for the rapid spread of charters, how district schools react to competition from charters, and what lessons Arizona holds for other states considering the charter option.

Unexpectedly, Charters Provide a Competitive Environment.   One key reason that the charter school legislation passed was that it was seen as a middle-of-the-road choice that would not completely alter public education. However, the rapid spread of charters had an unexpected overwhelming impact on Arizona education, and their quick emergence and explosion in numbers was aided by their very similarity to traditional public schools. Ironically, as noted in Chapter 6, charters in Arizona pose a more substantial competitive threat to district schools than private schools or means-tested voucher schemes.

Consequently, Arizona provides a natural experiment to see how district schools will react to competition. The competition is intense since the state government provides a per-pupil subsidy. As charter schools gain students, district schools lose subsidies.

The Reported Reactions of District Schools.   In theory, charter schools should improve district schools by forcing them to compete for dollars that follow students. Our interviews suggest that Arizona district schools have reacted to charter competition by:

(1) *Doing Nothing*. All Arizona public schools have grown quickly in recent years. From 1994–1995 to 1996–1997, enrollment grew by 6.3 percent. Accordingly, many districts were happy to have charters absorb overflow students, especially troubled or "at-risk" students. Interviews suggest that only the district schools in a few strongly affected regions (Mesa and other eastern suburbs of Phoenix; Flagstaff; Sedona–Oak Creek; Yuma; and, later, Tucson) show much concern about competition from charters. Sev-

eral state policy makers suggested the charter movement is still too small to provoke large-scale competitive responses, meaning that any effects at this point are likely to be subtle and to vary by district.

(2) *Improved Customer Service.* The Roosevelt Elementary District, an inner-city Phoenix district hit hard by competition from charters, sent letters to all the charter parents in the district to ask why they had opted for charters and to explain how the district would serve them better in the future. The nearby Isaac Elementary District required teachers and administrators to visit each parent living in the district to address any concerns.

The largest district in the state, Mesa, has responded with particular vigor to charters. On a regular basis, Mesa sends policy staff to the Arizona Department of Education's Charter Schools Administration Division to study proposed charters and "check up on the competition." Since 1994, Mesa has conducted customer service training for teachers and staff and developed a "Red Carpet Treatment" program for reintegrating charter parents wishing to return to district schools. Along with several smaller districts nearby, Mesa offered all-day kindergarten after nearby charter schools did so.

(3) *Advertising.* Interviewees believe that Arizona school districts are increasingly likely to advertise their options and awards in newspapers. The Flagstaff district, among others, issues leaflets comparing district cost and test scores with neighboring districts and with state averages. Mesa even advertises in local movie theaters. All the district officials interviewed suggested that charter schools had forced district schools to do a better job communicating their strengths. As one district administrator said, "It may be that we in the [district] schools have substance but are not very good at advertising. Maybe now we will get better at it."

(4) *Opening Magnet Schools.* The Mesa Unified District opened a new magnet school near an already existing charter school with essentially the same curriculum. A district official in Flagstaff noted, "We started our own magnet school to compete in a way with the charters. . . . People who didn't like the magnet schools in the past now are forced to compete by the charter schools." Interviewees suggest that the Phoenix Union High School District also opened a magnet to counter competition from charters.

(5) *Changing Curriculum.* Particularly in Mesa and in the nearby Queen Creek Elementary District, interviewees suggested that charters forced district schools to conduct in-service teacher training in phonics and increase the proportion of reading instruction using phonics. Indeed, Queen Creek won back more than a third of the students it lost to a charter school after taking this step. Similarly, the operator of a charter arts academy suggested that the competition from this charter school served to "protect arts programs all over the district" by forcing district schools to offer parallel opportunities.

(6) *Undermining the Competition.* As noted, competition sometimes has negative impacts. Charter operators insist that some district officials have used unethical means to squash competition. One charter operator is convinced that the local school district pressured the zoning board to prevent use of a particular building as a school. Others report that district secondary schools have been reluctant to accept transfer credits from charter elementary schools, though districts contend that this is because of quality control problems at some charters. As noted in Chapter 6, other charter operators report that school districts have spread negative rumors. Districts also have discouraged their teachers and principals from starting or teaching at charter schools and have ostracized those who have done so.

The Systemic Impact of Choice

More systematic data can help us interpret the significance of the anecdotal findings just discussed. Typically, studies of school effectiveness use student test scores to assess change, but we suspect scores will be slow to change, may be only indirectly impacted by competitive pressures, and will change only as a consequence of changes in school leadership and culture. Instead, we turn our attention to those changes in school and school system behavior that appear more likely to be a direct response to competition. The presence of behavioral effects at this level does not mean that competition will affect classroom teaching and learning, but we suggest that absent effects at this level are a strong reason to believe that competition will not impact classroom performance. We assess the impact on schools and school systems by surveying teachers, expecting teachers to be the observers best positioned to assess behavioral change.

To assess the impact of competition on traditional public elementary schools, we compare behavioral change in three groups of school districts during the 1994–1997 period. The first Arizona charters opened in 1995. The survey of school behavior was conducted in 1997 and asked teachers to compare current behaviors to those in 1994. Consequently, by comparing changes in behavior with the growth of charter school competition, we can develop an understanding of how competition may impact district behavior. The three groups are:

(1) Nevada school districts, which do not face charter school competition. Whereas Arizona has significant competition, Nevada had no charter schools during the 1994–1997 period. Competitive pressures were very low in Nevada.

(2) Arizona school districts in which less than 12 percent of all elementary schools were charter schools for the 1997–1998 school year. In most of these districts, there were no charter schools; hence the main type of com-

petition present in these districts is the *statewide threat of entry* by charter schools. We sampled twenty-one Arizona districts in this category. Competitive pressures are expected to be moderate for this group.

(3) Arizona school districts in which at least 30 percent of all elementary schools were charter schools. In these districts, *competition* exists between charter and the traditional public schools. We sampled twenty-four Arizona school districts in this category. Competitive pressures should be high for this group.[2] (However, because charter schools tend to be small, the *percentage* of public school elementary students attending charters is far less than 30 percent for most of these districts. The mean charter market share is 9.0 percent for this group.)

Comparisons between Nevada and Arizona schools were made particularly relevant by the demographic similarity of the two states (see Table 8.1). Although Arizona had more child poverty and a more diverse student body, the two states were generally very similar when samples were picked late in 1997. Each had a relatively small private school sector, spent a comparable amount on public education, had a similar ethnic makeup, and had grown very quickly in recent years. Nevada led the nation in growth in the 1990s, and Arizona placed second; their schools have faced serious challenges.

If competition from charter schools has a significant impact on district schools, teachers from the two Arizona groups should observe greater changes in district- and school-level behavior from 1994–1995 to 1997–1998 than the Nevada respondents. If there are significant differences, it is important not to assume that higher levels of change are necessarily positive (Hess 1999). We measured change on a series of school and district behaviors. Change was measured by asking teachers to report on the state of

TABLE 8.1   Comparison of Arizona and Nevada Demographics, 1997–1998 School Year

	Arizona	*Nevada*
Percent White	62	77
Percent Black	4	10
Percent Hispanic	26	8
Percent Native American	6	3
1990–1996 population growth	20.8	33.4
Per-pupil expenditure	$4,874	$5,095
Students per teacher	20	19
Percent in private school	8.3	7.8
Percent urban	87.5	88
Percent of children in poverty	21.4	12.9

SOURCES: Barone et al. 1998; URL: http://govinfo.library.orst.edu/sddb-stateis.html.

affairs in 1994–1995 and in 1997–1998, by aggregating those responses into the three groups identified above, and then by calculating the change over time for each group.[3]

Method. Teachers in ninety-eight Arizona traditional public schools and forty-five Nevada public schools were surveyed by mail in March 1998. For Nevada district teachers, the return rate was 73.9 percent (N = 451); for Arizona district teachers the comparable figure was 79.1 percent (N = 1065).

Survey questions were taken primarily from the widely used U.S. Department of Education School and Staffing Surveys (for details, see Chubb and Moe 1990). For purposes of this chapter, teachers responded to questions about school and system behavior using an agree-disagree scale of 1–6. For example, teachers responded to the item "I am encouraged to experiment with my teaching by my current principal" on a scale of "strongly disagree" (1) to "strongly agree" (6). All responses were aggregated, to generate an average response for both 1994–1995 and for 1997–1998. If an aggregate group rating in 1994–1995 was 4.5, but improved to 4.85 in 1997–1998, then the mean change was .35.

The dimensions of primary importance for examining the feasibility of the market hypothesis can be conveniently divided into two categories:

(1) Leadership dimensions. Teachers reported, for both 1994–1995 and 1997–1998, on the extent to which their principal: encourages experimentation in teaching; protects teachers from outside pressures that may adversely affect teaching; consults with staff members about decisions that may affect them; promotes the use of technology in the classroom; follows up on new initiatives and policies; and helps teachers upgrade and/or fine tune the school curriculum. Teachers also reported on the status of four central district policies in 1994–1995 and then in 1997–1998. The policies were: the extent to which districts inform parents about schooling options; the provision of full-day day care or kindergarten services; the use of flyers to inform parents about district services; and the extent to which in-service training and professional development are promoted by the district.

(2) Teacher involvement in school decisionmaking. Teachers reported on the change over time in the teacher role in seven elements of school governance: budgeting; in-service training; student grouping; curriculum; classroom discipline; class scheduling; and hiring new teachers.

Results. We tested the nature of systemic competitive effects by running an Analysis of Variance (ANOVA) test in which the level of competition in the three groups served as predictors and in which the school and system behaviors were the dependent variables. If the ANOVA F statistic was statistically significant at p < .05, we employed a post hoc test—the Bonferroni test—to determine the statistical significance of differences between pairs of means.[4]

Results for the ten leadership dimensions are reported in Table 8.2. Consistent with the competition hypothesis, the results suggest that more competition leads to larger changes in the variables of interest. The two Arizona groups reported that principals had shown a growing propensity to encourage teacher experimentation, protect teachers from outside pressures, and consult with staff members. In all cases, the Arizona high competition group showed the greatest change, with teachers reporting increased levels of activity. It is important to remember that change may not be desirable and may actually have negative impacts on school performance. However,

TABLE 8.2 Mean Changes in Recalled Leadership Dimensions for Arizona and Nevada School Districts from 1994 to 1997

Dimensions	Nevada	Arizona—Moderate Competition	Arizona—High Competition	F-Value
Principal (P) encourages teachers to experiment	$-.32^a$	$.13^b$	$.18^b$	$F(2,1318) = 15.61^{***}$
P protects teachers from outside pressures	$-.24^a$	$.09^b$	$.30^b$	$F(2,1311) = 14.46^{***}$
P consults with staff members	$-.30^a$	$.15^b$	$.31^b$	$F(2,1321) = 17.60^{***}$
P promotes technology in classroom	$.16^a$	$.15^a$	$.38^b$	$F(2,1318) = 5.16^{**}$
P follows up on new policies	$-.10^a$	$.12^{ab}$	$.29^b$	$F(2,1318) = 8.55^{***}$
P helps teachers upgrade curriculum	$-.14^a$	$.10^b$	$.20^b$	$F(2,1305) = 8.09^{***}$
District (D) informs parents of school programs	$.16^a$	$.18^a$	$.36^b$	$F(2,1310) = 8.43^{***}$
D provides all-day kindergarten/ extended care	$.26^a$	$.18^a$	$.49^b$	$F(2,1302) = 10.62^{***}$
D uses flyers to inform parents of services	$.05^a$	$.09^a$	$.22^b$	$F(2,1309) = 9.35^{***}$
D promotes in-service training	$-.01^s$	$.13^{sb}$	$.22^b$	$F(2,1257) = 6.30^{**}$

NOTES: Means with differing superscripts differ according to a Bonferroni post hoc test at p < .05.

***p < .0001 **p < .001

the behavioral changes produced by competition, such as increased consultation with faculty and support for broader use of technology in the classroom, do appear to be generally positive.

On three of the four district leadership dimensions, the high competition districts show significantly more improvement than both the Nevada and the moderate competition districts ($p < .001$). High competition districts were significantly more likely to have stepped up their efforts to inform parents of school programs, to provide all-day kindergarten or some kind of extended day care, and to use flyers informing parents of services. Both high and moderate competition districts were somewhat more likely to increase in-service training than were the low competition districts.

As Table 8.3 shows, the seven indicators assessing teaching involvement show similar competitive effects. As the level of competition increased, teacher involvement in school decisionmaking grew. Teachers in more competitive districts reported increasing influence over in-service training content, establishing the school curriculum, classroom discipline, and class scheduling. The low competition Nevada group in some cases showed a negative change, suggesting a decline in teacher influence. Again, although the desirability of any particular change cannot be assessed, at first blush, the changes in the high competition districts appear to be generally positive. Mean differences between the two Arizona groups were not statisti-

TABLE 8.3 Impact of Competition on 1994–1997 Changes in Teacher Influence in School Governance

Influence	Nevada	Arizona— Moderate Competition	Arizona— High Competition	F-Values
Determining the school's budget	.003	.04	.12	$F(2,1244) = 2.14$
Determining content of in-service programs	.06[a]	.23[ab]	.31[b]	$F(2,1243) = 5.76$**
Setting policy on tracking	.04	.06	.07	$F(2,1222) = .22$
Establishing curriculum	−.02[a]	.16[b]	.07[ab]	$F(2,1240) = 3.34$*
Classroom discipline	−.03[a]	.16[b]	.15[b]	$F(2,1240) = 6.21$**
Determining class schedules	−.12[a]	.003[ab]	.05[b]	$F(2,1240) = 4.57$**
Hiring new teachers	.09	.20	.11	$F(2,1244) = 1.26$

NOTES: Means with differing superscripts differ according to a Bonferroni post hoc test at $p < .05$.

*$p < .05$ **$p < .01$

cally significant for any of the seven indicators, suggesting that the level of competition has limited impact on teacher involvement in school governance in the short run.

Conclusions and Policy Implications

The results suggest that increases in competition do foster behavioral change in both school and district leadership. That said, this overall finding must be placed in context. First, the changes reported are generally slight to moderate, a finding consistent with Rofes (1998). Although competition has an impact, the short-run effect is not a massive one. Second, the observed changes may or may not be beneficial. Education scholars, for example, disagree over whether teachers should be encouraged to experiment with curriculum matters. Further, change itself may impede educational performance. That said, many of the changes observed— increased emphasis on in-service training, professional development, and greater involvement by teachers in school governance—appear likely to be positive if pursued consistently and implemented thoroughly.

There are multiple long-run scenarios consistent with these short-run results. It is possible that these short-run changes will intensify across time and will have an impact on the teaching and learning core. Alternatively, these initial changes may be the extent of the likely reaction; additional changes will not be forthcoming, and these changes may not impact the classroom core.

Careful study of the early data from Arizona and Nevada suggests that charter school competition has impacted traditional public school districts in ways likely to be positive. Arizona schools facing potential competition experienced greater change than Nevada schools lacking competitive concerns, and Arizona schools that faced higher levels of actual competition were the most likely to have changed in significant ways. These findings help fill out part of the picture in Arizona; however, future research is needed to determine the extent and true impact of such changes.

Notes

1. Hoxby (1996, 1998) and Smith and Meier (1995) are partial exceptions. Their work infers impacts on public schools from existing private school enrollments, and predicts impacts from expanded choice.

2. We attempted, roughly, to stratify districts by size (indicated by number of schools), geographic location, and demographic similarity. District size varied greatly, from one to 114 traditional public schools. We split districts into thirds, with "small" districts of four traditional public schools or under, "medium districts" of five to eleven schools, and "large" districts of twelve schools or more. We picked roughly equal numbers of districts from each third.

3. Our measurement at the individual teacher level greatly increases the degrees of statistical freedom; for example, usually at least 300 teachers provided data for a given dimension for all three groups. Measuring these changes at the district level is more difficult statistically due to inadequate statistical power; in particular, we have data from only fifteen Nevada districts.

4. Given the high N in our sample and thus the great amount of statistical power, the statistical significance of many of our tests is not surprising. However, the effects are in a clear and predicted pattern, something that would not occur were the findings random. We also chose the Bonferroni post hoc test because it used a more stringent criterion of experiment-wise error.

References

Armour, David L., and Brett M. Peiser. 1998. "Interdistrict Choice in Massachusetts." In *Learning from School Choice*, ed. Paul E. Peterson and Bryan C. Hassel. Washington, D.C.: Brookings Institution.

Barone, Michael, Grant Ujifusa, and Richard E. Cohen. 1998. *The Almanac of American Politics, 1998: The Senators, the Representatives, and the Governors: Their States and Districts*. Washington, D.C.: National Journal.

Boyer, Ernest L. 1992. *School Choice*. Princeton: Carnegie Foundation for the Advancement of Teaching.

Bryk, Anthony S., Valerie E. Lee, and Peter B. Holland. 1993. *Catholic Schools and the Common Good*. Cambridge: Harvard University Press.

Chubb, John E., and Terry M. Moe. 1990. *Politics, Markets, and America's schools*. Washington, D.C.: Brookings Institution.

Elmore, Richard F., Penelope Peterson, and Sarah McCarthy. 1996. *Restructuring in the Classroom: Teaching, Learning, and School Organization*. San Francisco: Jossey-Bass.

Fullan, Michael. 1991. *The New Meaning of Educational Change*. New York: Teachers College Press.

Greene, Jay P., Paul E. Peterson, and Jiangtao Du. 1998. "School Choice in Milwaukee: A Randomized Experiment." In *Learning from School Choice*, ed. Paul E. Peterson and Bryan C. Hassel. Washington, D.C.: Brookings Institution.

Hassel, Bryan. 1998. "Charter Schools: Politics and Practice in Four States." In *Learning from School Choice*, ed. Paul E. Peterson and Bryan C. Hassel. Washington, D.C.: Brookings Institution.

Hess, Frederick. 1999. *Spinning Wheels: The Politics of Urban School Reform*. Washington, D.C.: Brookings Institution.

Hoxby, Caroline Minter. 1996. "The Effects of Private School Vouchers on Schools and Students." In *Holding Schools Accountable: Performance Based Reform in Education*, ed. Helen F. Ladd. Washington, D.C.: Brookings Institution.

_____. 1998. "Analyzing School Choice Reforms That Use America's Traditional Forms of Parental Choice." In *Learning from School Choice*, ed. Paul E. Peterson and Bryan C. Hassel. Washington, D.C.: Brookings Institution.

Johnson, Susan Moore. 1996. *Leading to Change: The Challenge of the New Superintendency*. San Francisco: Jossey-Bass.

Lipsky, Michael. 1980. *Street Level Bureaucracy.* New York: Russell Sage Foundation.

Loveless, Tom, and Claudia Jasin. 1998. "Starting from Scratch: Political and Organizational Challenges Facing Charter Schools." *Educational Administration Quarterly* 34 (1): 9–30.

Millott, Marc Dean, and Robin Lake. 1996. *So You Want to Start a Charter School?* Seattle: University of Washington Institute for Public Policy Management.

Peterson, Paul, and Chad Noyes. 1997. "School Choice in Milwaukee." In *New Schools for a New Century: The Redesign of Urban Education,* ed. Diane Ravitch and Joseph Viteritti. New Haven: Yale University Press.

Rofes, Eric. 1998. "How Are School Districts Responding to Charter Laws and Charter Schools?" University of California at Berkeley: Policy Analysis for California Education.

Smith, Kevin B., and Kenneth J. Meier. 1995. *The Case Against School Choice: Politics, Markets, and Fools.* Armonk, N.Y.: M. E. Sharpe.

Sukstorf, Marla E., Amy Stuart Wells, and Robert L. Crain. 1993. "A Re-Examination of Chubb and Moe's *Politics, Markets, and America's Schools.*" In *School Choice: Examining the Evidence,* ed. Edith Rasell and Richard Rothstein. Washington, D.C.: Economic Policy Institute.

Tyack, David B., and Larry Cuban. 1995. *Tinkering Toward Utopia: A Century of Public School Reform.* Cambridge, Mass.: Harvard University Press.

Vanourek, Gregg, Bruno V. Manno, Chester E. Finn Jr., and Louann A. Bierlein. 1997. "Hudson Institute Charter Schools in Action Project: Final Report." October 24, 1997, URL: http://www.edexcellence.net/chart/chart1.htm.

Witte, John F. 1996. "School Choice and Student Performance." In *Holding Schools Accountable: Performance Based Reform in Education,* ed. Helen F. Ladd. Washington, D.C.: Brookings Institution.

Witte, John F., Christopher A. Thorn, Kim M. Pritchard, and Michele Claibourn. 1994. "Fourth-year Report: Milwaukee Parental Choice Program." Madison: University of Wisconsin–Madison.

9

Closing Charters: How a Good Theory Failed in Practice

GREGG A. GARN AND ROBERT T. STOUT

The Arizona charter school policy was based on economic theory rather than empirical research, and, not unexpectedly, a divide has occurred between theory and practice. This chapter examines the practical problems faced by the state agencies: the Arizona Department of Education (ADE), the Office of the Auditor General, and the state-level sponsoring boards—the Arizona State Board of Education (ASBE) and the State Board for Charter Schools (SBCS). The researchers found that in contrast to the rhetoric of charter school advocates, who viewed the program as relatively problem free, a lack of communication among the aforementioned entities deprived board members and parents of critical information about the performance of charter schools from 1995 through 1998. And without reliable performance information, a market system cannot function; thus the theory has not translated well into practice.

Introduction

Over the past two decades, policy makers in Arizona have grown increasingly weary of reforming the district public school system. Numerous policies aimed at improving the academic performance of pupils were enacted with the same dissatisfying results. As a result, state-level policy makers were receptive to plans for creating an entirely new system of public education in the form of charter schools. The central motivation behind this reform was the desire to create a public school system based on market accountability. Rather than requiring charter schools to follow a prescribed set of rules and employing bureaucrats to monitor compliance, the policy makers would force charter schools to attract students and maintain enrollment as their primary proof of effectiveness. In other words, charter schools would be accountable to customers (parents and students) rather than bureaucrats. State senator Tom Patterson articulated this market-based view: "Charter schools are in a way a test of an entirely different accountability method which is decentralized, which depends— rather than on bureaucratic rules and regulations—on first of all these being schools of choice. It's accountability that comes from the parents and the consumers" (Patterson interview 1998).

Arizona citizens were receptive to the fundamental argument that schools should be subject to market accountability mechanisms and forced to compete for students. Politicians further increased public support for this reform by using simplistic metaphors to justify the policy, in the absence of empirical research. A popular analogy was drawn to the American automobile industry. In the 1960s and 1970s, American automobile manufacturers dominated the world market. However, legislators argued that over time the monopoly allowed these organizations to become lazy, and as such, the cars they produced in the 1970s were expensive, inefficient, and unreliable. In the late 1970s, when Asia began to produce more efficient, reliable, and less costly automobiles, customers recognized a better product when they were offered a choice. U.S. automakers were forced to respond to the competition and did so by producing a higher quality product to gain back market share. In sum, competition in the marketplace forced the production of better quality automobiles.

Arizona policy makers applied this same faith in market ideology to the public school system and in 1994 designed a charter school policy. Legislators intended to promote competition among public schools by giving parents and students choices about which school to attend, rather than compelling them to attend the neighborhood district school. Policy makers argued that charter schools would break up the district school monopoly because parents would select the school that best met their children's educational needs. Thus, charter schools would have to respond to customer demands and satisfy parent expectations or risk losing students and the per-pupil allocations that followed each child. If charter schools lost enough students, they would be forced to close. Over time, charter school advocates argued, parents "voting with their feet" would create a system of high performing public schools.

Rarely does the rhetoric of ideologues translate smoothly into practice, and the establishment of charter schools in Arizona was no exception. Although policy makers focused intently on dismantling the bureaucratic entanglements for charter schools, they neglected to articulate how state agencies should deal with charter schools in a market-based context.

Legislators failed to consider the details of how this policy would be implemented and managed. As a result, the state sponsoring boards, the Arizona Department of Education, and the auditor general's office have struggled to translate the charter school legislation into a working program. This chapter focuses on the practical problems faced by these agencies.

Methods

Sources

The research questions in this study lent themselves to an exploratory and descriptive qualitative case study methodology. This case study employed three main research methods: document analysis, observations, and focused interviews. These multiple methods were used in concert to compensate for the strengths and weaknesses of each source. Documents proved to be a valuable data source because they contained systematic information relevant to the case. Although they were an incomplete source by themselves, documents complemented the other data sources well. Documents obtained from interviews, site visits, meetings, library searches, and public records were gathered and analyzed.

Specific document sources evaluated for this study include: newspaper articles from three prominent Arizona newspapers; the minutes of the Committee on Education for the Arizona state senate and the house of representatives of the 43rd legislature; charter applications from schools approved and operating during the 1995–1996 and 1996–1997 school years; Arizona Department of Education site visit monitoring notes; data from the superintendent for public instruction's annual report; charter school report cards; and the charter school statute, including amendments made through the 1998 session. These documents played three important roles. First, they were relatively easy to attain and provided background for interviews. Second, they guided observations of important actors. Third, the documents were used to verify and strengthen data from other sources as a confirmatory source after interviews and observations were conducted (Yin 1994).

Observation of key actors constituted a second data source. We observed essential actors in multiple contexts, such as meetings of the ASBE and the SBCS, in addition to Committee on Education meetings in the Arizona state senate and house of representatives.

The third and most important data source proved to be interviews with key actors. In this study, a focused interview style was used. Interviews lasted from thirty to ninety minutes and followed a semi-structured protocol. Information from other data sources was used to structure the interview protocol, and participants were given a chance to elaborate on topics central to the study.

Interviews were conducted with twenty-four persons selected from the following four groups: board members and administrators from the two state sponsoring agencies (the ASBE and SBCS); personnel from various divisions within the Arizona Department of Education, including the superintendent of public instruction; staff members from the auditor general's office; and legislators who served on the Arizona house of representatives and the Arizona senate Education Committees.[1] Sixteen of the interviews were recorded on audiotape and transcribed. Eight interviews were conducted over the telephone and were documented through extensive notes typed up immediately following the interview.

Data Analysis

Data analysis consisted of both coding and direct interpretation methods. When findings from these two methods conflicted, coded data were given more credence than direct interpretation. During this project, data analysis and collection occurred simultaneously. Our tentative understandings were continually tested against the rest of the data and verified or discarded. When data from one source were collected, they were coded and compared with data collected from the same source at another time, as well as with data collected from alternative sources, applying several of the internal validity standards of Miles and Huberman (1994). As this process continued, themes and patterns emerged and were refined.

Results

Factors Impeding Implementation

The origin of many practical problems faced by charter school entities can be traced back to a series of contextual factors that complicated the implementation of the charter school policy. Ineffective planning, a lack of funding for administrative personnel, and a reduction of staff at the ADE proved to be serious impediments during the implementation process. Consequently, the articulation of a proactive and coordinated charter school program was not feasible.

The first factor that hindered the implementation of charter schools was ineffective planning. The state legislature approved charter school legislation on June 17, 1994, and the statute took effect September 16, 1994, leaving little time to legitimately organize the program. According to Corinne Velasquez, the executive director of the ASBE:

> The day the legislation was signed by the governor—actually it was ninety days later when it [went] into effect. The day it went into effect, we [had] people in here with charter school applications who said, 'I am ready to start

a new charter school.' So there are two things that happened in the legislation. . . . One, there was no planning time for the [Arizona Department of Ed-
ucation] to develop the program; and, two, there was no appropriation tied
to the bill for the legislation. And here I have people lining up saying, 'I'm
all ready to open up my charter school now.' What are you going to do?
(Velasquez interview 1998)

From the day the statute took effect to the opening of the first school,
ADE staff had approximately eleven months to interpret the aims of the
charter school legislation and develop a series of policies that upheld the
intent. Because other states with charter school legislation had only a
few schools operating, the staff at the ADE did not anticipate that the response in Arizona would be any different, and consequently developing
the details of the charter school program was a relatively low priority.
Paul Street, a former associate superintendent of the ADE, recalls:

One person and a secretary that first year were trying to handle all of that, all
of the application proceedings and getting them answered, getting them to
board members. . . . And I remember it was pretty overwhelming. . . . It [the
charter school legislation] passed in June and went into effect ninety days
later. And so by early fall we were scrambling to get stuff in place and get the
procedures together and get the applications written up and those kinds of
things." (Street interview 1998)

Badly misjudging the number of people interested in opening a charter
school, the ADE failed to develop a predetermined strategy for holding
these schools accountable. Instead, ADE staff developed a triage mentality—deal with the most critical problem first, and then go on to the next
most serious issue:

When the ink was not even dry on the legislation that allowed charter schools
to take place, . . . there were people waiting with applications to have charter
schools. . . . It was many people. So they never had the opportunity to set
these systems up, and we haven't had a breather to be able to do it. Wouldn't
it be wonderful if we could just stop and use this year for planning and getting it all together, and then start chartering again? But I don't think that's
going to happen either. . . . It would be wonderful, but we'll never have that
luxury. (ADE administrative staff interview 1998)

Another problem with the charter school legislation was that although
it gave two state-sponsoring entities (the ASBE and SBCS) responsibilities
for approval and oversight of charter schools, it limited appropriations
for administrators to staff either of the state boards. This oversight left

both boards incapable of fulfilling basic obligations. Policy makers made an explicit decision to limit funding for administrators in an effort to discourage a new bureaucracy from developing around this reform. By default, the ADE was forced to share basic approval and oversight responsibilities during the first application cycle, without additional funding.

Concurrent downsizing at the ADE further complicated the implementation of the charter school policy. While the department was receiving additional responsibilities for charter schools, there was a reduction in staff:

> As close as I can tell, okay, I came in after that happened, and don't hold me to exact figures, but I want to tell you there were approximately, when Lisa [Graham Keegan] took office, there were 460 employees in the building. And when I got there at the end of her eighth month, they were down to 350, so it was like 110 people, about 27 percent reduction in an eight-month period. And that has pretty much stabilized. (Street interview 1998)

Time, funding, and staff reductions during the policy implementation process combined to hinder the development of a comprehensive plan to deal with charter schools. Consequently, contacts with charter schools evolved based on addressing immediate problems, rather than anticipating future ones. Corinne Velasquez:

> We have never been able to get out of the reaction stage, you know, we have never been able to think. We never had time to think far enough ahead to what is the next step that is going to come. . . . So every time we have been so involved with a particular stage of development that we have done no long-term planning or anticipating for what we have to do later. (Velasquez interview 1998)

Theory and Practice Diverge

The following three sections examine how the chaotic implementation of charter schools ultimately resulted in a series of practical problems that the state sponsoring boards, the ADE, and the auditor general's office had to face.

State Sponsoring Boards.   The charter statute endowed the ASBE and SBCS with general responsibilities for charter schools. The legislation gave the sponsoring boards the power to approve new charter schools, to sanction schools for minor infractions, and to revoke the charter of poor performing schools. Although the state-level boards had the potential to play an important part in ensuring charter school accountability through 1998, they fulfilled those responsibilities in name only. Both the ASBE and the SBCS have focused their limited energies on approving new schools and left monitoring responsibilities to parents. Consequently, the state sponsoring boards required little in the way of reporting and did even less monitoring of charter schools.

Neglecting oversight responsibilities, both state sponsoring boards concentrated on the application process. During the 1997–1998 application cycle, they developed a three-step procedure of completing the application, getting the application approved, and signing the charter contract to ensure accountability once the school opened. Interviews with board members and administrative staff confirmed that more time was devoted to the approval process than to any other area. In contrast, once the charter school opened, contact with the sponsor was rare and accountability requirements were superficial.

Both the ASBE and SBCS did require charter schools to complete an annual written report detailing outcomes achieved and progress toward the goals specified in the charter contract. *However, there was no prescribed format for the annual report, and it was up to the charter school operator to determine what information they would include in this self evaluation.* Moreover, the information in the report was neither evaluated nor verified for accuracy by board members:

> Actually, by law [charter schools] are required to [submit an annual written report to their sponsor]. They [the board] don't evaluate it in any way. I think . . . this is the first year we have . . . asked for that report. The report is basically there for the board to look at. . . . The [written] report is basically almost like the [oral] presentation where it's information you want to tell us, but it also talks budgets and finances. . . . But we don't nail them with anything. (SBCS administrative staff interview 1998)

A former board member confirmed that the annual review was not rigorous. "It was just a formality, just 'We got the report, here is what it says.' . . . But I don't ever recall there being—we just got the reports in and some board member saying, 'Well, I've got some real concerns about this.' I don't remember ever hearing that kind of thing" (Street interview 1998).

Additionally, the SBCS required charter school operators to make an oral report to the board as well as the written report. Similarly there was no prescribed format, and it lacked an external evaluation component. As Mary Gifford, the former executive director of the SBCS said:

> Part of [the oral presentation] is, "This is the time to showcase your school. Get up here and tell us good things that are going on at your school." It also allows us to drop in questions. Some of them are softball questions that are just interesting, that we'd like to know. It allows us to get the problematic

things up there, and that forms some of the questions to hopefully get at the roots of their problems. . . . If they're in trouble or we suspect they are in trouble, if we get a [large] volume of complaint calls and we can't put our finger on the problem, we may have them come and do their annual report, and we get to the root of the problem with them there. It's the best time of the year, because most times we get to hear the good things. A lot of them bring their kids in. . . . For most schools, it's the best time, and for most board members it's the best time. (Gifford interview 1998)

In addition to the annual reports, administrative staff of both boards had an informal goal to visit the schools on a yearly basis. The visits were unstructured, informal, and aimed at showing off the successful aspects of the operation, much like the annual reports. In the 1997–1998 school year the SBCS staff and board members followed through with this unwritten policy; however, the ASBE was still determining how to implement a similar plan as the 1997–1998 school year ended. High profile individuals on the ASBE had little spare time for making site visits to charter schools.

The annual reports and the site visits allowed the charter school directors complete discretion over what information they provided to the state sponsoring boards. Moreover, the information that was provided was not evaluated by board members in any systematic manner. Therefore, and in keeping with the rationale that parental monitoring was favorable to bureaucratic monitoring, the application process, not the annual reports, proved to be the primary accountability mechanism employed by the state sponsoring boards to evaluate Arizona charter schools.

Arizona Department of Education. The disorganized implementation process also contributed to the lack of communication among divisions within the ADE, which in turn limited the information provided to the sponsoring boards about problems in charter schools. The charter school policy explicitly reduced the bureaucratic reporting requirements for charter schools and altered the roles of ADE staff members. Because charter schools were primarily accountable to the sponsoring boards and parents, the ADE's primary function was to inform the boards of potential or actual problems in charter schools. With that performance information, the sponsoring boards were expected to reward or sanction charter schools appropriately. Therefore, faced with a series of problems presented by the charter schools, the various divisions within the ADE developed independent strategies for dealing with charter schools, and the transfer of performance data to state sponsoring boards was negligible.

The Exceptional Student Services Division of the ADE provides one example of how the communication breakdown limited information.

Arizona Revised Statute (ARS) 15-183E7 (http://www.azleg.state.az.us/
ars/15/183.htm) requires charter schools to comply with all statutes relating to the education of children with disabilities in the same manner as
district schools. Consequently, Exceptional Student Services staff members established some oversight mechanisms to ensure compliance with
federal and state laws.

Interviews with staff members in the special education division indicate they had little interaction with charter schools during the first year of
operation (1995–1996). Special education staff responded to specific complaints but lacked a systematic program to monitor compliance among
charter schools. During the following school year an outreach program
was initiated that monitored a sample of charter and district schools for
compliance.

However, with the growing number of charter schools and the limited
staffing provisions, special education staff only monitored twenty-five
charter schools each year. Charter schools from the sample were subjected
to a group evaluation, whereby a team of staff members visited the charter school, evaluated the program for students with disabilities, and provided technical assistance when required. Special education staff documented their findings in a corrective action plan. Interviews with special
education staff and State Board for Charter Schools administrative staff
members confirmed that information from the corrective action plans was
not passed on to the state sponsoring boards. The poor communication
between the Exceptional Student Services Division and the state sponsoring boards from 1995 through 1998 deprived board members and parents
of critical performance information about charter schools.

Academic Support, another division within the ADE, provides a second example of the faulty communication system. Staff in this division
monitored programs for special needs students with many risk factors,
including financial deprivation and language barriers. Federal programs
within this unit include Indian Education, Early Childhood Development, Title I and VI, Bilingual Education, and the Dwight D. Eisenhower
program. Academic Support programs apply only to charter schools that
chose to take advantage of supplemental federal funds provided for at-
risk students. Although many charter schools in Arizona targeted at-risk
students, most of the charter schools in general did not receive federal
subsidies.[2]

The reasons for not applying for supplemental federal funds were apparent to ADE staff:

> Over half of the charter schools do not participate. Some don't do it because
> we allocate on a per-pupil basis and they are too small, and it's not worth-
> while, and others are philosophically opposed. They started their school to

get away from the bureaucratic rules and regulations. (personal communication, ADE Title I administrative staff 1998)

Personnel from Academic Support are required to monitor charter schools that receive federal grant money, so, much like the special education monitoring visits, these schools were examined for procedural compliance. Unfortunately, also like the special education staff, Academic Support personnel reported that the information collected was not passed on to the state sponsoring boards:

> Numbers are checked against other departments within the Academic Support Division. If lots of variance is identified, then more extensive follow-up is done; we contact the school immediately and sometimes go out into the school. We can catch most of the problems with those checks. To the best of my knowledge, this information has not been passed on to the sponsor. I think in the future it will be a good idea to write a two-page letter to the sponsor and summarize our findings. (personal communication, ADE Title VI administrative staff 1998)

In short, the Academic Support Division collected important data that the sponsoring boards could have used to examine the performance of charter schools. The recurring problem of getting information to the state sponsoring boards again limited information about charter school performance.

The third and most egregious example of the inadequate transfer of information from the ADE to the sponsoring boards is a department-wide charter school monitoring program introduced during the 1996–1997 school year. The program was initiated after the department received a large number of complaints from charter school faculty and parents:

> I think it was initiated because there were some of us internally who were concerned that there was no monitoring going on, that nobody really knew what was happening out there in the field. We would hear horror stories, or parents would call in with these unbelievable tales of stuff, and nobody really knew what was happening, nobody knew if the schools were delivering what they said they would. Were they complying with their charter or not? Nobody really knew. . . . We just kind of took it into our own hands and kind of went to the superintendent with the plan, and she said, "Yeah, okay, it sounds good." (Street interview 1998)

Two ADE staff members worked full time on the monitoring project and coordinated the effort. "We elicited support from about 50 people . . . in total. Most of the department in various divisions and some were external, either charter school people, or public [district] school people, or

[Arizona State] University people, or whatever volunteered" (ADE administrative staff interview 1998).

The monitoring process began informally as ADE staff members responded to specific complaints. Technical advice and constructive comments were provided to charter school operators in an attempt to remedy troublesome issues. By fall 1996, a more systematic monitoring program was initiated, and a site visit protocol was developed:

> We basically took every piece of legislation that was referenced in law for charter schools. It took all the assurances that were advised, and it basically interpreted all of those into certain action plans or behaviors that we wanted to look for in schools. We did not do a programmatic audit, in that we did not look at quality or the process of education, or the programs that they were actually implementing. What we were monitoring were those things that have either legal or statutory compliance or charter compliance, meaning that they were doing things that either weren't in their charter, or they weren't doing things that were in their charter. So we looked for the compliance in state and federal statutes. (ADE administrative staff interview 1998)

The Department of Education monitoring teams were required to examine seven general areas outlined in the protocol: (1) purpose of the charter; (2) special area emphasis/curriculum design/innovation; (3) student assessment program; (4) operational structure; (5) parent/student/satisfaction; (6) school finance/reporting/enrollment/verification; and (7) statutory/statement of assurances review. An additional eighth section allowed responses from the charter school directors.

To facilitate the process, the ADE sent out the protocols to charter school directors several weeks before a site visit. Directors were required to type out, on the monitoring protocol forms, how they were meeting the requirements in each of the seven areas. When ADE monitors arrived, they commented on the degree to which their observations equated to the charter school directors' claims. When the visit was over, all artifacts collected during the visit were stored in a file folder for each charter school. The evaluators' notes from the site visits were either written directly on the monitoring instrument or taken on separate notepads. That information along with other data collected from the visit were to be combined and typed into a comprehensive record by support staff:

> The plan was that the secretaries would be typing the reports and putting them on file. . . . In the meantime there were secretaries that left and came and went and came and went, and the bottom line is that the reports, the majority of the reports, unless they were the ones that were in severe trouble or that needed to have records that were going to go to a hearing or whatever,

then I personally typed those. . . . Otherwise all the notes were left in file
folders. (ADE administrative staff interview 1998)

In sum, few monitoring notes were ever typed; the information from the
reports was never passed along; and neither the state sponsoring agencies
nor the charter schools received information about the monitoring visits.

When the reports were made public eventually, they were still in the
form of handwritten notes. The last page of the protocol included a summary sheet for the monitor to complete. This allowed the evaluator to
summarize comments on charter and statutory compliance, to determine
if a follow-up was necessary, and if so to indicate how soon it needed to
be completed. Based on the severity of the violation of any state or federal
statute, or the terms of the charter, the ADE evaluator was supposed to
complete the summary sheet. However, the summary sheets were blank
or missing from twenty of the thirty-two monitoring visit reports analyzed for this study. Of the twelve that did have comments in the summary area, nine required follow-ups because the school was out of compliance with either their charter or relevant statutes. Significantly, the
sponsors never asked for or received that critical information.

The monitoring program was quietly phased out after one tumultuous
year, and the results of the program were particularly dismal. Superintendent Keegan stated that ADE staff members would not continue the charter school monitoring program. Rather, the sponsoring boards would have
to assume monitoring responsibilities in the future. Both state boards publicly stated they would take over the monitoring responsibilities after the
1997–1998 school year. However, development of a monitoring program by
the sponsoring boards was behind schedule. Moreover, with a total of five
administrative staff members among both boards (including secretaries)
and a steadily increasing number of charter schools, it remained unclear
how monitoring by the state sponsoring boards would be accomplished.

ADE personnel failed to create a functional system for transferring performance information to the state sponsoring boards, and communication
remained uncoordinated and disorganized through 1998. The practical
result was that board members assumed charter schools were problem
free. Furthermore, parents, who were ultimately responsible for monitoring, were again deprived of important performance information.

Auditor General.   The Office of the Auditor General was the final government entity to play a notable role in charter school accountability. Staff
members from this office were given the responsibility to ensure that
charter schools were not misspending public tax dollars. Like the other
state agencies, the auditor general's office absorbed the additional responsibilities for charter schools under the existing budget allocation.

Unlike the other government bureaus, this office did establish a formal line of communication with the sponsoring agencies. However, policy actions of the SBCS have decreased the financial monitoring role for the auditor general.

By 1998, the auditor general's office assumed important responsibilities for financial oversight. Arizona Revised Statute 15-183E6 required charter schools to follow the same financial reporting system as district schools—the Uniform System of Financial Records (USFR). This statute also stated that the auditor general could conduct financial, program, or compliance audits to ensure charter schools were following the USFR correctly; that statute formally brought the auditor general into the charter school accountability system. Subsequently, ARS 15-183E6 (http://www.azleg.state.az.us/ars/15/183.htm) was amended and allowed charter schools to follow an alternative financial reporting system. Staff members from Financial Services who wrote the district USFR guidelines were given the responsibility for modifying and simplifying a version for the charter schools—the Uniform System of Financial Records for Charter Schools (USFRCS).

A 1997 amendment by the state legislature, known as the Single Audit Act, placed an even greater burden on staff at the auditor general's office. This act required all charter schools to conduct annual external financial audits:

> The governing board of a charter school is required to comply with the Single Audit Act, plus [it] must contract for an annual financial and compliance audit, with financial transactions subject to the Single Audit Act. . . . There was no provision in the charter school statute for our office or CPAs [Certified Public Accountants] to do audits. That was added later—the [single] audit requirements. (auditor general staff interview 1998)

Prior to the Single Audit Act, most charter schools were covered by legislation that required all non-profit organizations to conduct yearly audits. However, for-profit charters, about 25 percent of the total number of charter schools in Arizona, were exempt from any external auditing requirements. The Single Audit Act required all charter schools (including the for-profit charter schools) that expend more than $300,000 to complete a federal compliance audit as well as a financial statement audit. These audits combined were referred to as a "single audit." Charter schools that did not exceed $300,000 in expenditures were still required to complete the financial statement audit; however, they were exempt from the federal compliance audit.

Staff members from the auditor general's office were involved in many aspects of the audit. Their role was to ensure that the audits were completed appropriately and to check the results of the audit opinion, rather than to perform the formal audit itself. After the director of a charter school selected a CPA firm and the contract was approved, staff members from the auditor general's office continued to monitor the process. ARS 15-271 (http://www.azleg.state.az.us/ars/15/271.htm) required the auditor general to inform any charter school failing to meet the requirements (as prescribed by the USFRCS) that it had ninety days to correct the deficiencies. In order for the auditor general to make such a determination, external auditors completed a USFRCS compliance questionnaire along with a legal compliance questionnaire. When the audit was completed, the auditor general's office performed a working-paper review of the audit to check the quality of the CPA's work, as well as to ensure that the charter school was financially sound.

First, the audit opinion was analyzed. Second, the financial statement and the corresponding footnotes were examined. Third, the internal controls of the charter school were evaluated, and, finally, the compliance and legal questionnaires, completed by the CPA, were examined. If the external examination identified problems based on the audit information, the charter school operator received a letter from the auditor general, explaining the specific requirements and the ninety day deadline to resolve any deficiencies. A copy of the letter also was sent to the sponsor. After the ninety-day period, staff from the auditor general's office followed up to make sure that the necessary corrections had been completed, and they documented their findings in a second letter that informed the sponsor of the charter school's compliance status. At that point, the responsibility fell upon the sponsor to act.

The executive director of the ASBE describes the process as follows:

> They [auditor general's office] send us [the school's sponsor] a letter that says they have found a school to be not in compliance with the USFRCS, and . . . the state board determines that they are not in compliance with the USFRCS, and they must request a hearing before the board. And if they don't request a hearing, the superintendent [of public instruction] is allowed to withhold their funds. So 100 percent of the time people will request a hearing. . . . So we pretty much assume there is compliance unless we hear contrary to that. And that is the same with district schools. (Velasquez interview 1998)

Depending on the progress made toward fixing the problems, the sponsoring board could grant an extension to the school, or they could withhold funds. In sum, the sponsor, not the auditor general's office, had enforcement power over the charter schools.

The relationship between the auditor general's office and the sponsoring agencies changed between 1994 and 1998. Initially, the main contact was through ninety-day letters that provided basic information about the financial health of the charter schools. However, in the 1997–1998 school year, the SBCS granted twenty-two charter schools waivers from the US-FRCS. This ruling dramatically decreased the role of the auditor general. For the charter schools that received a waiver from the USFRCS, the sponsoring board assumed responsibility for monitoring financial compliance. The charter school legislation was specific that the auditor general was required to notify charter school staff if they did not comply with the USFRCS, and the staff members from the auditor general's office established a formal line of communication with the sponsoring agency through the ninety-day letters. But, if the charter school did not have to follow that accounting form, the auditor general lost jurisdiction, and the SBCS assumed responsibility for financial oversight. Whether or not the administrative staff for the sponsoring boards had the training or whether board members had the time or expertise to monitor the financial health of charter schools was unclear. However, they clearly did not have the same level of skills or time as the professionals who performed this work in the auditor general's office.

Conclusion and Recommendations for Policy Makers

In a market-based system customers need reliable information to make sound purchase decisions. For example, an individual would be in a better position to purchase an automobile if s/he had basic safety, quality, and performance data from an independent evaluator rather than from a salesperson in a showroom. From 1995 through 1998, safety, quality, and performance information about Arizona charter schools was in short supply. Key political actors, including Senator Huppenthal, the chairman of the senate Education Committee, recognized the performance reporting problem:

> To make that purchase decision something that means something, they have to have maximum information, so the things that I focused on that we don't have yet are academic productivity and quality ratings and, to a lesser extent, student quality ratings and teacher job satisfaction. If you know those things, I think you know a tremendous amount about the quality of the school. Right now, we don't have any of that data. So right now, in terms of any kind of data that's available on schools, almost all of the data that we have now in my mind is worthless, so right now we have no way of keeping score. None of the methods right now, none of the data we have right now coming in has a whole lot of value for someone making a purchase decision. (Huppenthal interview 1998).

Test scores, however fallible, were one source of information about school performance available. Parents and sponsoring board members can determine how the students in a charter school scored on a standardized test. However, the usefulness of test scores was reduced in the first years of charter schools because of changes in testing policy. Arizona first administered the Iowa Test of Basic Skills but then switched to the Stanford Nine during the second year of the charter reform. This change in testing policy disrupted the collection of trend data and negated measurements of school improvement or decline.

A second potential source of charter school performance information is a mandatory school report card required of all public schools. From this document, the ADE collected various types of information about schools: school organization and philosophy; academic goals; number of school days; average daily instruction time; school honors; instructional programs offered; grades served; enrollment; school site council composition and duties; school and parent responsibilities; staff information (including number of administrators, teachers, and teacher aides); transportation policy; resources available at the school site; school safety; food programs; attendance rate; mobility rate; retention rate or dropout rate; and academic indicators. The school report card seemingly covered the general information parents would need to know before enrolling their children in a charter school. However, because report cards were so incomplete, they were much more useful as a sound bite for policy makers than as information for a parent trying to make a decision about which school to select for his/her children.

Three problems surfaced with regard to the report cards. The first was that not all schools returned them, and even fewer returned completed ones. There were no sanctions for not sending this information to the ADE, so, not surprisingly, some public schools (charter and district) failed to comply. A second problem was that the report card information was posted on the ADE's web site (http://www.ade.state.az.us/). This web site was frequently down and not accessible even to individuals who had access to the World Wide Web.[3] A third and even less soluble problem was a large percentage of parents who did not (and still do not) have access to the Internet. In fact, Arizona governor Jane Hull has recently admitted these problems and called for better access to information about charter schools (Nowicki 1998).

Given our findings, we believe improved communication would translate directly into greater accountability for bureaucrats and, more importantly, parents. The theory of a free market requires the free flow of certain minimum amounts of information concerning the effectiveness of the product. Arizona policy makers need to improve the quality and quantity of information about charter schools operating around the state.

The fact remains that 20,000 students were enrolled in Arizona charter schools from 1995 through 1998, with very little performance data about the schools. Moreover, to our knowledge, there are no current plans for improving the system of communication. Charter school advocates call the policy a success. Yet, no charter schools are likely to be closed (short of being caught in the act of major fraud) because parents and sponsoring board members lack the necessary data to make any evaluative judgments. In sum, the rhetoric of advocates has not lived up to the practical results.

Notes

1. We gave our interviewees the choice of releasing their identity or protecting it. Most participants allowed us to present their real names, especially legislators and sponsoring board members, who were interested in getting credit for their opinions and ideas. Others were less interested in the publicity and, consequently, names were withheld and/or altered to protect their anonymity. In these instances a job title was substituted in place of a name to convey a respondent's background and insight.

2. Seeking subsidies tends to be diametrically opposed to the typical charter philosophy of less bureaucracy. Moreover, according to financial data from the annual report of the superintendent of public instruction for the 1995–1996 school year, the forty-six schools sponsored by the ASBE and SBCS spent a total of just over $500,000 on special needs services. One single school (Carmel Community) spent over $200,000 of that total. Clearly, most charters did not take advantage of special education funds.

3. The authors needed to access the ADE web site frequently for the study and were often frustrated with their inability to get necessary information from the site. According to personal communications with several other researchers, this web site's dysfunction was a common problem during that time.

References

Miles, M. B., and A. M. Huberman. 1994. *An Expanded Sourcebook: Qualitative Data Analysis.* 2d ed. Thousand Oaks, Calif.: Sage Publications.

Nowicki, Dan. 1998. "Governor Aims at Charters: Says Schools Need More Oversight from State, Better Business Plans." *Tribune*, August 28.

Yin, R. K. 1994. *Case Study Research: Design and Methods.* Thousand Oaks, Calif.: Sage Publications.

10

Nothing New: Curricula in Arizona Charter Schools

ROBERT T. STOUT AND GREGG A. GARN

Among the claims made by Arizona charter school advocates was that charter schools, freed from bureaucratic constraints placed upon district schools, would provide significant curricular innovation. Advocates claimed that creative individuals of all persuasions and from all sectors would produce an enormous richness of school choice. In turn, Arizona would become a national repository of new and exciting ways in which schools could address the twenty-first-century needs of children and young adults. The ideas planted and germinated in Arizona, the argument went, would be transplanted to district schools and even to other states.

We conclude in this chapter that the claim for curricular innovation is not supported by current data. We also conclude that evidence of significant improvements in achievement among students in charter schools is absent at present. Although time may alter our conclusions, the current status of innovation in charter schools is not favorable for charter school advocates.

The Evidence Bases for This Chapter

This chapter is based on evidence from five sources: (1) the applications of the first 50 charter schools, filed with and approved by either of the two state agencies authorized to grant charters; (2) the 1996–1997 *Annual Report of the Arizona Superintendent of Public Instruction*; (3) the annual report cards filed with the Arizona Department of Education

by the schools and available on the World Wide Web at http://
www.ade.state.az.us/rcweb/search.asp; (4) reports of school achievement test results from 1997 as reported by the *Arizona Republic* (the largest
circulation daily newspaper in Arizona) and available on the World Wide
Web at http://www.azcentral.com/news/schoolscores; and (5) site visits
to about 30 of the schools. (For the names and locations of all the schools
included in this analysis, see the list appended to this chapter.) In all,
we believe that we have moderately reliable data on approximately 75
schools, operating on 125 different sites, and enrolling nearly 14,000 of
the about 17,000 students reported to have been enrolled during the
1996–1997 school year. For comparative purposes, 780,000 students were
enrolled in district schools during the same period.

Although we have every confidence that we know a great deal about the
curricula of these schools, we are not absolutely sure that we know all of
the details. The reader is thus warned to exercise some caution in interpret-
ing our work. The reader also should be warned that in our collective experience we have discovered errors in the databases. They are all at least
one year old (and the landscape of charter schools in Arizona changes
rapidly); many are not entirely complete; and we have discovered inaccu-
racies. Nonetheless, we believe that the overall conclusions of this chapter
will stand serious scrutiny when displayed against the prevailing data.

Curricular Innovation—An Arizona Context

Although the meaning of a "curriculum" is debated routinely by scholars,
most persons can agree that a "curriculum" is composed of sets of interactions between and among teachers, students, some academic or other
content, and a collection of actions designed to allow students to learn the
desired content (Eisner 1991; Goodlad 1984; Curti 1935). In this respect,
variations can occur across a host of dimensions and the "curriculum"
can change rapidly. Thus, differences exist among ideas about what is to
be taught/learned, how it is to be taught/learned, what involved people
say about these matters, and what the same people actually do.

The expected academic and other content in Arizona curricula are influenced substantially by state mandates. Arizona has a list of "essential skills"
that students are expected to master at each grade level and in each subject.
The list has been in place for several years, and policy makers expect
schools to structure academic experiences around the skills as enumerated.
Arizona is well along in developing a set of academic standards, which
eventually may supplement or supplant the list of essential skills. In addition, Arizona is developing an examination to test whether students have
mastered the new standards. This test, the Arizona Instrument to Measure
Standards (AIMS), is intended to be a "high-stakes" examination such that

high school graduation will depend on its successful passage, as may promotion in the lower grades. Consequently, school personnel (both in district and charter schools) will ignore the essential skills and the standards at their own risk, since "success rates" are expected to be widely publicized.

Further, all applicants for charters are expected to show how their curricula are designed to address the state mandates. Therefore, we may see less, not more, variability among the schools with respect to what they declare they intend to teach and what, in fact, they do teach.

The state context for charter schools still leaves room for variation in how school personnel structure the teaching/learning environment. And it is here that we have found differences in approach, philosophy, and "audience" among the charter schools.

The Categories of Schools

Although we have chosen to classify schools in a particular way for ease of analysis, other schemes might be appropriate for other purposes. Our scheme puts schools in categories as follows:

- Schools designed to serve "at-risk" adolescents and young adults
- Schools designed for college-bound high school students
- Schools designed to address some special focus or to teach in a particular way

Within the last category we have "clustered" schools according to what we believe are similarities in approach or philosophy. In the following sections we will present a general analysis of the curricular offerings in the category. Subsequently we will discuss curricula that we have deemed "interesting" or out of the ordinary for each type of school.

Schools Serving At-Risk Youths

We have classified 17 schools serving about 4,000 at-risk students at 38 different sites. One of the schools in the group operates at 13 sites, and four others operate at multiple sites as well. Our analysis indicates little variation in the operating modes and in the kinds of students the schools are designed to serve. They advertise themselves as places where students who have not been successful in regular school settings can achieve sufficient academic success to gain entry to good jobs. Although most are designed for self-selection by students, some are places to which adolescents are sent as a condition of parole, probation, or other adjudication by a court. Some are "freestanding," and some are agents of a state or county authority. They operate in quite similar ways.

Students are under some form of performance "contract" and attend school for four hours a day (either on the A.M. or the P.M. "shift"). They are helped to find entry-level employment for times they are not at the school. Instruction is primarily computer-aided or computer-assisted, using nationally available "packages" of courses in the basic disciplines. Instructors are available to help individual students with the computer-based courses and to facilitate various forms of group activity for such matters as basic job skills, interviewing technique, workplace etiquette, and the like. In addition, the instructors are available to students to help them with personal problems and to lend encouragement. Students move through the computer courses at their own speed and accumulate academic credit by passing the tests associated with the computer programs. Some of these schools have open entry and open exit provisions. Others have arrangements with businesses and industries, and at least two have arrangements with a local community college for vocational preparation. Most ready a student for successful completion of the requirements for a GED, and they award their own H.S. diplomas.

College-Preparatory High Schools

We have classified seven college-prep high schools, which enroll approximately 800 total students. The classification is not entirely self-evident because four of the seven schools are sister schools to a K–8 entity, and six of the seven enroll students as early as grade 6. Strictly speaking, they are not high schools, but they serve a population with clear college-bound expectations. Among other similarities are their small sizes. They range in size from about 40 students to about 200 students. The schools have small classes, teach standard college-preparatory courses, utilize seminar formats, stress high academic achievement, and have all of the marks of recognizable college-prep institutions. In fact, at least three of the seven were independent college-prep high schools before being granted charters.

Special Focus Schools

In this section we analyze schools that enroll students in grades K–8 or some combination, schools that enroll students in grades 6–12 or some combination, and schools that enroll students in grades K–12. This classification is somewhat "messier" than the other two for obvious reasons, but some trends are clear.

Child-Centered Schools, K–8. Educators routinely use terms such as "child-centered" and "content-centered" to describe the prevailing philosophy of a school (e.g., Dewey 1988; Lamm 1988). The categories are rough but useful for purposes of our analysis, since the two types of school almost exhaust the options among the K–8 schools that declare their curriculum has a special focus. The first group of schools we discuss are "child-centered." We have placed 15 schools operating at 19 sites and enrolling a total of about 2,000 students in this group.

Of the 15 schools in the group, six are full Montessori schools, and two more are Montessori-like or "based on" Montessori principles. The rest are similar, in that they emphasize child development principles; active or experiential learning; multi-age groupings; learning by doing; projects; integrated and thematic courses; individualized learning; collaborative or cooperative learning; and opportunities for children with different learning modalities to experience the curriculum fully. They may use an ungraded or continuous progress approach. Student assessment routinely includes portfolios, and students are expected to be accountable for their work and for appropriate behavior in the school community.

Brief excerpts from the applications for charter will serve to demonstrate the curricular orientations of this group of schools. In one application we find, "Childhood is a journey not a race." In another we find, "We believe in practicing the precepts of a democratic society . . . thus preparing them [students] to be good citizens." Another promises that the school will provide an environment for "joyful learning." Most seek close cooperation with parents, and all are relatively small, ranging in size from about 40 to 250 students.

Content-Centered Schools, K–8. At the other end of the child-centered to content-centered curriculum continuum are 15 schools enrolling about 2,700 students. These schools stress high academic standards, high behavioral/discipline standards, rigorous classes, homework, and other earmarks of a "back-to-basics" approach. Some schools are more exact in their language about what that means than others, but all clearly signal to students and parents that the business of the school is to prepare students for high academic achievement in the context of a formalized environment. Two examples of exact language will suffice to give the reader the flavor of schools we have placed in this category. One asserts that the school is "designed to provide a back to basics program for parents who wish to be very involved with their child's education. It will emphasize phonics based instruction, strict discipline, high academic standards, mandatory homework, and a dress code." Another application says of the school that "it promotes a return to old-fashioned values. Several generations ago children of all ages gathered in a neighborhood school house where a respected teacher forged lives in a small classroom." These schools are places where parents can expect teachers to be in charge, students to be industrious and well behaved, and the courses to be filled with rigorous academic content.

Other Schools, K–8.   We have given seven schools in the K–8 category a kind of residual classification. Among them they enroll about 1,000 students. Two schools have a bilingual (Spanish/English) emphasis, and one is based on confluent education, described in the application as an emphasis on "learning how to learn." One has an arts-based curriculum, though not fully performing-arts based, and utilizes some packaged computer courses. Another has as its avowed emphasis "authentic learning" in a "working farm environment" with a focus on "sustainable agriculture." Finally, one is modeled after the Waldorf School of the early 1900s, developed by Rudolf Steiner in Germany.

Junior and Senior High Schools.   The second group of special curricular schools comprises those that enroll some combination of students in grades 6 through 12. We have classified ten schools in this way. They enroll about 1,800 students, but that number is a bit deceptive because about 1,000 of the 1,800 students attend one of two schools emphasizing Native American language and culture; one has a Hopi and the other a Navajo emphasis, and both are located on the respective reservation. Three of the ten schools are performing arts schools. Three others, which enroll a very small number of students, are for severely troubled adolescents, and two of those are full therapeutic communities, but not hospitals. The last two in the group are linked to community colleges and will be discussed in a later section.

K–12 Schools.   Finally, in the group of schools that declare a special curricular focus are those that enroll students in grades K–12. This category is a bit confusing because the schools may not currently enroll students in all grades. They have been granted charters to do so, however, and that is why they are included in this category. One of these schools has an Indian languages and culture focus (not Hopi or Navajo as already discussed) and two of the schools are designed as quasi-therapeutic communities for children with behavioral or emotional difficulty.

Some Schools of Interest

In this section we present a closer analysis of four schools. Our criteria for selection are not exact, nor are they particularly scientific. We have found the curricula of these schools to be interesting, among the more innovative, and they represent the categories of the charter schools in Arizona. For obvious reasons the authors of this chapter must take full responsibility for the choices, and for obvious reasons we are accountable to those who would argue that our selection does not do justice to the full range of curricular innovation. We admit to the criticisms, but counterargue that our selection is not a poor one. Also for obvious reasons we apologize to any school director or advocate who believes that her or his school deserves special mention. Finally, we do not name the individual schools, although they are among the ones listed in our Appendix.

The first school of interest to us springs out of the Waldorf School developed by Rudolf Steiner in the early part of this century in Germany. The school enrolls students in grades K–4. The first Waldorf School in a public setting in the United States was established in Milwaukee in 1991. About 600 schools worldwide identify with the Waldorf model. The mission statement of the school states, "It is the mission of [the school] to develop free, creative, independent, responsible, principled, and fulfilled human beings who are 'able of themselves to impart purpose and direction in their lives.'" The curriculum is anchored in a set of assumptions about developmental stages in a child's life. The teaching methods begin with encounter, then pass through experience to the crystallization of abstract concepts. The school integrates all of the arts into all subjects, using movement, music, storytelling, visual arts, and rhythm. The whole language approach is used to teach reading, and much is made of experiential learning. Multicultural studies and the humanities, along with all of the classic liberal arts, are prominent in the curriculum. The curriculum is tightly structured around the Waldorf model, and teachers are expected to be trained in it.

An interesting correlate to the curriculum is found in the contract for teachers, which states, "It is understood that as a colleague in the [school] you join a group of teachers who work under the direction of the College of Teachers with the philosophy, purpose, and curriculum of Waldorf modeled education and who seek excellence in the teaching of children."

The second example of interest to us is a pair of linked schools with similar missions and philosophies. One of the schools serves children in grades 1–3 and the other children in grades 4–8. Each school asserts that it has interest in the full development of a whole child. Language such as the following is infused throughout the materials from both schools. "We promise our students:

to reengage the disengaged
to revitalize the complacent
to stir the imagination
to spark critical thinking
to nurture a love of learning
to develop the citizen within
to dare to risk
to be an entrepreneur."

Other language identifies the multiple intelligences base of the teaching methods, as well as the "real world" and experiential nature of the curriculum. The schools are designed as micro learning communities in which students are assigned to small groups called "cottages". Each cottage has attached to it an academic and experiential curriculum. "Cottage enterprises" are activities in which students engage in practical tasks derived from academic themes. Printed materials include, for example, the plant nursery cottage in which young students learn a science (e.g., biology), the methods of science (observation, experimentation, recording of data, and drawing conclusions), and the applications of science (writing, discussing, and presenting orally). Some form of planned activity or the production of some good or service serves as the unit's culmination.

The third school of interest in this analysis is attached to a community college. Like others in the category of high schools for "at-risk" students, this school utilizes a package of computer-based courses, an open entry mode, individualized programs based on successful completion of the computer-based courses, and requirements for time on task during each week. Students can complete assignments at their own pace, but they must attend and must progress. They must have earned the equivalent of two years of high school credit to enroll and must declare themselves interested in careers in technical or health-related fields. What is of interest to us, however, is that students may also enroll concurrently in the community college. Secondarily, what is of interest is that the school offers English courses through the Great Books programs. Students read, analyze, and write about the books contained in the various series.

The emphasis in the school is to treat the students as much like adults or college students as they wish to be treated. This means that the students must want the experience, must want to do the work, must show up to do it, and must demonstrate that they are making progress. The program can be quite accelerated depending on the commitment of the student. For example, a typical "course" is designed to be completed in four weeks, and even the Great Books experiences are tightly structured and linked, in part, to a computer-based English course.

The last school in this section is of interest not so much for its curriculum but for its purposes and history. In 1967 an individual established a program for employment and academic skills training for unserved or underserved rural Arizonans. The historic programs included adult basic education, GED test preparation, English as a second language, and other offerings designed to give youth and adults practical skills that would allow them to achieve employment above poverty levels. Students are aged sixteen to twenty-one but are not required to have any certifiable academic skills. The curriculum in use was developed by the California Department of Education, Youth Adult Alternative Education Services

Division and is called the California Employability Competency System. Based on entrance testing, a highly structured and computer-based curriculum, and individualization, the effort is designed to allow students to move fairly rapidly from entry to some established goals. The school operates in about a dozen sites, mostly in rural Arizona, consistent with its initial mission.

The Origins of the Schools

One of the early claims or hopes of the advocates of charter schools was that the open environment would invite a host of new players onto the stage of providing schooling. That has happened, of course. But what may not have been anticipated was the opportunity for existing providers of varying kinds of education and education-related services. Of the 75 schools analyzed in this chapter, 25 existed prior to the charter legislation. In 1996–1997, of the 13,000 students enrolled in the charter schools described in this chapter, about 5,000 were enrolled in charter schools that had prior existence. In effect, these entities rolled over existing programs into the charter opportunity. By doing so, some reduced their dependence on tuition or fees for income (the Montessori schools are examples); some added the opportunity to grant a high school diploma to their existing ca pacity to prepare persons for the GED (programs serving high school dropouts or other students at risk); and some altered their funding bases to supplement the Jobs Training and Partnership Act (JTPA) or other program funding with state funding. The argument that many charter schools show little in the way of curricular innovation is made with the knowledge that many charter schools already existed in form and function prior to the enabling legislation.

A Cautionary Note on Achievement

What follows must be read with great caution on two counts. First, no trend data are available because the Arizona Department of Education changed test mandates, so that only one year (1997) of test data (The Stanford Nine) can be presented in the analysis. Second, the available databases are incomplete in many respects: Some schools did not give the test; some did not report the results; some had very few students taking the test; and some did not enroll children in grades that were tested. As a consequence, we have data that we believe are moderately reliable from only about 40 schools, and only for students in grades 6 and 11. In addition, we have combined some categories and show scores only for high schools serving "at-risk" students and schools with some kind of special curricular focus.

High Schools for "At-Risk" Students

We have data for 14 schools in this category, shown in Table 10.1. As the reader can see, we have no reported scores above average in at-risk charter high schools on any test. Of the forty-two reported average scores (3 tests x 14 schools), thirty-three are reported as below the 30th percentile. We cannot conclude from these data that charter high schools for "at-risk" students have made significant inroads into the historic low achievement test performance of those students.

Special Focus Schools

We have data for 20 schools enrolling K–8 students in this category. Some of them are child-centered, some content-centered, and some were schools with an existence prior to the charter legislation. We report data on students in grade 6 because it allows us to include the largest number of schools.

As is seen in Table 10.2, this category has substantial variation. This wide discrepancy is not entirely unexpected, given that some of these schools were formerly tuition-receiving, that some are experimental in character, that most are new, and that the expectations embedded in the standardized test may not be those that the school embraces. But the majority of schools lie in the 40 to 70 range, a distribution of what one would expect and observe in district schools. Therefore, we cannot conclude that these charter schools are producing exceptional student achievement.

We have only three high schools in this category for which we have scores. The scores reported from them for grade 11 students are all in the 4–60 range. Again, these scores mirror district high school scores.

Our general, but tentative and cautious, conclusion is that student achievement as measured by the Stanford Nine test looks just about the

TABLE 10.1   Average Scores for Students in Grade 11 (Number of Average School Scores in Each Decile)

Decile	Subject Area		
	Reading	Math	Language
0–9	1	0	2
10–19	5	7	4
20–29	4	5	5
30–39	2	2	3
40–49	2	0	0

TABLE 10.2   Average Scores for Students in Grade 6 (Number of Average School Scores in Each Decile)

| Decile | Subject Area | | |
	Reading	Math	Language
10–19	0	0	1
20–29	0	1	1
30–39	1	2	4
40–49	3	4	5
50–59	4	4	4
60–69	3	3	1
70–79	4	2	0
80–89	2	1	1

way one would expect, given the audiences of the schools, and very much like scores reported in district public schools.

Conclusion

We began this chapter by cautioning the reader on several counts. We know a great deal about these schools, but we know more about what they claim to accomplish than about what they actually practice. Further, our site visits gave only small glimpses into what they actually do. We do not have data on all of the charter schools in Arizona, and not all of the data available to us were complete. Consequently, we have pieced together information from multiple sources, and not all sources have even the same kinds of data. Nonetheless, we are confident that we have provided a solid overview of the rapidly changing landscape of Arizona charter school curricula. We are willing to conclude from our analysis that little is occurring in instruction that merits the attention of those seeking new and powerful ways to engage children and youth in learning.

There are some obvious advantages to charter schools, though. They tend to be small and have clear focus. This allows parents to have a sense of intimacy with the school and to expect to know what their school is doing with and for their children. But this is not new in our collective experience, only different from most district schools in Arizona, which, given the requirement to serve all comers, tend to be large, with diffused missions.

The content-centered schools in the group are "good, old-fashioned, back-to-basics" schools. Few district schools have the luxury of so proclaiming and structuring themselves. The child-centered schools clearly spring out of the progressive education movements of the early part of this century. Again, few district schools could sustain such an environment.

The schools for "at-risk" youth are obviously serving students who, for whatever reasons, were not happy in a district school. Whether these students are being well-prepared for adult life is not clear, but they are in some form of academic environment from which they can be expected to take something.

All of these schools are based on the belief by someone or some group that what is being offered is better than what was thought to be available in district schools. Only at our peril would we conclude that they are mistaken. We do not. But we do conclude that nothing particularly startling surfaces when viewed in the larger framework of curriculum on a national or world scene.

A second conclusion follows from the first. The rhetoric of curricular innovation is much more interesting than the reality in Arizona. Future debates, we hope, will occur with less pretentious language. Charter schools probably are not providing curricular innovation of greater variety than are district schools. But they are doing it more visibly and with tighter focus. This is not to conclude that such innovation is not useful, only that the claims for it are overblown.

A third conclusion is that little evidence currently exists to show that all of the charter school activity leads to clear paths for increasing student achievement. Based on what we know from these schools, we still do not know in a general way how to insure high achievement among all students.

Finally, we conclude that adults and students probably are getting from these schools what they expected to get when they chose them. "At-risk" youth are getting a second or third chance, or sometimes a last chance, to attain a certificate of accomplishment. Parents of younger children are getting the kind of education they think best for their children. Teachers and others are getting a chance to see whether their educational visions can be realized. If adults and students choose what they want, and if no serious consequences occur (and we have no evidence to suggest otherwise), then over time some good ideas may emerge. That may be the most that can be expected.

Appendix: The Schools Included in This Analysis

SCHOOL	LOCATION(S)
ABC Alternative Learning	Phoenix
Academy of Lifelong Learning	Phoenix
ACE Charter High School	Tucson
American Grade School	multiple

Arizona CALL-A-TEEN	Phoenix
Arizona Career Academy	multiple
Arizona Montessori Charter	multiple
Arizona Montessori	Prescott
Arizona School for the Arts	Phoenix
ATOP Academy	multiple
AZ-Tech High School	Yuma
Benjamin Franklin Charter	multiple
Bennett Academy	multiple
Bright Beginnings	Chandler
Calli Ollin Academy	Tucson
Carmel Community Integrated Arts	Chandler
CASY Country Day School	multiple
Center for Academic Success	multiple
Children's Academy of Arizona	Tucson
Copper Canyon Academy	Glendale
Discovery Academy	St. Johns
Eco-Tech Agricultural	Chandler
Educational Opportunity Center	Yuma
EduPreneurship	Scottsdale
EduPrize Charter School	Gilbert
Esperanza Montessori	multiple
EXCEL Center	multiple
Flagstaff Arts and Leadership	Flagstaff
Flagstaff Junior Academy	Flagstaff
Foothills Academy	Cave Creek
Franklin Phonetic Primary	Prescott Valley
Gan Yeladeem	Scottsdale
Gateway Community High School	Phoenix
Grey Hills Academy High School	Tuba City
Heritage Academy	multiple
Hopi Jr.-Sr. High School	Keams Canyon
Horizon Charter School	Chandler
Intelli-School	multiple
Kachina Schools	multiple
Khalsa Montessori	multiple
Kingman Academy of Learning	Kingman
Lake Havasu Charter	Lake Havasu City
Lake Powell Academy	Page
Laurent Clerc	Tucson
Life School College Preparatory	Mesa
Mesa Arts Academy	Mesa
Mingus Mountain Academy	Dewey
Mingus Springs Charter	Chino Valley
Montessori Day Public School	multiple
Montessori Ed Centre	Mesa
Montessori Schools of Flagstaff	multiple

Mountain School, Inc.	Flagstaff
New School for the Arts	Scottsdale
Northern Arizona Academy	multiple
PCAE-Edge	Tucson
Pimeria Alta High School	Nogales
PPEP-TEC	multiple
Pine Forest Charter	Flagstaff
Presidio School	Tucson
Scottsdale Horizons	Scottsdale
Sedona Charter	Sedona
Skyview School	Prescott
SRPMI Community School	Scottsdale
Success School	multiple
Teen Choice Leadership School	Phoenix
Tempe Prep Academy	Tempe
Tertulia	Phoenix
Triumphant Learning Center	Safford
Valley Academy	Phoenix
Ventana Academic School	Cave Creek
Victory High School	multiple
Villa Montessori	multiple
Young Scholar's Academy	Bullhead City

References

Curti, M. 1935. *The Social Ideas of American Educators*. New York: Charles Scribner's Sons.

Dewey, J. 1988. "The Psychological Aspects of the School Curriculum." In *Curriculum: An Introduction to the Field*, ed. J. R. Gress and D. E. Purpel. Berkeley: McCutchan Publishing Corporation.

Eisner, E. W. 1991. "Should America Have a National Curriculum?" *Educational Leadership* 49 (2): 76–81.

Goodlad, J. 1984. *A Place Called School: Prospects for the Future*. New York: McGraw-Hill.

Lamm, Z. 1988. "The Status of Knowledge in Radical Concepts of Education." In *Curriculum: An Introduction to the Field*, ed. J. R. Gress and D. E. Purpel. Berkeley: McCutchan Publishing Corporation.

11

How Arizona Teachers View School Reform

FREDERICK HESS, ROBERT MARANTO,
SCOTT MILLIMAN, APRIL GRESHAM

Teachers are pivotal in school improvement efforts. One of the great hopes of charter school advocates is that charter schooling will free good teachers from administrative and bureaucratic handcuffs. How do teachers feel about the reforms bandied about in Arizona? In particular, how do they feel about choice-based reforms relative to other kinds of school reform? Further, what explains why different teachers support or oppose various proposed reforms? These are the questions we will explore in this chapter.

Education researchers agree that the success of school reform depends largely on the teachers charged with implementing the changes in classrooms. Historically, reforms lacking the support of personnel in the classroom core have seldom managed to improve schools (Sarason 1991, 1996). Consequently, among the keys to improving teaching and learning are increasing faculty commitment, cultivating teacher expertise, and attracting and retaining committed faculty (Elmore et al. 1996; Fullan 1991; Johnson and Pajares 1996; Murphy 1991; Odden 1991).

Disappointment with pedagogical and curricular reform efforts has increased the attention given to choice-based reforms. Yet we know little about what teachers think about education reforms, whether they be traditional changes or more drastic efforts. In this chapter, we will examine the views toward various reforms from three groups of teachers: Arizona charter school teachers, Arizona district school teachers, and Nevada district school teachers.

An extension of the market hypothesis offered in Chapter 8 is that teachers will play a large role in the greater competitive environment that may result from a more comprehensive choice framework. At least in the short term, the receptivity of teachers to choice-based approaches will have significant effects. For instance, public school teachers are often the most ideal people to teach and/or operate charters, yet peer pressure among teachers will likely affect whether they would leave their traditional public school for a charter. Also, teachers, as links between district schools and potential charter parents, may communicate damaging information about charters, particularly if they do not believe in the fundamental nature of the reform. Thus, assessing teachers' views toward such reforms is important. However, little is known of their views apart from anecdotal stories.

Determinants of Teacher Attitudes

Another key question concerns which personal and institutional characteristics may be associated with particular views of reform among teachers. We know very little about what shapes teachers' opinions toward any kind of reform. Previous research rarely has attempted to isolate those variables that make teachers more or less receptive to particular reform efforts. Instead, studies of reform generally have used observation and interviews to explore teacher responses to a particular reform in one school or a handful of schools. The few surveys that have been done have found that some general characteristics appear to influence teacher attitudes.

A study of 12,000 Chicago teachers that examined the impact of the Chicago School Reform Act of 1988 found that teachers in schools with shared decisionmaking, strong leadership, teacher collegiality, and community support are more likely to support reform than teachers not in such schools (Sebring and Camburn 1992). Ellen Katz and her colleagues (1994) found that receptivity to state reform increased with in-service training, increased resources, and job security. Jane and Fred Page's (1989) survey of state teachers of the year found significant differences between secondary and elementary teachers, older and younger teachers, and teachers with different educational backgrounds. A previous Page and Page (1988) study surveyed ninety-seven social science teachers and found that they were most receptive to reforms that increased salary and funding, used mentor teachers, and increased school partnerships with universities.

The most frequently discussed determinants of teacher receptiveness to school reform are the teacher's length of service and the nature of the local school culture. Veteran teachers become cynical about reform because they have seen numerous reform efforts come and go and may view new reform efforts as transitory impositions (Hess 1999; Tyack and Cuban 1995; Wagner 1994). Veteran faculty also have more time, energy, and self-regard invested in the current state of affairs. Consequently, veteran teachers should be less supportive of reform.

Second, research suggests that school cultures are tenacious, tending to perpetuate traditional work arrangements and the attitudes that underlie them (Cuban 1984; Tyack and Tobin 1994). Teachers in schools with negative cultures are likely to develop a preference for the security of routines that insulate them from the worst frustrations (Downs 1967; Lipsky 1980). Therefore, we expect that teachers in schools with negative cultures will be less likely to support choice-based reforms, regardless of the length of time the teacher has taught.[1]

Third, teacher union opposition to school choice may reflect or influence teacher opinions. The NEA (National Education Association) and AFT (American Federation of Teachers) strongly oppose vouchers and often oppose public school choice (Harmer 1994; Lieberman 1997; Milbank 1998). Institutionally, teachers' unions are powerful political actors that benefit from their control of the labor force and therefore have a strong interest in maintaining the monopoly position of the districted public schools. We hypothesize that teachers who belong to unions will be more likely to oppose school choice, particularly private school choice.

Fourth, partisan beliefs may influence policy attitudes. We predict that, perhaps due to a positive correlation with religious values (Hunter 1991) and more likely to an affinity for market structure, politically conservative teachers, more than liberal ones—and Republicans more than Democrats—will embrace market-based public policy.

Fifth, it is likely that teachers who majored in education will view choice less favorably than teachers who did not. Education majors, with a greater investment in the certification requirements implicit in public education and, perhaps, with fewer career options outside of K–12 schooling (Ferris and Winkler 1986; Monk 1989), may have more to fear from a competitive environment.

A final factor that may influence teacher opinion on public school choice—the direction of which is unclear—is the extent to which teachers already work in competitive environments. Does actual exposure to public school choice increase or decrease teacher support? Little empirical work has been done on this issue, but the policy implications are significant. In particular, if teacher support for public school choice increases with exposure to competition, then this will facilitate implementation of the policy, but the opposite will occur if exposure has negative effects.

The Survey

Examining Teachers' Opinions of Seven Reforms

Chapter 8 describes the survey we used, including numbers and response rates—the response rate for Arizona charter teachers was 63 percent (N = 125). We asked teachers to use rating scales ranging from 1 ("strongly oppose") to 5 ("strongly support") to record their opinions of seven commonly discussed education reforms:

- statewide education standards
- vouchers for secular public or private schools
- merit pay for outstanding teachers
- magnet schools
- site-based control over curricula
- charter schools
- site-based control over hiring and firing of teachers

These options can be divided into three main categories. First, reforms of education standards and site-based control over curricula do not substantially alter the current public school structure. Teachers' attitudes towards these weaker reforms are shown in Table 11.1. In contrast, merit pay, site-based control of personnel, and magnet schools, all shown in Table 11.2, would clearly alter the existing arrangements within public school districts (arguably, to the disadvantage of teachers) but would leave those districts fundamentally intact. Finally, Table 11.3 includes teachers' reactions to the most extreme reforms, vouchers and charter schools, which have the potential to radically reform or even eliminate the existing public school system.

Pedagogical and Curricular Reforms.   Overall teacher support, not surprisingly, is relatively high for pedagogical and curricular reforms, measures that leave more room for teacher autonomy than the other reforms examined. On the least radical reform—statewide standards—district and charter school teachers agree. One teacher wrote a comment capturing this view, "I believe that one of the biggest evils in public education is the practice of social promotion." Despite their great support for state-level standards, teachers in all three samples want more site-based control over curricula.

As seen in Table 11.1, a comparison between the three groups (Arizona charter teachers, Arizona district teachers, and Nevada district teachers) shows that about 75 percent of teachers in Arizona and Nevada district elementary schools favor "more individual school control over curricula," and nearly 90 percent of charter school teachers agree.

TABLE 11.1 Arizona Charter, Arizona District, and Nevada District Elementary School Teachers' Support for Curricular and Pedagogical School Reforms (in Percentages)

	Arizona Charter School Teachers		Arizona District School Teachers		Nevada District School Teachers	
	Support	Oppose	Support	Oppose	Support	Oppose
Statewide education standards	86	8	84	11	84	10
More individual school control over curricula[a]	89	5	76	17	74	18

[a] $X^2(8) = 46.809, p < .00001$

Moderate Reforms.   Non-pedagogical reforms that do not alter the structure of schooling received somewhat less support, but the mixed teacher response was still generally positive. Merit pay received a mean rating of 2.99; magnet schools received a 3.33; and greater individual school control over hiring and firing teachers received a 3.63. Again, a higher rating indicates more support for the reform.

Despite the implications for their own job security, just as most teachers supported site-based control over curriculum, most supported "more individual school control over hiring and firing of teachers." Table 11.2 shows that this item was supported or strongly supported by 58 percent of Nevada elementary teachers, 65 percent of Arizona district teachers, and 86 percent of charter school educators. Merit pay gained the support of nearly three quarters of Arizona charter teachers, a very slim plurality of Arizona district teachers, and was opposed by a plurality of Nevada teachers. Notably, as Chapter 8 suggests, greater union influence in Nevada might explain Nevada teachers' opposition to merit pay. The far greater support for merit pay among charter school teachers may reflect a general market-based orientation among such teachers. Whereas just over 50 percent of Arizona and Nevada district teachers supported magnet schools, nearly nine of ten Arizona charter school teachers did so.

Charter School and Voucher Reforms.   The least popular reforms were those choice-based reforms that explicitly mandate broad institutional change. Teachers generally opposed these reforms, with vouchers receiving a 2.17 rating and charter schools a 2.43. Both of these reforms could potentially trigger significant, unpredictable changes in teacher pay and working conditions, as well as changes in the overall structure of public

TABLE 11.2 Arizona Charter, Arizona District, and Nevada District
Elementary School Teachers' Support for Moderate Level School
Reforms (in Percentages)

	Arizona Charter School Teachers		Arizona District School Teachers		Nevada District School Teachers	
	Support	Oppose	Support	Oppose	Support	Oppose
More individual school control over hiring/firing teachers[a]	86	4	65	20	58	23
Merit pay for outstanding teachers[b]	74	15	47	44	38	49
Parents choose among magnet schools with different curricula[c]	86	1	52	22	51	24

[a] $X^2(8) = 77.77, p < .0001$
[b] $X^2(8) = 74.8, p < .0001$
[c] $X^2(8) = 122.61, p < .0001$

schools. Teachers may shy away from these reforms for self-interest and/or for ideological reasons.

The most controversial reform items were those that would significantly alter or even end conventional public school systems, and for these choice-based reforms, Arizona charter school teachers held views sharply at odds with their counterparts in district schools. Table 11.3 shows that, whereas large majorities of Arizona charter school teachers support vouchers, a large majority of Nevada district teachers and an even larger majority of Arizona district teachers oppose vouchers. Not surprisingly, 92 percent of Arizona charter elementary school teachers support charter schools, but a plurality of Nevada district teachers and a large majority of Arizona district teachers oppose them. Interestingly, the greater support for market-based reforms among charter school teacher cannot be explained by their political views. As Table 11.4 shows, charter school teachers are no more Republican than Arizona district school teachers, though they are slightly more likely to be political independents.

Determinants of Teacher Preferences

Length of Service. Why is there so much variation in how teachers view the desirability of these reforms? First we looked at how *length of service* af-

TABLE 11.3   Arizona Charter, Arizona District, and Nevada District Elementary School Teachers' Support for Charter School and Voucher Reforms (in Percentages)

	Arizona Charter School Teachers		Arizona District School Teachers		Nevada District School Teachers	
	Support	Oppose	Support	Oppose	Support	Oppose
Charter schools (which can be started by teachers or parents and are largely autonomous schools with open admission)[a]	92	4	25	58	33	36
Vouchers for all nonreligious schools, public or private, for all parents[b]	56	19	19	65	25	52

[a] $X^2(8) = 488.19, p < .0001$
[b] $X^2(8) = 148.43, p < .0001$

TABLE 11.4   Partisan Affiliations of Arizona Charter and District Elementary School Teachers (in Percentages)

	Strong Republican			Independent		Strong Democrat	
	1	2	3	4	5	6	7
Charter teachers	9	16	10	28	9	17	10
District teachers	9	19	12	16	16	17	11

NOTES: $X^2(6) = 13.79, p = .03$

Respondents were asked to rate their partisanship on a seven-point scale: 1 = strong Republican; 7 = strong Democrat.

fected views of these reforms. To do this, we split our sample of Arizona district teachers into three groups: teachers who started teaching before 1989; those who started teaching from 1989 to 1994; and those who started teaching in 1995 or after. We did not include Nevada teachers or charter teachers in this sample because we wanted to focus on a coherent group of opinions, such as those in a particular state, and because charter status was somewhat correlated with length of service.

TABLE 11.5   Length of Service As Related to Arizona District Teacher Opinions
of School Reforms (in Means)

	0–3 Years	4–9 Years	At least 10 Years	ANOVA (F-test)
Merit pay for outstanding teachers	3.42[ab]	3.45[a]	2.89[b]	$F(2,1025) = 10.65, p < .0001$
Vouchers	3.00[a]	2.35[ab]	2.11[b]	$F(2,1021) = 6.62, p < .001$

NOTE: Means with differing superscripts differ according to a Bonferroni post hoc test at $p < .05$.

Table 11.5 shows the only two reform variables whose support is significantly related to length of service, according to our analyses of variance and post hoc Bonferroni tests. More experienced teachers were significantly less willing than teachers with four to nine years of service to support one moderate reform—merit pay—and were significantly less likely than new teachers (zero to three years of service) to support the relatively extreme reform of vouchers. However, no significant differences related to length of service were found on the other five reforms we asked teachers to consider.

School Culture.   We next investigated the impact of *school culture* on teacher attitudes, with questions taken or modified from Chubb and Moe (1990). We asked respondents whether they agreed with the following statements: (1) "Goals and priorities of the school are clear"; (2) "I feel I am treated as a valuable employee"; and (3) "I usually look forward to each working day at the school."

The resulting index ranged from 3 to 18, with a negative school culture suggested by a lower composite. We segmented teachers into two groups—those with a score ranging from 3 to 9 (a negative school culture), and those with a score of 16 to 18 (a very positive school culture)—and then compared mean ratings for the two groups using t-tests. As in the case of teacher experience, support for some reforms varied little between the two groups. The reforms on which there was little evidence that culture mattered were: allowing individual schools to have greater control over curricula, merit pay for outstanding teachers, the hiring and firing of teachers, and school vouchers.

On the questions of statewide standards, magnet schooling, and charter schooling, however, moderate differences did emerge between the two groups. These differences are presented in Table 11.6. Interestingly, the effects were generally not in the direction predicted by the hypotheses. In particular, teachers working in negative school cultures were 7.75

TABLE 11.6   School Culture As Related to Teacher Opinions of Various School Reforms (in Means)

	Negative Culture	Positive Culture	t = test
Statewide standards	3.88	4.14	$t(464) = 2.24, p = .025$
Magnet schools	3.51	3.26	$t(464) = 1.9, p = .06$
Charter schools	2.58	2.27	$t(466) = 2.0, p = .05$

percent more likely to favor charter schools and 6.25 percent more likely to favor magnet schools. At the same time, they were 6.5 percent more likely to oppose statewide standards. These differences, although not large, suggest that teachers working in a negative environment appear more willing to entertain some reforms that could produce substantial changes in the structure of school governance. Perhaps this is because these teachers believe that their school culture will improve or that they will enjoy new opportunities to relocate to a more attractive school setting. On the other hand, teachers in positive school cultures have an incentive to maintain the status quo, and they may see standards-based reform as a way to quiet public fears and ensure quality control, thus strengthening the current system.

Union Membership.   For four reforms, union members did differ significantly from non-union members. The results are shown in Table 11.7. Union members favored statewide standards more than nonmembers. However, union members were significantly more negative than their non-union counterparts about the other three reforms: merit pay, and the school choice reforms of vouchers and charter schools.

Since both of the nation's teacher unions (the National Education Association and the American Federation of Teachers) are suspicious of school choice measures, we expected that their membership would be more hostile to vouchers and charters than would other teachers. The data support this hypothesis. Non-union members were significantly (10.25 percent)

TABLE 11.7   Union Membership As Related to Teacher Opinions of Various School Reforms (in Means)

	Non-Union	Union	t = test
Statewide standards	3.97	4.14	$t(1013) = 2.69, p < .01$
Merit pay	3.22	2.84	$t(1023) = 3.88, p < .001$
Charter schools	2.58	2.33	$t(1022) = 2.91, p < .01$
Vouchers	2.42	2.01	$t(1019) = 4.87, p < .001$

less hostile to vouchers than were union members. Union members were also somewhat more likely to oppose charter schooling.

Partisan Beliefs. One individual variable of interest is a teacher's political views; thus, we examined how partisan beliefs influence teacher attitudes on reform. In particular, we tested whether Republicans, who may place more faith in market processes, are more likely to favor charter schools and vouchers—the choice-based reforms—than are Democrats. In the survey, we asked respondents to rate their partisanship on a seven-point scale (as previously seen in Table 11.4). We then drew from the teacher sample two smaller groups—partisan Republicans (with a 1 or 2 rating) and partisan Democrats (with a 6 or 7 rating)—and compared their mean ratings.

The results shown in Table 11.8 offer some support for the hypothesized relationship: Partisan Republicans were 14.25 percent more likely to favor vouchers then were partisan Democrats. Notice, however, that Republican teachers still refused to lend positive support to voucher proposals. On the question of charter schooling, the difference between the two groups was rather small, although Republicans viewed charters slightly more favorably. Interestingly, support of charter schools remained low for both groups, despite the fact that charter schooling enjoyed significantly more support among the population and political leaders in Arizona than did school vouchers.

Education Majors. Do teachers who majored in education while in college view proposed reforms differently than teachers who majored in other fields? We address this question by comparing ratings between teachers whose primary major was in an education field with those with a primary major in another field.[2] Contrary to our predictions, no major differences occurred between the two groups. College preparation does not appear to play a significant role in shaping teacher responses to school reform.

Exposure to Charters. Finally, we explored whether teachers are more likely to accept reforms with which they have had contact or with which

TABLE 11.8   Partisan Beliefs As Related to Teacher Opinions of Various School Reforms (in Means)

	Conservative Republican	Liberal Democrat	$t = test$
Charter schools	2.53	2.33	$t(497) = 1.81, p = .07$
Vouchers	2.47	1.90	$t(523) = 4.98, p < .001$

they are familiar. This question is particularly interesting in the case of charter schooling. If teacher familiarity breeds acceptance, then the charter school movement could win greater support as charter schools spread.

Our evidence in the case of charter schools is mixed. On the one hand, if a teacher has considered taking a job at a charter school, or knows someone else who has, then support for charter schools increases significantly. For example, teachers who had looked at jobs in charter schools rated charter schooling a 3.42, whereas teachers who had not considered a charter school job rated charter schools a 2.28, $t(1026) = 10.33$, $p < .001$, a difference of 28.5 percent. These same teachers are also significantly more likely to support vouchers (M = 2.75) than the others (M = 2.07), $t(1024) = 5.18$, $p < .001$.

Similarly, teachers who knew another teacher who had considered a charter school job rated charter schools 7.8 percent higher (M = 2.66) than did teachers who did not know someone who had considered a job in a charter school (M = 2.27), $t(1024) = 4.72$, $p < .001$. Teachers who knew another teacher who had considered a charter school job also were slightly less hostile to vouchers (M = 2.26) than those teachers who did not know anyone considering a charter school job (M = 2.10), $t(1022) = 1.9$, $p = .06$.

Although correlation never can determine causation, these data would be consistent with the hypothesis that knowing someone in charters leads to a more positive attitude.[3] However, other data suggest the opposite finding. As previously shown in Table 11.3, Nevada teachers rate charter schools more highly by 12 percentage points than do teachers in Arizona (2.91 versus 2.43). Since Nevada has no charter schools, these data suggest that exposure to charter schools could actually be associated with reduced acceptance. In addition, for Arizona, as the percentage of students in a district who attend charter schools increases, there is no significant change in how teachers in that district view charter schooling.

Conclusion

There is significant variation in support for various kinds of school reform across the different groups of teachers surveyed. Depending in particular on the nature and ambition of the reforms considered, traditional district teachers and charter school teachers tend to have very different views of the desirability of certain reforms. In particular, charter school teachers are more likely to support market-based reforms.

We also have found that various characteristics have predictable effects on the ways in which teachers respond to certain kinds of reform proposals. Traits such as political affiliation, union membership, experience, and school culture have a particularly significant impact on how teachers respond to more ambitious reform proposals.

It should be noted that although we found statistically significant differences in teacher attitudes based on a number of factors—length of service, union membership, school culture, and partisan beliefs—these differences generally were not very large. For example, although non-union teachers were more favorably disposed to the two school choice reforms than were union members, nevertheless both groups still opposed both vouchers and charter schooling. Overall, the evidence suggests that the teachers surveyed generally shared similar views on most education reform issues.

Notes

1. It is possible that environmental factors tend to concentrate veteran teachers in more negative school environments. However, in our sample, teacher experience and school morale were uncorrelated (Pearson's r of .00). Consequently, the analysis is able to examine independently both hypotheses.

2. Most of the teachers with education as their primary major had a degree in either early childhood or else elementary education, but there was a scattering of other education majors (such as educational leadership, art education, and curriculum and instruction). Teachers with non-education majors were widely scattered, although many had traditional liberal arts majors (such as English or biology).

3. There are two other equally valid interpretations that must be considered: Teachers with more positive attitudes toward charters are more likely to befriend those working in charters, and a third variable (e.g., few years in service) may actually lead to both.

References

Armour, David L., and Brett M. Peiser. 1998. "Interdistrict Choice in Massachusetts." In *Learning from School Choice*, ed. Paul E. Peterson and Bryan C. Hassel. Washington, D.C.: Brookings Institution Press.

Bryk, Anthony S., Valerie E. Lee, and Peter B. Holland. 1993. *Catholic Schools and the Common Good.* Cambridge, Mass.: Harvard University Press.

Cuban, Larry. 1984. *How Teachers Taught: Constancy and Change in American Classrooms: 1890–1980.* New York: Longman Press.

Chubb, John E., and Terry M. Moe. 1990. *Politics, Markets, and America's Schools.* Washington, D.C.: Brookings Institution Press.

Downs, Anthony. 1967. *Inside Bureaucracy.* New York: Little, Brown.

Elmore, Richard F., Penelope Peterson, and Sarah McCarthy. 1996. *Restructuring in the Classroom: Teaching, Learning, and School Organization.* San Francisco: Jossey-Bass.

Feistritzer, Emily. 1992. *Who Wants to Teach?* Washington, D.C.: National Center for Education Information.

Ferris, James, and Donald Winkler. 1986. "Teacher Compensation and the Supply of Teachers." *The Elementary School Journal* 86(4): 389–403.

Finn, Chester E. 1997. "The Politics of Change." In *New Schools for a New Century: The Redesign of Urban Education*, ed. Diane Ravitch and Joseph Viteritti. New Haven: Yale University Press.

Fliegel, Seymour, and James McGuire. 1993. *Miracle in East Harlem: The Fight for Choice in Public Education*. New York: Times Books.

Fullan, Michael. 1991. *The New Meaning of Educational Change*. New York: Teachers College Press.

Greene, Jay P., Paul E. Peterson, and Jiangtao Du. 1998. "School Choice in Milwaukee: A Randomized Experiment." In *Learning from School Choice*, ed. Paul E. Peterson and Bryan C. Hassel. Washington, D.C.: Brookings Institution Press.

Harmer, David. 1994. *School Choice*. Washington, D.C.: Cato Institute.

Hassel, Bryan. 1998. "Charter Schools: Politics and Practice in Four States." In *Learning from School Choice*, ed. Paul E. Peterson and Bryan C. Hassel. Washington, D.C.: Brookings Institution Press.

Henig, Jeffrey R. 1994. *Rethinking School Choice: Limits of the Market Metaphor*. Princeton: Princeton University Press.

Hess, Frederick M. 1999. *Spinning Wheels: The Politics of Urban School Reform*. Washington, D.C.: Brookings Institution Press.

Hoxby, Caroline M. 1998. "Analyzing School Choice Reforms That Use America's Traditional Forms of Parental Choice." In *Learning from School Choice*, ed. Paul E. Peterson and Bryan C. Hassel. Washington, D.C.: Brookings Institution Press.

Hunter, James Davidson. 1991. *Culture Wars: The Struggle to Define America*. New York: Harper Collins.

Johnson, Margaret J., and Frank Pajares. 1996. "When Shared Decisionmaking Works: A Three-Year Longitudinal Study." *American Education Research Journal* 33: 599–627.

Katz, Ellen H., Sharron Dalton, and Joseph B. Glacquinta. 1994. "Status Risk Taking and Receptivity of Home Economics Teachers to a Statewide Curriculum Innovation." *Home Economics Research Journal* 22 (4): 401–421.

Lieberman, Myron. 1997. *The Teacher Unions*. New York: Free Press.

Lipsky, Michael. 1980. *Street Level Bureaucracy*. New York: Russell Sage Foundation.

Loveless, Tom, and Claudia Jasin. 1998. "Starting from Scratch: Political and Organizational Challenges Facing Charter Schools." *Educational Administration Quarterly* 34 (1): 9–30.

Maranto, Robert, Scott Milliman, and Frederick M. Hess. 1998. "Does Public Sector Competition Stimulate Innovation? The Competitive Impacts of Arizona Charter Schools on Traditional Public Schools." Paper presented at the American Political Science Association annual meeting, Boston, Mass., September 3–6.

Milbank, Dana. 1998. "Schoolyard Tussle: John Kerry Takes on the Teachers' Unions." *New Republic*, December 14, 22–25.

Millott, Marc Dean, and Robin Lake. 1996. *So You Want to Start a Charter School?* Seattle: University of Washington Institute for Public Policy Management.

Monk, David. 1989. *Educational Finance*. New York: McGraw-Hill Companies.

Murphy, Joseph. 1991. *Restructuring Schools: Capturing and Assessing the Phenomena*. New York: Teachers College Press.

Nathan, Joe. 1997. Charter *Schools: Creating Hope and Opportunity for American Education*. San Francisco: Jossey-Bass.

Odden, Allen. 1991. "The Evolution of Education Policy Implementation." In *Educational Policy Implementation*, ed. A. Odden. Albany: State University of New York Press.

Page, Jane A., and Fred M. Page. 1988. "Proposed Reform in Education: Views of State Teachers of the Year." Paper presented at the annual meeting of the Mid-South Educational Research Association, Louisville, Ky., November 8–11.

_____. 1989. "The Teaching Profession and Educational Reform: Views of Social Science Teachers." Paper presented at the annual meeting of the National Social Science Association Conference, New Orleans, La., November 2–4.

Peterson, Paul E., and Chad Noyes. 1997. "School Choice in Milwaukee." In *New Schools for a New Century: The Redesign of Urban Education*, ed. Diane Ravitch and Joseph Viteritti. New Haven: Yale University Press.

Ravitch, Diane, and Joseph P. Viteritti. 1997. "New York: The Obsolete Factory." In *New Schools for a New Century: The Redesign of Urban Education*, ed. Diane Ravitch and Joseph Viteritti. New Haven: Yale University Press.

Rofes, Eric. 1998. *How Are School Districts Responding to Charter Laws and Charter Schools?* Berkeley: University of California at Berkeley, Policy Analysis for California Education.

Sarason, Seymour. 1991. *The Predictable Failure of Education Reform: Can We Change Course Before It's Too Late?* San Francisco: Jossey-Bass.

_____. 1996. *Revisiting the Culture of School and the Problem of Change*. New York: Teachers College Press.

Sebring, Penny A., and Eric M. Camburn. 1992. "How Teachers Are Engaging Reform in Chicago: Differences Among Schools." Paper presented at the annual meeting of the American Educational Research Association, San Francisco, Calif., April 20.

Tyack, David B., and William Tobin. 1994. "The Grammar of Schooling: Why Has It Been So Hard to Change?" *American Educational Research Journal* 31: 453–479.

Tyack, David B., and Larry Cuban. 1995. *Tinkering Toward Utopia: A Century of Public School Reform*. Cambridge, Mass.: Harvard University Press.

Wagner, Tony. 1994. *How Schools Change: Lessons from Three Communities*. Boston: Beacon Press.

Witte, John F. 1996. "Who Benefits from the Milwaukee Choice Program?" In *Who Chooses? Who Loses? Culture, Institutions, and the Unequal Effects of School Choice*, ed. Bruce Fuller and Richard F. Elmore. New York: Teachers College Press.

PART THREE

Practitioners Look at Arizona Charter Schools

12

The Empowerment of Market-Based School Reform

LISA GRAHAM KEEGAN

These are exciting times in public education, and with charter schools and school report cards, Arizona is in the forefront of national education reform. It is no exaggeration to say that in ten years public school systems across the nation may look a lot like the system we are putting in place in Arizona. We are particularly proud of how quickly our state's charter schools have taken off and largely succeeded. Every school district in the state knows that a charter school may come in and win over a certain number of parents, making Arizona a fascinating place to compare with other states.

Many thought that charter schools would be a big-city phenomenon, but some of the really innovative, exciting charters are in rural counties. For instance, PPEP TEC (Portable Practical Educational Preparation Training for Employment Centers) has numerous sites in both rural and urban areas. Their parent corporation, PPEP, has a long history of providing adult education, social services, and health care to farm workers and the rural poor. Opening charter schools in communities they were already serving was a logical and welcome extension of their original mission.

Reasons for the Charter School Explosion

Drafting the Charter School Law

The idea for the charter law came from other states, but those of us in the Arizona state legislature who favored education reform were not sure how well charters would work. Before we passed the state charter law in

1994,[1] only one state (California) had more than fifteen charter schools, not a pervasive presence. In fact, the current comprehensive presence of charters in Arizona is a consequence of the vouchers debate. A law that would have provided vouchers to low-income parents for use at private schools of their choice narrowly lost in the state legislature in 1994.[2] In the course of the debate, state legislators who thought vouchers too extreme agreed to support charter schools. As public schools, charters presented a moderate alternative that assured parental choice but also kept choice within the public sector, so that admission could not be selective and tax dollars could not go to support religious education.

Multiple Sponsoring Boards

In drafting the charter law, ARS 15-183, we on the house Education Committee closely studied charter legislation in other states, particularly Minnesota.[3] Politically, Minnesota was a hotbed of charter activity, but it had few charter schools. Why? Charter school entrepreneurs had to go before their school board and basically say, "I divorce you. Now please approve my new school." We did not make the same mistake in Arizona, whereby people who propose charter schools have to rely solely on the good graces of district school boards, although we did enable charter entrepreneurs to choose this avenue if they saw fit. Rather, we set up a separate State Board for Charter Schools whose *sole* purpose is to charter those schools that meet the basic requirements. We also gave the Arizona State Board of Education power to approve charter schools.

The State Board for Charter Schools differs from the Arizona State Board of Education in several ways. First, it is not overwhelmed by other missions and issues in the education community. The only purpose of the State Board for Charter Schools is to create and oversee charter schools. It's what they do. Just as a hammer finds nails, they find charter schools. Second, the majority of their members come from outside the education community. In fact, the original push for the board came out of the Hispanic community. Many Hispanic parents felt that too few Hispanics won election to school boards, so their children's needs were not being met. We initially stipulated a minimum of three board members from low-income areas, but, unfortunately, the law was later amended to remove that provision. A final, unexpected, benefit of having a separate board for charter schools is the healthy competition that has emerged between the Arizona State Board of Education and the State Board for Charter Schools, regarding the support and approval of charters.

Fewer Bureaucratic Requirements

The two state-level chartering authorities are not the only reason we have a large number of charter schools. We also expedited rule-making for charters. I ran for superintendent of public instruction in 1994 partly because I feared that the charter impetus would get bogged down in bureaucracy. In fact, in the summer of 1994, the Arizona Department of Education announced an "18-month rule writing period." Fortunately, we were able to speed that process up once I was elected and minimize further paperwork. Among all the states, Arizona probably has the least invasive state management of charter schools. I believe that we in the Department of Education oversee public schools, period, and thus we oversee charter schools. All public schools have unreasonable reporting requirements, and we are committed to making the fulfillment of those requirements easier rather than more difficult, for *all* public schools, including charters.

Parental Demand for Charters

Yet we never anticipated the ready supply of charter operators and teachers and the burgeoning demand of parents. On the supply side, in fall 1995 there were 105 applications. Application after application just kept coming in, and we thought, "Who *are* these people?" Mainly, they were teachers rather than profit-making enterprises.[4] The Department of Education, particularly the special education division, had to put in long hours to instruct new operators how to comply with federal requirements.[5]

The enormous parental demand for alternatives to district schools may have been predictable, but we did not predict it. After all, it takes a great deal of courage for parents to enroll their children in a new, untested charter school when there is a nearby district school whose program is a known quality. I think the huge number of charter applicants shows there is a wide gulf between parental satisfaction and parental loyalty. Even though many parents are satisfied with the school their children attend, if another school opens up next door, and they can make a comparison, they may leave. Given the opportunity to choose a better school, they will say, "OK, I'll go over here." Given a choice, relatively few parents have absolute loyalty to the school their child is in right now. There is a huge market for schools that address kids' needs in different ways.

Although there are definite stresses to starting up as quickly as we did—the *Wall Street Journal* (Stecklow 1996) calls us the Wild West—there is no question in my mind that it was the right thing to do. My philosophy is that you should not thwart a market that wants to move.

The Empowerment of Charter Schools

Parental Empowerment

Charter school parents are fascinating people and are the real key to charter school success. Every time we think we have exhausted the pool of

motivated parents, we see more poring over the charter school applications in our office to see what type of schools are available for their children. I wonder what frustration in their previous school drives them to
actively make a choice to place their children in a charter school.

Now it seems absurd, but those opposed to charter schools often argued in public meetings about charters that such schools would cream
the elite kids, who would profit from academies. In fact, the market for
schools is in *dis*satisfaction, so it concentrates in low-income, minority
communities and around kids with special needs—wherever parents feel
their child is not being served, for whatever reason. It angers me to hear
the argument that in a free-market system of education, the loser is the
poor family with no capacity to choose. I see that as a very offensive argument. The location of charter schools shows clearly that the motivation
to move kids is just as high or higher in low-income communities.

When we first had to close a charter school for financial misconduct on
the part of the leadership, many of the parents were resistant and loyal to
their school. (Editor's Note: See Chapter 13 for Mary Hartley's account of
the Citizen 2000 charter school.) I had a most incredible meeting with the
parents of the children in that school. They came with their kids, and we
brought in pizza and sat with these parents for three hours and talked about
what happened. The one point I kept hearing over and over was the parents' explicit desire for their kids to go beyond where they were. You rarely
see that ambition, so much a part of America, so starkly expressed today.
Those parents said, "We knew there was fraud going on. That didn't matter
for us. What mattered was that our children were noticed; they knew our
children's names. There was a vision for our children that had never been
expressed for them before." The leader of the school was African-American,
and that was a huge factor in the parents' choice of the school.

Another important thing I remember is that regardless of the problems
at the school, it was doing well academically. The teachers themselves
were dedicated; the parents were incredibly motivated; and the kids were
learning. The parents were wonderful; they told us, "This is basically a
private education for our children we thought we could never access.
They were treated like children at a private academy." And most of those
parents came right back the next day, went through charter school applications, and put their children right back in charter schools. Charter
school parents are not calm parents, and I find them fascinating. These are
Ninja parents. They are not going to be placated, and, for whatever reason, the traditional district schools are not making them happy. In this
case, most of the parents did not send their children back to the districts.

The Human Face of Charters

There are a lot of those Ninja parents out there. One of the most interesting aspects of Arizona education is that the number of charter schools is

such that everybody knows somebody who goes to a charter school, and that puts a human face on it rather than just a newspaper face. With over 30,000 charter students statewide, most of us in Arizona know about what's going on in a charter school firsthand or secondhand, not just from the papers. There are so many charter schools that the media can't camp on the doorstep of every single charter school waiting for it to do something wrong. In states where there are ten charter schools, every day of the week they've got some reporter asking them, "Are you doing X, Y, or Z?" Here, there's no way the media can microscopically inspect 272 schools. Still, as of December 1998, our 272 charter schools have received more media attention than the 1,150 district schools.

Charter Competition with District Schools

I believe that, understandably, school districts have embraced a monopolistic mind-set that is bad for our children. If one walks into a school and says, "I'm interested in putting my child in your school," you would think this is a great market moment. After all, you are an interested consumer. But the answer you get is, "Where do you live?" In other words, you are either entitled to go to this school or you aren't, and that is the beginning and end of our conversation. What if instead you said, "I want to put my child in your school," and the answer was "Fabulous! Let us tell you about the school. Who is your child?" If that change is the only one that charters make in education today, the nature of public education would *transform* immediately because right now the mind-set is: "We have to take you anyway, even if we don't want to. We're crowded, and we're not necessarily happy that you're here." There's no money attached to the child. If she's quiet and nice, then they're happy, but the child doesn't bring to the school the money she's worth. The whole dynamic is inhuman, sterile. If we can only capture the dynamic of excitement going on when parents choose a charter school and spread that to parents' choice of any school, charter or district, our children will greatly benefit.

Even a fairly good school district may not be safe from competition. You have to impress your parents. Our largest school district lost 5,000 kids in two years. They used to be a growing district, and now they're flat. They responded well to it, considering the difficulty that any bureaucracy has responding to change. The first year they had a program to welcome new parents into the school district. They were being nice! The following year, they decided that being nice was not enough, so they now affirmatively advertise. They are making genuine efforts, but the next step has to be to ask why the children are in school. Peripherals such as a welcoming night for parents are fine, but you have go beyond advertising and outreach and get down to the classroom level to find out why these kids are leaving. This district has some very good ideas on handling this.

Now they are working with the Edison Project to revamp their curriculum. In the end, it is our children who benefit from these reactions.

The Accountability of Charter Schools

The major benefit of a charter school is freedom—freedom to hire and fire staff, freedom to choose a curriculum, and freedom to say, "We're not going to follow this rule just because it's there. We only follow rules that exist for a reason." If the public knows the performance of the school, and if we can demonstrate legitimate and sane use of the public's money, that's all we need to know. Other than that, charter schools must have the freedom to work. But along with this freedom, which is the crucial catalyst for innovation, comes accountability to the state, to the teachers, and, most of all, to the parents and children. For example, the state board approved teacher certification standards that do not require attendance at a college of education. Increasingly we're saying—to teachers as well as charter schools—you can prepare yourself however you want, so long as you meet the standards.

Statewide Academic Standards

Our department requires all schools to be accountable. We oversee the schools. We examine their academic core, and we monitor their funds. We determine whether the school is teaching to the state standards, and we are developing a criterion reference test to do so. In fact, the Thomas B. Fordham Foundation ranked Arizona's 1997 science standards fourth among thirty-six states; and mathematics fifth out of forty-six states and the District of Columbia. The foundation previously ranked Arizona's language arts standards fourth nationally, making Arizona, as the only state to score in the top five of all three core content areas, first overall.[6]

Closing Down Charter Schools

Not every charter school is up to the challenge. In 1995 the Department of Education repeatedly predicted that seven or eight charter schools would fail the first year, and that prediction inoculated us when Citizen 2000 had to be closed in 1996. As of December 1998, five other charter holders have been closed, which is all the media wants to talk about. Fair enough. It is terrible to have to close a school. But one must remember that for the first time in the history of the state, we are closing failing schools. There are many schools that deserve closing, but we don't have the authority to close them unless they are charter schools. Those who harp on the fact that a few charter schools have closed should ask which schools formerly had these children. Where must they have been before, that they would come to such an unsatisfactory setting and call it superior? Certainly there are parents who are very satisfied with traditional schools, and I'm one of them, with two of my children in district schools. That's not true for all. It's my goal to enable parents to make informed choices about schools that best fit their children in order to forestall such tragedies.

Informing Parents

Key to accountability is parental choice, but, for true choice to exist, parents must be informed. To inform parents, the 1994 law forced all schools to report objective information to the state which is recorded on the school report card. The report card is sent to all parents of children attending that school. The report card idea came from dissatisfaction with the districts' traditional annual reports on their performance. As a parent, you couldn't glean much information about your particular school from those reports, nor were they particularly objective. They were more like year-end stock reports. It was difficult or impossible to find anything bad anywhere in the state. In addition, we realized that with the onset of charter schools, parents needed to be able to compare one school to another. But most people didn't even know which district had their school, much less how the individual school was doing. The school report cards, available on the Web at http://www.ade.state.az.us/schools/reportcardpage.htm, report a variety of objective indicators verified by the Department of Education. Report cards include standardized test scores (along with district and statewide comparisons), disciplinary and criminal infraction statistics, attendance figures, personnel information such as the numbers of certified and uncertified teachers, and the school calendar.

Importantly, report cards also include the school curriculum and mission statement. Ideally, the mission statements would give you a sense of what goes on in schools. All too often, however, the mission statements in school report cards are prime examples of education gobbledygook. I have no idea what some of them mean! It would be interesting to catalogue those over time. As parents ask more questions, school mission statements seem to be evolving. District schools started out advertising their high self-esteem and their ability to work with all people in an open and collegial way for the benefit of mankind. That's fabulous, but it means absolutely nothing. Increasingly, school mission statements talk about math, phonics, and reading ability. Now they advertise kids' awards for academic achievement.

Reading the report cards tells me the key difference between charter schools and district schools: Charter schools use report cards to market externally, whereas many district schools use them to speak to their internal environments. The districts are speaking to their teachers. They're talking about themselves. This is a very traditional educational view ("Who do we feel we are at the academy?"). The charter schools are trying to get people to come to their school, so they're focused differently. I believe that parents look at the report cards and respond to that difference.

The Future: Money Following Students

In order for a healthy market system to work in education, we must have freedom to innovate, rewards for creativity, accountability for failure, and informed choice. We also must have bottom-up funding based on the individual child, not top-down funding that starts at the state level, moves to the district level, then the school level, and finally the level of the student, with bureaucracy siphoning off a percentage at each and every level.

We must change the way we fund schools, not just in Arizona but across the nation. The current system of appropriations based on local property taxes and bonds is not consistent with the ability to create schools and innovate. It limits the ability of parents to reward successful schools and leave unsuccessful ones. In addition, current funding practices are wholly unequal, and in the long run the courts will not allow them.

In Arizona, we want to reconstruct school finance to mirror the funding mechanisms in charter schools. We want the capital monies to be portable, to move with the kids to the schools they choose. As of 1998, the biggest difficulty for charter operators is getting capital to get started, whereas district schools already have their buildings and can ask the voters for approval of school bonds. Corporate charters such as the Edison Project are capitalized, but the mom and pop schools are teaching students while trying to figure out who will rent them a building and how they will get the basic materials to operate. They are doing superhuman work. If the funding for capital and operations were available to charter schools, their growth would be even more explosive.

Conclusion

In short, these are indeed exciting times in public education. For the first time in awhile, we are seeing change in the public school system, not inch by creeping inch, but in leaps and bounds, as the new market system takes over. By fall 1998, charter schools were a proven success in Arizona, as evidenced by the over 30,000 children attending them. Because they are successful and we want them to continue to grow and prosper, we will look for ways to make our law better. Charter schools are a prime example of the benefits of parental choice. Expanding parental choice continues to be a major objective in Arizona and many other reform-minded states because we look at charter schools as the beginning of parental choice, not the end.

Of course, there are growing pains that accompany this extraordinary new growth. Accountability mechanisms, although in place, are not as effective yet as they could be. We are working to improve them. And not all charters are perfect; who would expect they could be? We live in an imperfect world. I keep seeing in my mind's eye those Ninja parents ready to take on the world and the traditional educational system to give their child a better chance than they themselves had. We are doing everything we can to help those parents and their children reach that goal. But to do that we need to change the financing system as well, so that smaller schools like the charters are no longer punished financially. That is the future for Arizona, and perhaps the nation.

Notes

1. *School Improvement Act of 1994,* 41st Arizona State Legislature, 9th special session.

2. HB 2505, 41st Arizona State Legislature, 2d regular session.

3. The Arizona charter school law is more fully known as ARS 15-183, 41st Legislature, 9th special session, chapter 2.

4. The fact of the matter is that Arizona schools operate on a pretty low margin. If you're going to try to make money from the per-pupil subsidy, Arizona is not the easiest place to be. Try Boston.

5. Special Education is an important issue for charter schools. Although charters accept special education kids, no sane person could withstand the sheer volume of regulation involved. Of course, district schools have the same bureaucratic requirements, but charter schools seldom have the resources to hire a special education coordinator. Thus, charter schools often contract with districts or private contractors simply to assure that they are in legal compliance.

6. Chester E. Finn Jr., Michael J. Petrillia, and Gregg Varnourek, "The State of State Standards," *Fordham Report* 2 (July 1998): 1–39.

References

Stecklow, Steve. 1996. "Start-Up Lessons: Arizona Takes the Lead in Charter Schools for Better or Worse." *Wall Street Journal*, December 24.

13

A Voice from the State Legislature: Don't Do What Arizona Did!

MARY HARTLEY

Arizona has acquired quite a reputation for its charter school movement. Often proponents tout our state as having the strongest charter school legislation in the country. However, critics point out loopholes the size of the Grand Canyon and an increasing number of problems that plague these schools. If I may offer a cautionary note to those of you who are thinking of using Arizona as a model for your own charter school statutes—think twice, then think it through again. Make sure you scratch below the surface and recognize that there is significant tarnish on the bright future of charter schools.

Background

Let me give you a little background on how we got where we are today. The first serious debate on charter schools began during the 1993 legislative session. The chairman of the house Education Committee, now our superintendent of public instruction, introduced a bill that took a meat ax approach to education reform. The bill would have repealed all of the laws regarding schools and replaced them with a handful of statutes outlining responsibilities of parents, students, teachers, principals, school councils, superintendents, and governing boards. It also contained a small section on charter schools. The uproar over the wholesale repeal of the education laws overshadowed the debate on charter schools. That bill died, and a modest senate bill that dealt only with charter schools passed the senate but was never heard in the house.

During the 1994 legislative session, "education reform" was resurrected in the 114-page amendment to House Bill 2505 proposed in a late-night conference committee. That bill (HB 2505) contained a provision for private school vouchers. Democrats noted in their minority report on House Bill 2505 that all the conference committee discussion was on vouchers and that, consequently, "there was inadequate discussion and limited analysis of the provisions governing charter schools, decentralization, open enrollment, and twenty-first century schools."[1] The "voucher bill" died.

That summer, an election year, the governor called the legislature back into a special session to deal with education reform. Realizing there were not enough votes to pass a voucher bill and feeling political pressure to do something, the legislature, with a bipartisan vote, passed an education bill that included charter school provisions.[2]

That legislation exempted charter schools from all laws and rules relating to schools except those relating to health, safety, civil rights, and insurance, and those specifically enumerated in the new law. Charters could be held by for-profit as well as non-profit entities. The legislation allowed charters to exist for five years and then to be renewed for seven years at a time. Finally, it specified that charter schools were to receive the same amount of per-pupil funding as standard public schools, including the additional funding given to small schools.

With the signing of that law, Arizona's charter school experiment began. Perhaps "experiment" is the wrong word. It implies that there will be some examination of the results, some testing, some hypothesis to prove or disprove. So far the Arizona legislature has steadfastly refused to even take a peek at whether our charter schools are working. Maybe charter school "binge" is a better description of Arizona's experience.

Shifting into high gear, the charter school board and the state board of education hastily developed an application process—one that has been less than adequate and has led to a very rocky start for that first crop of fifty-one schools. Forty-six schools were chartered by the two state boards, and five were chartered by individual school districts. At the end of that first year, the actual enrollment was 6,300 students, and in 1996–1997 it grew to 16,500. The best estimates for the 1998–1999 school year are 34,000 students at 272 school sites. As of this writing, the estimate for the 1999–2000 school year is anybody's guess, but for budget purposes we in the senate have estimated that enrollment will grow to 40,000 students at a cost to the general fund of around $192 million.

If $192 million sounds like a lot of money, that is because it *is* a lot of money. Although Arizona puts public schools on a starvation diet, we feed our charter schools champagne and caviar. Instead of "doing more with less," as in the rest of the nation, Arizona's charter schools do "less with more"—a lot more. In some circumstances their funding can be $600–$700 more per student than the funding for students in standard public schools.

The first wave of generosity came in 1996 when the Department of Education found that half of the charter schools overcharged the state for their transportation allowance by a total of $3.6 million. Arizona's funding formula reimburses the transportation costs of standard public schools on a per-mile basis. At best, school districts break even on this part of their budget. Charter schools were abusing this formula by paying parents $.30 a mile to transport their own children to school, charging the state the bus rate of $1.95 per mile, then pocketing the difference. The legislature resolved this issue by giving them a flat $174 per student for transportation expenses, whether they provided any transportation or not. Most charter schools do not provide any transportation, so the extra money is just gravy.

During the 1997 legislative session the legislature debated capital funding for all schools. The Arizona Supreme Court decided in 1994 (*Roosevelt v. Bishop*) that our system for funding the capital needs of schools was not "general and uniform" as required by our state constitution, because it relied almost solely on property taxes that varied dramatically from district to district. The legislature attempted to fix the problem by giving low property-wealth school districts extra funding, based on a formula. At the time, charter schools were provided an additional $146 per K–8 student and $219 per high school student to meet their capital needs. Shortly thereafter, the formula funding for standard public schools was repealed when the Arizona Supreme Court said it was not sufficient to satisfy the constitutional requirement (*Hull v. Albrecht* 1997). The extra $146/$219 for charter schools, however, stayed in effect.

In 1998, when faced with a court-imposed deadline that would shut down all public schools, the legislature got serious about fixing its capital funding system. It passed the Students FIRST plan, which provided standard public schools an additional $50 per student for soft capital, such as computers, telephones, and other equipment with a relatively short life.[3] The plan also included some formula-driven funds for building maintenance and a commitment to bring all schools up to building adequacy standards that have yet to be developed. In addition, the plan promised to build new schools when the available square footage per student was smaller than certain statutory requirements.

In the Students FIRST plan, charter schools were exempted from the requirement to be brought up to standards, a constitutionally questionable provision, and they were excluded from the soft capital, building maintenance, and new schools funding. In exchange charter schools received a whopping $400 increase in their per-student allocation. To make matters worse, in the 1999 legislative session, legislators gave charter schools operated by a nonprofit entity the ability to apply for industrial develop-ment bonds. With no debt limit, these low-interest loans will tempt char-ter school operators to go further into debt at the public's expense.

This means that a charter school annually receives $570/$643 per each K–8 or high school student that standard public schools do not ($174 transportation, plus $146/$219 capital needs, plus $400 Students FIRST, minus $50 soft capital, minus $100 estimated building renewal). To put this in perspective, a classroom of thirty charter high school students has $19,290 more funding than a standard public school classroom—almost enough to pay the teacher's salary!

Granted, most of the extra money is supposed to compensate for the fact that charter schools do not have a property tax base to construct buildings, but most of the charter schools are so small it is unlikely they would have such high capital expenses. Many small rural and remote standard public schools find themselves in like circumstances and have never received any state monetary aid despite their lack of bonding ability. For the 1997–1998 school year, 38 percent of the charter schools had less than 100 students en-rolled. Constructing an entire school for 100 students simply does not make economic, or any other kind, of sense. As a result, most of the schools operate out of churches, strip malls, or portable buildings.

Arizona has paved the way, however, for those charter school operators who do want to make large capital investments. Amazingly, Arizona al-lows charter school holders to keep their school assets and any other capital equipment they acquire during the time they operate as charter schools. The attorney general gave that practice his blessing. For example, consider Basis School. The charter holders planned to purchase a $2.2 mil-lion estate in a historic residential area for use as a charter school site. Neighborhood outrage prevented them from getting the necessary zoning, but had they been successful, they could have reconverted the 'school' into a plush, taxpayer-funded personal residence upon the expi-ration of their charter. Quite a nice retirement plan, I'd say. A public in-terest attorney has threatened to sue the state over what he considers to be an unconstitutional gift of public funds.[4]

In 1996 charter schools began complaining that they could not get loans to make capital investments because their charters extended for only five years. The legislature came to their aid by extending their charters to fif-teen years, with "reviews" every five years. What does this mean? Al-though it hasn't been tested because charters have been in business for only four years, I believe the State Board for Charter Schools would be forced to allow a charter school to operate for the full fifteen years, even if their test scores plummet or they experience other major problems dur-ing that time.

Furthermore, in our short four-year "experiment" with charter schools we have experienced numerous problems. Let me give you some examples from newspaper reports and from personal conversations I've had over the last couple of years.

The Numerous Problems with Arizona's Charter "Experiment"

Although our federal and state constitutions guarantee that publicly funded schools will not provide religious instruction, it has crept into our charter schools.

- An advertisement for Life College Preparatory in Mesa was placed in a Mormon newspaper, promising that students would have religious mentors to help prepare them for entering LDS-affiliated universities. The same school placed a similar ad in the *Catholic Sun*, but altered it to contain only general information. According to editorials in the *Arizona Republic* (June 10, 1998) and the *Daily Star* (June 16, 1998), it did not advertise in any secular publication.
- The Heritage Academy in Mesa had a curriculum that included teaching creationism in lieu of a sound science program. The headmaster told a newspaper reporter, "There is no law that says you cannot teach creationism as an idea. Don't we believe in academic freedom around here?" After the State Board for Charter Schools began an investigation, the headmaster claimed they would not teach anything about the origin of man (Kull 1996).
- During a visit to NFL-YET Academy in South Phoenix, a charter school board official made them remove a prayer and a picture of the Virgin Mary from their office wall (Pearce 1998).

Parents of disabled students have complained that charter schools practice both subtle and overt discrimination against their children in the hopes of not having to provide the more expensive services required by both federal and state law. Last June Ms. Jerri Katzerman, an attorney for the Arizona Center for Disability Law, stated that her office had received more than 200 calls from charter school parents since the previous October (Tapia 1998). For example:

- A child disabled by AIDS was denied admittance to the Phoenix campus of the Children's Academy of Arizona because it was not wheelchair accessible (Creno 1998).
- Three boys with learning disabilities were expelled from Eagle's Aerie School, ostensibly because their pants were too short. An

independent hearing officer found that the expulsion was un-
warranted (Todd 1998b).

- The Children's Academy of Arizona in Tucson, with twenty-two
  special education students, had seven complaints filed with the
  Department of Education for everything from failing to evaluate
  children to failing to provide them with services (Tapia 1998).

Funding is based on enrollment, so some charter schools have been accused of caring only about the number of students. For these schools, education of students is an afterthought.

- An April 27, 1998, a *U.S. News and World Report* article described
  how Life School College Preparatory offers franchises for $1,000
  per student, which the founder modeled after Amway franchise
  schemes. Teachers recruit their own students and receive com-
  mensurate increases in their salary (Toch 1998).
- That same article described an "American Literature through
  Cinema" course at Apache Trail High School where students lis-
  tened to the soundtrack from the movie *Last of the Mohicans* (Toch
  1998).
- One parent complained to me that Paramount Life Academy
  used their students during school hours to distribute flyers promoting the school (personal communication, May 1998).
- The State Board for Charter Schools found that a school in Lake
  Havasu City had no books or instructional materials and that
  students spent the day watching Arnold Schwarzenegger movies
  (*Arizona Republic,* January 14, 1997).

Nepotism, which is not against the law for our charter schools, also
runs rampant. Board members routinely hire family members for other
positions in the school.

- A charter holder of Ventana Academic School was arrested for
  sexually molesting her former students. The governing board
  did not see any warning signs, possibly because two of the three
  board members were her parents (Harker 1998).
- A NFL-YET Academy charter holder hired one brother as budget
  director, another brother as 'spiritual development' director, his
  mother as an administrator, his father as a carpenter, and his
  sister as a teacher (Toch 1998). The now-bankrupt Citizen 2000
  School (described below) also hired several relatives.
- When a board member of the Sequoia Charter School realized his
  school was going to buy a piece of property, he asked his parents

to buy it first. The school eventually bought the property, and their $500 investment netted a $90,000 profit (Mitchell 1998a).

The financial problems that some of the schools have had are another subject of great concern. By December 1998 six charter holders had closed, often in the middle of the school year, leaving hundreds of children academically stranded. The worst case was when the founder of Citizen 2000 declared bankruptcy and was subsequently indicted on thirty-one counts of theft, fraud, and misuse of $125,843 of public money (Matthews 1998). In my opinion, allowing charters to be "for profit" is comparable to issuing medical licenses to snake oil salesmen.

Many of these problems could have been avoided if the legislature had recognized and utilized the infrastructure already in place throughout the state in the offices of our county school superintendents. The superintendents are elected to provide administrative assistance to the school districts within their county. School districts rely on the superintendents for a variety of financial services such as administering their payroll, paying vouchers, and investing funds.

My preference would have been for charter schools to be sponsored by the school board (for schools within their boundaries) or the county school superintendent (for schools within the county). Applicants who were denied would be able to appeal to the elected County Board of Supervisors. This structure would have preserved local control, allowed for more than one chartering entity, and provided a natural accountability process through the election process.

Three Solutions for Arizona

So how does Arizona work its way out of this mess? I propose three solutions: restrict the number of new charter schools, make them more accountable, and increase parental rights, including the right to have accurate and timely information.

Restrict New Charter Schools

As of 1999 the Arizona State Board of Education and the State Board for Charter Schools may each charter twenty-five schools a year. The board of education has limited itself to the number it can reasonably supervise. Given its other responsibilities, it only chartered ten last year. The State Board for Charter Schools, which is more interested in promotion than oversight, has consistently approved its maximum and has begged the legislature to increase its limit.

Equally important is that any single school district governing board can charter as many charter schools as it wants, and the charter schools do not have to be within their attendance border. Experience has already taught us that allowing unlimited charters is a bad idea. Window Rock, a remote five-school district on the Navajo Reservation, was the first to sponsor twelve charter schools, almost all of which were in distant urban centers. Two years later, after financial problems and allegations of mismanagement at some of its schools, Window Rock gave notice to its charters that it would no longer sponsor them after June 1999. Days later, Ganado Unified School District, also on the Navajo Reservation, told its seven charter schools that it would have to find new sponsors. Those school district governing boards realized it was impossible for them to provide the oversight needed.

Those concerns have not deterred Higley Elementary School District, a small rural district on the edge of the Phoenix metropolitan area. Although it has only 250 students of its own, it decided to charter twenty-eight schools with an enrollment of more than 5,500 beginning in the fall of 1998. The superintendent, who on occasion has had to drive a bus and teach physical education in his small district, has vowed to visit each charter school quarterly, although many of them are in remote rural areas hundreds of miles away (Riordan and Todd 1998).

Doubts about the ability of Higley Elementary School District to handle this responsibility deepened when the state auditor general put the district on notice, noting that its own accounts were not in compliance with the Uniform System of Financial Records. Higley claimed that there would not be similar problems with its charter schools because it was hiring an accounting firm that specialized in charter schools to monitor them. According to a newspaper report, the accounting firm, which brought in business by convincing school districts to accept charters previously rejected by other boards, was in fact $400,000 in the red (Mitchell 1998b). Still, there is nothing in the law to stop Higley from venturing in over its head.

You may ask what would be the motivation for Higley to open so many charter schools. The answer is the same as for many other charter school operators—MONEY. Higley is charging its charters $9,600 to $100,000 apiece. It plans to use the money to buy computers and improve technology for its 250 students and to prepare for substantial growth in size as new housing developments take hold in that district (Todd 1998c).

I believe we should limit the number of new charter schools until we do two things: fix the problems with our current schools and determine whether or not charter schools have been a success. There has not been a single study or report that will help us evaluate how our experiment is going. I am probably as familiar with charter schools as any legislator, yet I cannot even guess what percentage of charter schools are doing a better than an average job. My hunch is that the most promising ventures jumped in right away and have already received their charters. This leads me to believe there would be no sacrifice in the overall quality of our charter schools if we reduce the number of new charters for the next few years. In fact, there are signs that in some areas of the state we have reached market saturation, yet additional charters are still being granted.

I would like to eliminate permanently the ability of school districts to charter schools outside their borders and to limit the board of education and the board for charter schools to a combined total of fifty charters over the next three years. In addition, new charters would not be issued for more than five years, phasing out the fifteen-year contracts.

Increase Accountability of Charter Schools

During this moratorium, Arizona should increase the accountability of its charter schools. The current oversight is abysmal, mainly because the legislature strictly limited the reporting requirements and never provided funding for oversight. The superintendent of public instruction voluntarily cut the Department of Education budget dramatically shortly after charter schools were first instituted, even though the department retains the responsibility for ensuring compliance with general state and federal mandates, such as special education. Up until fiscal year 1997–1998, the State Board for Charter Schools, which chartered 146 schools, had only three employees. In fiscal year 1998–1999, the legislature gave them three more. For fiscal year 1999-2000, the board is slated to receive two more employees for the purpose of performing auditing functions that previously belonged to the auditor general.

This lack of funding was not inadvertent, nor was it a result of fiscal conservatism. It was due to the belief held among the superintendent of public instruction, the charter school board, and most Republican legislators that the marketplace is the ultimate form of accountability. In other words, they believe that because parents can yank their kids out of charter schools the moment they are unhappy, charter schools have a higher level of accountability than even our standard public schools. I disagree. Just as there always have been people who fall victim to other scams and frauds, there always will be parents who will unknowingly send their children to inferior charter schools.

Accountability for charter schools should encompass these two things: *financial accountability* that demonstrates that public money was spent in a prudent manner and in accordance with the terms of the contract (i.e., the charter) and *educational accountability* that demonstrates that the education of pupils is superior, or at least equal, to what they would have received in the standard public schools.

Our financial accountability is minimal. When charter schools first complained about the difficulty of complying with the Uniform System of Financial Records (USFR), the legislature required our auditor general to develop a different system more suited to small charter schools. We required this despite the fact that Arizona has many small, standard school districts in similar circumstances that have always complied with the USFR and have never asked to be exempted. In response, the auditor general developed a Uniform System of Financial Records for Charter Schools (USFRCS). When charter schools continued to complain about the paperwork, the legislature allowed the chartering board to exempt the schools from that system all together in return for a promise to abide by generally accepted accounting principals for financial record keeping. These exemptions are routinely granted upon request, and subsequently the auditor general checks only that an outside audit has been done and that the charter school complies with laws relating to open meetings, publication of budgets, procurement and enrollment calculations. It is up to the chartering board to determine the financial condition of the school—something they have no expertise in.

Unfortunately, measures were approved during the 1999 legislative session that further weaken financial accountability in our charter school system. For schools sponsored by the Arizona State Board of Education or the State Board for Charter Schools, new financial oversight provisions transfer auditing authority from the auditor general to the board that chartered the school. In addition, charter schools will now have the ability to write financial accountability exceptions into their charters. Therefore, instead of having a neutral auditor, charters' accountability will now be judged by the motivated self-interest of the entity responsible for the problem's creation.

Although our financial accountability is minimal, our educational accountability is even worse. Charter schools sponsored by the state are required to file an annual report with their chartering entity, but the board members admit that they do not evaluate them. Their staff is too limited to provide any oversight.

The Arizona Department of Education is responsible for monitoring compliance with state and federal laws, such as those relating to special education. Unfortunately, the department's oversight is disjointed, that is, each division conducts their reviews independently of other divisions, and there is little exchange of information between them. What is more disturbing, the department does not regularly inform the chartering entity when it encounters a problem at one of the schools (Todd and Mitchell 1998).

After receiving a large number of complaints from charter school teachers and parents, the Department of Education undertook an ambitious monitoring program of every charter school during the 1996–1997 school year. About fifty department employees participated in this effort to determine if there were any health and safety issues and whether the school complied with both state and federal laws and their charter.

When the employees returned to the office, their notes were put into a file a cabinet. In fact, the notes were never even typed up, and the Department of Education never released a report on the evaluation. When an attorney for the Arizona School Boards Association asked to see the reports, the Department of Education refused. Finally, after threatening a lawsuit, the attorney was given access to the files, but only after the handwritten notes were removed. Some notes were returned to the original evaluators, but others were lost or destroyed. The Department of Education quietly dismantled the monitoring program, and to date there has been no further monitoring done by either the Department of Education, the Arizona State Board of Education, or the State Board for Charter Schools (Garn 1998).

Test scores are the only other measurement we have of the performance of our charter schools. According to a computer analysis performed by a local newspaper, the charter schools' 1998 Stanford Nine Achievement Test scores were either the best or the worst in the state (Pearce and Konig 1998). Despite a state law requiring charter schools to increase student academic achievement, standard public schools seemed to have done an overall better job.

For example, public schools scored a 65 percent increase in math from 1997 to 1998 in most grade levels, whereas charter schools weighed in with only a 38 percent increase. Several charter schools actually came in with a decrease in Stanford Nine scores. NFL-YET Academy tallied a whopping 38 percent decrease in reading scores from 1997 (Pearce and Konig 1998).

According to an *Arizona Republic* article (July 11, 1998), charter school proponents blame the polar scoring on the fact that some charter schools are geared for the academically gifted and some for at-risk students. That may be true, but it's the middle I'm worried about. They are the ones whose parents are sending them to these schools, and the state is funding them, in the hopes of a better education. According to these statistics, chances are they would have learned more by simply remaining in conventional public school.

There are a number of changes that are necessary. Limiting charters to five years and requiring that renewal of those charters be based on evidence that students who attended during those years showed significant signs of academic improvement would be beneficial in achieving a greater level of accountability in this area as well. Charters should be operated by nonprofit organizations only. All charter schools should be subject to the USFRCS, and their annual audits should be reviewed by the auditor general. Furthermore, the chartering entity should be required to visit the charter school annually and complete an evaluation of the school's compliance with all federal and state laws, as well as with its charter. That evaluation also should be reviewed by the auditor general. To calculate the effectiveness of our charter schools and to make recommendations for improvement, the legislature should contract for an independent study of the charter school program.

The success of all this accountability hinges on parental access. Although charter schools are left to live or die by the market, it is a market that does not include accurate disclosure of information in a timely fashion. There is currently no resource that provides parents with objective and necessary information to evaluate these schools critically.

As it now stands, families are left to vote "with their feet." I would, however, submit that in reality this is a devastating experience for the students it affects. Parents in these cases have discovered that their children have learned little and are now academically stranded in the midst of a school year. In the meantime, charter schools are free to "advertise" and "market" themselves to a new set of parents with little regard to any "truth in advertising."

Increase Parental Influence on Charters

Clearly, legislative remedies are called for. The bills I have introduced would have increased parental influence, not governmental control, through the most powerful oversight mechanism of the market—information. For example, according to state law, charter schools are required to establish a governing body to determine policies with no further guidance. Therefore, there is no requirement on behalf of charter schools either to include parents on the governing body or to inform parents of the governing structure to allow legitimate access. The governing body has the power to amend the educational mission of the charter school without parental input. I believe it is necessary, and perfectly reasonable, to require charter schools, through their charter, to inform parents of how the schools are governed, of the process for selecting the governing body, of how the public may provide input into the selection process, and of how to appeal decisions of the governing body. In addition, I believe it is sound public policy to require charter schools to disclose the qualifications of their instructors and to adhere to open meeting, public records, conflict of interest, and anti-nepotism laws.

Conclusion

Although limitation of new charters, increased accountability, and clearly defined parental rights would go a long way toward resolving our current problems, these changes are not likely to happen any time soon. Our Republican-controlled legislature has refused steadfastly to do anything charter school supporters would be opposed to. However, I predict that the cost of these schools will eventually force these legislators to take notice.

Arizona's economy is going strong now; only a fool would expect it to last forever. We have initiated hundreds of millions of dollars in tax cuts, many of which have been phased in, that eventually will hamper our ability to provide needed services to our citizens. In addition, Arizona has just assumed responsibility for funding all of the capital needs of our schools, including building all new schools and bringing old schools up to building adequacy standards. When we have our next fiscal crisis, we will have no choice but to evaluate the escalating costs of our charter school movement.

Two factors may accelerate the problem. First, standard public school districts may start to charter their existing schools. In exchange for a little bit of paperwork, they could get the extra $600–$700 per student that charter schools now receive. Second, the supreme court may require charter school buildings to meet the same adequacy standards as existing public school buildings, which would require tens of millions more dollars of capital investment by the state.

As it stands now, however, the Arizona charter school movement is heading for a train wreck, and the legislature is asleep at the wheel. Ultimately it is my belief that Arizona's experiment has done more harm than good to the national effort to reform education.

Notes

1. *School Financing Act of 1994*, 41st Arizona State Legislature, 2d regular session.

2. *School Improvement Act of 1994*, 41st Arizona State Legislature, 9th special session.

3. *Students FIRST*, chapter 1, 43rd Arizona State Legislature, 5th special session.

4. Timothy M. Hogan, Executive Director, Arizona Center for Law in the Public Interest.

References

Arizona Daily Star. 1998. Editorial, June 16.

Arizona Republic. 1997. "Valley News in Brief: State Threatening to Shut Down School," January 14.

Arizona Republic. 1998. Editorial, June 10.

Creno, Cathryn. 1998. "Suit: Charter Closed to Boy With Aids," *Arizona Republic*, June 25.

Garn, Gregg. 1998. "The Accountability System for Arizona Charter Schools." Ph.D. diss., Arizona State University.

Harker, Victoria. 1998. "Charter School Director Sued, Parents Accused Her of Molesting Boys: $26 Million Sought." *Arizona Republic*, April 24.

Kull, Randy. 1996. "Creationism Gets Equal Treatment: School Flouts Court, State Law." *Arizona Republic*, September 30.

Matthews, Paul. 1998. "Hundreds in Lurch When Schools Close." *Tribune*, August 25.

Mitchell, Kirk. 1998a. "$500 Down, $90,000 Profit: Windfall from System Legal, Auditors Say." *Tribune*, August 23.

_____. 1998b. "Shaky Charters' Cheerleader: Accounting Firm Helps Schools Past Rejections." *Tribune*, August 23.

Pearce, Kelly. 1998. "Church-State Controversy." *Arizona Republic*, June 6.

Pearce, Kelly, and Ryan Konig. 1998. "Charter Schools High, Low in Tests." *Arizona Republic*, July 11.

Riordan, Nikki, and Cece Todd. 1998. "East Valley Now Charter Schools King: Small District Builds Sponsorship Empire." *Mesa Tribune*, May 10.

Tapia, Sarah Tully. 1998. "Schools Balk at Bucks Needed for Special Education." *Arizona Daily Star*, June 28.

_____. 1998. "Parents Say Charter School Wouldn't Meet Kids' Needs: Academy Is Target of Complaints." *Arizona Daily Star*, June 28.

Toch, Thomas. 1998. "The New Education Bazaar." *U.S. News and World Report*, April 27.

Todd, Cece. 1998a. "Higley Has Tight Rein on District Charters." *Mesa Tribune*, September 27.

_____. 1998b. "Disabled Students Left Behind: Federal, State Laws Demand Compliance." *Mesa Tribune*, August 25.

_____. 1998c. "East Valley Now Charter King: Funding Keeps Dazzling Idea Underground." *Mesa Tribune*, May 10.

Todd, Cece, and Kirk Mitchell. 1998. "High Price for Haste: State's Rush for Charters Invites Abuse." *Mesa Tribune*, August 23.

14

Public Schools and the Charter Movement: An Emerging Relationship

LEE L. HAGER

This chapter examines the relationship between traditional public schools and public charter schools, in the view of this educator.[1] What follows are my own views, which do not reflect those of all district school teachers and officials, who are a diverse group. I will cover the six stages of Arizona charter schooling: (1) traditional public schools before the new wave; (2) the emergence of charter schools; (3) public school reaction to charter schools; (4) how the traditional school establishment stopped fearing charter schools and learned to work with them; (5) benefits of charter school and public school collaboration; and, finally, (6) future predictions.

Public Schools Before the New Wave

Traditionally, public schools' competition was private education, but few private schools were started to replace a failing public school system. Though private schools did compete with public schools, that was not their focus. Most were organized to express religious beliefs that could not be taught in public schools, or to allow wealthy children to socialize with children of their socioeconomic status. The numbers of these private schools remained constant, or even declined due to increased costs (Bryk et al. 1993; Cookson 1994).

I believe that in Arizona the first real challenge to public education came from the home-school movement. Some families chose to educate their young at home to promote their own religious values or to avoid problems in the public schools. Reaction to home-schooling was very similar to the initial reaction to charter schools. Public schools first ignored, then avoided, and eventually accepted and worked with the parents of home-school students. Arizona schools learned that home-schoolers who attend a certain portion of the day at public schools are revenue sources. Many home-school parents faced with more challenging upper-level classes realized they needed the support of a public school for advanced curricula. In fact, districts who began to work productively with home-school parents and their associations found that many of these students began to attend public schools more frequently. This finding is consistent with Gallup polls that have found that parents and community members who are more informed about their public schools rate them more highly (Gallup and Lowell 1998).

The magnet schools movement was another challenge to traditional public schools. Like many states, Arizona has a number of successful magnet schools. Unfortunately, magnets cost more money. Traditional schools first thought magnet school successes were based on specific magnet programs, including such exotic ones as flight training, advanced dance programs, professional level arts and crafts, and science and engineering programs using the most current technological equipment. How could a traditional public school with a traditional budget compete with such expensive programs? Not very easily. Yet I suspect that although magnets were appealing, the main reason parents and students selected a magnet school was that, for the first time in public schools, they had a *choice*.

Charter Schools in Arizona—Their Emergence

As Chapters 6, 12, and 13 show, Arizona's 1994 charter school law in effect said: "Abracadabra—instant schools!" The leaders of the Arizona charter movement were interested only in information that supported charters and moved their agenda forward. Many of them had long supported the investment of public funds in private schools. In many cases their sons and daughters already attended these schools for considerable tuition. When the public-monies-in-private-schools movement failed, the same legislators began viewing charter schools as another way to achieve their goal. In fact, some longtime private schools became charter schools to gain public funding and end the tuition burden for parents whose children already attended. Perhaps the initial emergence of charter schools in Arizona was less about improving schools and more a frustrated attack on public schools perceived to be failing.

As a result of the rush to implement the charter law, many details were left out. As the previous chapter shows, some charter schools have misused or lost state funds (Mattern 1997). Some have closed overnight, leaving students and parents stranded during the school year. In Flagstaff, an administrator for the American Grade Schools closed his school, but, since he retained his charter, later opened schools in the Phoenix area!

In spite of the numerous problems brought on by haste, many charter schools are successful, in part because of the support of state-level regulators, but also because of their dedicated staff and administrators. Charter schools have tried to maintain lower class sizes. Yet as they grapple with the business operations of schools (i.e., accounting, food service, transportation), operators often find that they must either hire more support staff or else contract with public school districts to provide the services. These additional costs reduce charters' ability to lower class sizes, just as with other schools, both public and private. After all, Arizona is ranked near the bottom of the fifty states in funding of education (Schnaiberg 1998).

In my view, Arizona's best charter schools were founded by public school employees or else hired public school employees to administer and teach. Often, charter school entrepreneurs are public school employees who were unable to use their creativity within the traditional public school system. Charter schools have made good use of their skills, ideas, and creativity. They truly may represent what futurist Joel Barker calls "paradigm pioneers," those who break with the old at a time when the new is unproven. Their desertion may call into question the organization of traditional public schools.

Those charter schools employing creative public school employees with a desire to do something new have had great success in Arizona. They have been able to balance the creativity behind the creation of the charter schools with the necessary detail work of implementation. In the business operation of a school, regardless of size, the devil is in the details. This has been a hard lesson for many of the charter school operators, specifically those who are inexpert in school operations. Many well-intentioned charter school founders have overlooked the laws that regulate all public schools. In some cases, Arizona charter schools have had to be held accountable regarding special education laws, as well as those requiring due process for discipline hearings (Schnaiberg 1997).

Public School Reaction to Charter Schools

Most of the teachers and administrators in traditional public schools believe that if they were given the lack of regulations that charter schools enjoy, they too would be as creative and as successful. Yet Arizona has a long-standing procedure for waiving rules and regulations that appear to impede educational excellence. These petitions are taken to the Arizona State Board of Education under the auspices of the chief state school officer. One would think that if regulations and bureaucratic red tape were keeping the traditional educational system from achieving the perceived success of the charter schools in Arizona, the waiver process would have been used often. Yet very few petitions ever have been submitted for waiving mandates on traditional public schools; thus, the traditional schools' lament concerning charter schools' unfairly advantageous freedom appears unfounded.

However, a "woe is us" attitude of public school employees continued for some time after charter schools were established. The support for charters combined with low education funding to convince many of us that the charter movement was a step toward dismantling public education. For many, the legislation demonstrated lack of respect for the efforts made by public school employees on behalf of the students. The perceived "unqualified support" of the state legislature for charter schools again posed the question of whether charter schools improve the educational system by providing choice for parents, or whether they are yet another method to shut down the traditional public educational system that some have found unsatisfactory. Charter schools advocates back the first assertion, whereas the initial reaction of many public school employees would support the second. Many Arizona public school employees believe the powers that be give unqualified support to charter schools even though some high profile charter schools have been found out of compliance in a number of areas. Although these examples lend credence to traditional public school support, the press tends to use the worst examples to make a point. I have no reason to believe these examples represent most charter schools.

In short, initial public school reaction to the charter movement can be summed up as a perception that public school employees are underfunded, underpaid, overworked, and have to deal with all of society's ills; yet we continue to provide a challenging curriculum with high standards. Recently, Arizona standards received a rare "A" from the U.S. Department of Education (1998). Perceived under-appreciation put most public school employees and their supporters at odds with the charter movement. In particular, those who left district schools to start or work in charters were viewed with suspicion by their former colleagues. Perhaps traditional public schools missed an opportunity by failing to tap into this creativity and energy when it had existed in the traditional setting. Previously unrecognized, it blossomed in charter schools.

How We Stopped Fearing Charter Schools and Learned to Work with Them

When the initial sting of the charter school movement began to subside, the pride that traditional educational employees and their supporters felt began to emerge in competitive reactions to charter schools. The traditional educational establishment began to pose important questions. What is it about charter schools that attracts parents and students? What do charter schools have that the public schools do not have? Do they provide better educational opportunity? These questions are best examined on two levels.

The attraction of charter schools seems aligned with the ability of families and students to choose their own educational program, instead of "one size fits all." In almost all educational systems throughout the United States, students are able to make many choices. In many cases, the programs highlighted in a charter school are offered in a traditional one. Part of the attraction lies in the marketing of charter programs and, most importantly, in the ability of families to choose their educational setting, as opposed to having that choice dictated by the neighborhood in which they live.

In my opinion, there is no *clear* evidence that charter school students perform any better or worse than traditional public school students. The issue of possible selection criteria for charter schools enters into this discussion. Is the educational testing playing field level or not? Answering this question would require research comparing the profiles of charter and public school students.

As public school supporters asked these and other insightful questions, they noticed something else about the charter school movement. The initial wave had passed; the drain of students from the public setting had peaked; and the sky had not fallen. Once emotions had subsided on both sides, both traditional and charter schools focused on new issues. Many charter school founders realized that they needed the institutional support of local school districts with respect to transportation, food service, accounting, school law issues, and placement of special education students. Simultaneously, traditional public education supporters adopted the charter notions of choice and of specific programs within a single educational setting. They also realized if they were going to compete and demonstrate their competence, they had much to learn from the charter movement.

Primarily, traditional schools had to offer parents and students choice in the content and location of educational programs. Secondly, they needed to market specific programs that competed with charter schools. In some cases, this involved additional courses and programs that allowed students to identify a pathway through the curriculum that would help them demonstrate their competencies and pursue their interests within a comprehensive educational program. The "pathways" innovation in the Flagstaff Unified District is discussed below.

Once the emotional dust had settled, creative individuals within the traditional public school setting began to generate ideas and programs. Perhaps these individuals were akin to the charter school pioneers who left the traditional public schools. In many educational settings, for the first time, individuals felt a renewed energy to look at the traditional public educational setting and suggest change and true innovation. Oddly, the movement that had angered and frightened many may have in fact liberated those creative individuals within the traditional setting to pursue educational innovations.

Benefits of Charter School and Public School Collaboration

Some of the early advocates for charter schools who had been less interested in true innovation and more focused on attacking public school systems now focused their energies into more positive actions—supporting charters rather than damning traditional public schools. Thus, some of the relentless criticism of public education was diluted. In 1998, an interesting development brought about in part by these critics is a tax credit to funnel dollars to *all* schools. This program allows an individual to donate $200 to any school of their choice. Their Arizona state tax bill is then actually reduced by $200. The funds must go directly to the school, not to the district, and they must be earmarked for a specific program: a sports program, a music program, the academic decathlon, and so on. Many believe this tax credit will be a real boon for *all* schools, whether charter, traditional, or private; yet it would not have been possible without promotion by traditional critics of public education.

Another important public school benefit from charter schools is that often large public school programs are confronted with students who simply do not fit. Even though public schools have attempted to move away from "one size fits all" to "several sizes may fit most," some students still do not fit traditional public schools. Charter schools may offer a reasonable alternative for some of these students. This development in the relationship between traditional public schools and charter schools is a quantum leap from the initial stage of fear and hostility just a few years ago.

Further, there may be an ebb and flow of students both to and from charter schools. Some charter schools find that older students requiring technology training and expensive equipment-based educational programs would be better off in the traditional public school (which usually has better supplies for laboratory sciences and vocational arts). Charter schools cannot provide sports programs, large music programs, or any program requiring a significant number of students. As a result, charter schools sometimes encourage their students to attend a traditional educational program for all or part of the day. The monies follow the student. Just as in the relationship between traditional public schools and the home-schoolers, such relationships can result in partial payment to both institutions serving the student.

Another crucial benefit from the collaboration between the traditional public school and charter schools is the re-thinking of the whole notion of choice. Choice is truly a liberating experience for parents, as they begin to select schools both for location and program. We know the schools and the programs that families select are the ones they support. This has been demonstrated for years within the traditional public educational setting.

Recently the Flagstaff Unified District opened its first school of choice with an emphasis for middle school students on fine and performing arts or science and technology. It filled up and faced a waiting list almost immediately. I interviewed a number of parents who made this selection, and they explained to me that it was not so much that they cared about the specific area of emphasis as they did about being asked, "Which one do *you* prefer?" Many parents who did not select this particular opportunity called to say that, although they weighed the benefits of the choice school and turned it down, they were pleased to have a choice. Thus, this "district school of choice" created a great deal of support among parents, leading them to feel better about the entire Flagstaff Unified District. I suspect this scenario has played out across Arizona, where these choices have been provided.

Another innovation within the Flagstaff Unified District that has been driven by the charter movement is our "pathways" program. The emergence of charter schools sparked discussions concerning those aspects of charter schools that people found appealing. Our high school staff started discussions concerning adjustments to both the substance and the marketing of their educational program. Clearly, some charter schools have strong marketing but lack educational substance. Staff at Flagstaff high schools considered such charters' drawing power and noted that we need to change not only program substance but also communication with our clients.

We looked at the comprehensive high school and began to distinguish classes that all students must have (either by state law or for good citizenship) from the elective side of the curriculum. These conversations were held in collaboration with parent and educator site councils, which have taken on many of the responsibilities for governance within schools across Arizona. As with many educational innovations, labeling became an impedance to discussion. Do we call options magnet schools? Schools of choice? Should we charter them? After initial frustration with defining the plan for improvement, we decided to look at the entire program within a high school and began to identify "pathways" in which students could concentrate while taking required courses.

We found that some realignments and adjustments to the master schedule were in order, but only minor additions were needed to round out these pathways. With few resources, we produced a high quality, specialized program offering choice to families within a traditional educational setting. In fact, the traditional educational system already has a support system to efficiently operate a school, unlike a new charter school.

As parental involvement in the educational program increases through special programs and choice, the community is brought closer to the public school fold. This rapprochement is evidenced by an innovative program in which members of the Chamber of Commerce interviewed a representative sample of high school graduates from each of the three high schools in the Flagstaff Unified District. Community members were able to hear firsthand about the positive or negative impact of the educational programs. Also, these community leaders were able to hear from graduating students what the community should be doing to support the educational process.

It is important to note charter schools' impacts on the entire discussion concerning choice and innovative programs. The "pathways" in the high schools differ from school to school. The initiation of many innovative programs varies from school to school across the district. Schools no longer have to feel that change has to be "all or nothing," across the entire district. These school-within-a-school programs may exist at only one school. Educators throughout the Flagstaff Unified District are now empowered and energized to evaluate and reform their specific school—a far cry from the traditional way of doing things.

The charter movement, with all its many problems, became a catalyst for true educational innovation and a liberating force. It pushed school systems to value grassroots innovation that team parents, family members, communities, and students to deliver on the promise of educational excellence. This catalyst has moved us away from systemic change. By breaking down many of the barriers that large, traditional educational systems create, we can focus now on the classroom and the vital interface of the teacher and the student.

Conclusion: The Future

As charter schools continue to live or die based on the notion of a free-market school system, those that survive will become stronger and catalyze change in traditional public educational systems. Charter proponents were right to advocate competition so that only the good schools survive. The idea that Americans are better off when Ford has "true competition" is true—no longer can schools offer parents any color of their choice so long as it is black. Yet is important to remember that we are not speaking of a commodity when we refer to the education of young people. We cannot allow mediocre schools to survive, whether traditional or charter. There is only one opportunity for a young person to go through an educational system. We cannot put them back, melt them down, and build them better the next time.

If educational entities—public, private, home-school, charter, or the next variation—can learn from one another and become strong through amalgamation, everyone will benefit. If any innovation is seen as "the one best way to educate our youth," we will find ourselves with another lock-step system that allows little individuality or creativity.

As educational institutions continue to develop new programs, including choice and areas of concentration, the system that some would have dismantled will make the necessary adaptations based on sound research and good practice. The transformation will come, not in a sudden revolution but as a well-planned evolution. Traditional educational systems will continually be poked and prodded by innovations such as charter schools. If these innovations can be seen as a benefit instead of an attack, the process of collaboration can begin much sooner and the students will benefit more quickly from the creativity generated by the entire community. Of course, such collaborations could come more quickly, if it were not for foes of public education who espouse what I call the "tobacco road" of school innovation: blow it up and start all over again.

I believe that in part because of the Sturm und Drang brought on by the charter movement in Arizona, the agenda for school reform and sensible innovation has a new look. Now is the time for critics and pundits to participate in meaningful discussions with students, parents, and professional educators, or else get out of the way of true reform. Within the charter movement or the traditional educational setting, programs must be fluid and flexible and offer choice. The charter school movement in Arizona has brought about a transformation for traditional public education that no member of a think tank, writing articles and critiques, could have ever engineered. Some of the charter schools will be successful and thrive, and many will not. However, public education in Arizona has been permanently impacted by this catalyst for reform.

Notes

1. Throughout this chapter I will refer to public schools in the traditional sense and refer to charter schools separately, although by law, charter schools in Arizona are considered public schools. Charter schools are, however, exempt from many of the regulations for traditional public schools.

References

Bryk, Anthony S., Valerie E. Lee, and Peter Holland. 1993. *Catholic Schools and the Common Good*. Cambridge: Harvard University Press.

Cookson, Peter G. 1994. *School Choice: The Struggle for the Soul of American Education*. New Haven: Yale University Press.

Gallup, Alec M., and Lowell C. Rose. 1998. "The 30th Annual Phi Delta Kappa/ Gallup Poll of the Public's Attitudes Toward the Public Schools." *Phi Delta Kappan* 80 (1): 41–56.

Mattern, Hal. 1997. "Charter School Founder, Aide Indicted: Counts Include Theft, Fraud, Funds Misuse." *Arizona Republic*, March 25.

Schnaiberg, Lynn. 1997. "Special Education Rules Pose Problems for Charter Schools." *Education Week*, February 19.

———. 1998. "A Dose of Competition." *Education Week: Quality Counts*, January 8.

U.S. Department of Education. 1998. *National School Report Card*. Washington, D.C.: U.S. Department of Education.

15

Whose Idea Was This Anyway?
The Challenging Metamorphosis from Private to Charter

JIM SPENCER

In January 1988, my wife and I began operating a private Montessori preschool in Flagstaff, Arizona. Before that time, we had intended to do other things in our personal lives and in our careers, but our community's demand for quality child care was so strong that by 1994 we were serving over 200 children ages 2–9 in a three-site elementary program.[1]

Our program was very small, for three related reasons. First, the expense of starting a completely equipped and staffed Montessori elementary program is quite high. Second, Flagstaff lacks the wage base that would allow us to charge the private school tuition necessary to support a new high caliber program. Third, being "poor but proud," we couldn't bring ourselves to offer and advertise a second-rate program. Consequently, the elementary students we had were limited to those children who had been with us for several years.

Lexus: The Relentless Pursuit of Perfection

The relentless pursuit of perfection that characterizes the Lexus luxury sedan somewhat imperfectly parallels our own experience. When it first hit the marketplace in 1989, the Lexus was immediately crowned by *Consumer Reports* as the best car on the road. I'd like to say it was the same with us, but it would be more accurate to say that we started out as a rusted Yugo. However, even our critics would have to say that we have improved every year that we have been in business. I'm blowing my own horn here, but we did grow from an original student population of forty and a staff of five to our present student body of 270 and staff of thirty-five because we've done something right in our own pursuit of excellence.

We opened our school years ago when our community wanted an alternative to traditional child care and elementary education, and since that time we have worked to provide an ever-improving product. I emphasize "ever-improving" because we've worked very hard to upgrade every aspect of our school (and later, our schools) year after year. Each year, our facilities are cleaner and newer; our classrooms are better equipped and furnished; our programs are educationally stronger; and our staff is better trained and more highly motivated. Excellence does not just happen, and we did not "just grow." We knew what we wanted when we started. We've worked extremely hard and sacrificed a great deal— profit, vacations, new "stuff," family time, and sleep, among them—to pursue it. Excellence may take another few years to finally arrive, but we'll keep pushing towards it.

One might expect that our plans include continued growth into a giant school system with 400 sites and thousands of students. Nothing could be farther from the truth. Our vision is based on the adage that "small is beautiful." This vision has been echoed by the Edison Project's fundamental principles of "schools within schools," but we had this vision long before the Edison Project (http://www.edisonproject.com/schooldesign.html) developed its approach.

We're adding a grade a year, limiting growth so that we can concentrate on getting the best possible fit the first time. We expect to grow to a maximum of 450 students at four sites. We will limit growth when we have three primary schools serving children from age 2 through kindergarten plus an elementary school. We will have three schools within a school, each with no more than thirty children and at least two permanent teachers in every classroom, supplemented by "specialists" in areas such as languages, art, music, chess, computers, and gardening. By establishing relatively small sites, we enable our administrators to operate their educational programs autonomously, with only general guidance.

We do centralize financial operations of the schools and the maintenance of the facilities, however, for two reasons. First, we believe each site should be uniformly operated. Second, our administrators must be free to concentrate on educating children, rather than budgeting, accounting, and "fixing things." Each site is a small community managed by a single person, and no site is so large that it loses its personal approach. Every teacher at every site knows every child and every parent at that site, which really makes a difference. At each site, the teachers and administrators meet frequently to discuss how to achieve our shared goals. In this way, we all know each other and we can work together in our "relentless pursuit of excellence."

After the state legislature passed charter school legislation that was arguably the most progressive of its kind in the country, we applied for a charter by the end of 1994. As private individuals, we could apply to the state for the authority to operate a public school, and we recognized our opportunity to offer Flagstaff a real Montessori elementary program. Shortly thereafter, we were among the first applicants approved by the State Board for Charter Schools, and we were the first charter school in Flagstaff.

Although we were ecstatic about our new status, we had no idea what we had done. What's more, I'm reasonably certain that we weren't alone. Probably most Arizona charter operators with a background in private education have had second thoughts about whatever prompted us to give up the good life. Why we have thought thus is the story that follows.

Private Is Just That

Imagine yourself the owner of a hardware store. You took out a second mortgage on your home and borrowed money from Aunt Edna to start the store. You ate a lot of beans for a lot of years to get to the point where you were your own boss. You charged what you could to cover the costs of doing business, expensed everything you could to keep your taxes down, and ran the whole thing with a one-write check system and a one-page spreadsheet. No one else but Uncle Sam knew how much you made, and no one else knew how you made it. It was *private.*

Moreover, if you'd done half your job, you had developed a way of doing things that worked for you, given your circumstances and your temperament. Your procedures were tailored to these circumstances, and, generally speaking, your policies were "flexible" and had been developed as needed. Then, imagine how you felt the day that the folks from Ace Home Centers approached you with a buyout offer. It boiled down to sell or risk losing the business to the "big boys." Actually it sounded like a pretty good deal: a lot more money coming in, a chance to expand, and they wanted you to stay on as general manager.

All of a sudden you find yourself working for someone else who doesn't understand *your* business, who has his or her own set of rules that you must now follow, who treats *your* customers like cattle, who now wants *your* business analyzed for him or her six ways from Sunday, and who has eleven different programs from eleven different head office departments that are all designed to implement "company policy."

Your friends ask, "Why did you do it?"

You reply, "It sounded like a good idea at the time."

We're Not in Kansas Anymore:
Differences Between Private and Charter Schools

Every analogy breaks down eventually, so let's not carry this one too far. Suffice it to say that being a charter school is not like being a private school. In our arena of private Montessori education, the success of our schools has rested largely on our ability to create the best class of students from those who applied for admission. It's never been a policy of "take the best, reject the rest" (as suggested by some), but rather an approach that asks in every case who will best benefit from this educational methodology, and who can contribute to the environment shared by the other children.[2]

When it works right, private Montessori education operates a lot like the shop of a craftsman who makes fine violins, one at a time. I believe one key strength of private schools is that most of them have the luxury of addressing students individually rather than like widgets coming off an assembly line. Don't mistake me, I'm not about to harangue and bash traditional public schools. After all, I, too, am a product of conventional public schools and did not even enter my first private school until the graduate level. At the same time, if I thought our traditional public schools had all the answers, I'd be doing something else with my life.

First Big Difference

As a charter/public school we are required to take everyone who comes to us on a first-come-first-served basis regardless of whether we feel they will benefit from the experience or not. We are experienced professionals, yet we cannot tell a parent, "Your child would be better served by the Waldorf Charter School down the street." Nor can we ask, "Given what you have told us about your background and your desires for your child, have you considered Lamb of God Christian School?" Such professional advice is not permitted. It is the parent *alone* who decides where his or her child goes.

Consider the impact on a former private school classroom. Presume we are able to accept only twenty-four children. Perhaps three of the first twenty-four to apply can't control themselves in the relatively unstructured openness of the Montessori classroom or are over-stimulated by the presence of so many learning aids. These students then disrupt the classroom and the individual work environments of twenty-one other children. The classroom focus shifts to these three; they become discipline problems, are labeled (if only in the minds of the teachers) as problem children, and "fail" in their first experience in a charter school. The teachers are frustrated, at least three children are frustrated, and each of three sets of parents are unhappy with the school, their child, or both. In the end, a very successful private school may have its reputation diminished among both parents and potential teachers.

Second Major Difference: Drowning in Paper

Remember the one-write check system and the one-page budget? They are gone with the wind. It seems like everyone in the Arizona Department of Education wants to know something about what you are doing. Many want to know the same things, but they don't share information between offices very well. Consequently, the time you used to spend at your son's Little League games is now spent filling out reports, creating lists, and completing tables. Yes, you just told somebody that last week, but this time someone else wants to know about it sideways!

It would be wrong, however, to cast all the blame on the "head office." We mustn't forget all the pollsters, professional information crunchers, and doctoral students of education. I swear every doctoral student in education seems to be doing a dissertation on charter schools, the "in" topic in the education field. Each of these students has a survey that will take *only* forty-five minutes to complete.

Third Difference: There Is No Privacy

Public is public. It seems like everyone has access to everything. Unless you can prove that it violates some other law to do so, you are obligated to share every bit of what used to be private information with anyone who asks for it, from the curious to the malicious. For example, when we first started, my wife and I were unaware that we had to notify and invite the media and all outsiders every time we discussed our charter school. Taken literally, we had to invite the world to every one of our family dinners! When we realized this problem, we added three more people to our board, but we found it hard to adjust to our lack of privacy in discussing matters concerning our school.

Fourth Difference: Some People Hate You

Anytime you get involved in something new that changes or adversely affects any well-established institution, you make enemies. When we were a private school, we were left alone and ignored by those who did not believe in our program. However, when we began "siphoning" off public tax dollars (paid by the parents of the children we educate) and competing with traditional schools, we were called names in the grocery store and personally slandered at public meetings. Sadly, I am not exaggerating.

Then there is the local newspaper reporter who is convinced you got into this "racket" to destroy public education and who sees it as his or her task to ask you just the right questions in just the right way so that he or she can prove it to one million loyal readers. With hundreds of vendors constantly mailing me for my business, even the *mailman* has expressed his ire at having to stuff about three times as much mail into the larger mailbox I had to buy.

Fifth Difference: Beware False Profits

I wish I had a dollar for every time I heard someone make reference to all the money charter school operators were making. My CPA will testify that I haven't benefited financially. The bottom line is that if you are thinking about becoming a charter school to make more money than you do as a private school, you would do much better by opening a liquor store.

Sixth Difference: Big Brother Is Watching You

This difference is almost self-explanatory. As a private school, the parents of your enrolled children watch you. If they don't like what they see, they stop watching because they have moved their children somewhere else. As a public school, not only does Big Brother watch, but so does Big Sister, Big Aunt, Big Uncle, Big Second Cousin Twice Removed, and so on. Everybody watches, and everybody has an opinion, a comment, a criticism, and an investigative reporter for a brother-in-law. The Democrats watch because they believe charter schools are getting away with murder and killing the traditional public schools; the Republicans watch to prove that the Democrats are lying. The traditional public schools watch to find weaknesses in charter schools on which they can capitalize in order to reclaim their lost sheep. The Department of Education watches because they have to; it seems like everybody at the Department of Education has to watch. The media watches because that's how they eat, whether what they say is true or not. In fact, you'd be hard pressed to find any identifiable group that doesn't have an interest in watching charter schools. When we were private, it was just the parents of our children who watched.

Seventh Difference: The Question of Fit

Private schools with methodologies that are nontraditional must change their approach or add another one. Montessori children, to cite only one example, are individually monitored and evaluated in every subject area every day by their teachers. For this reason, Montessori students rarely take tests. As a result, they are unfamiliar with test-taking strategies and are at a disadvantage in standardized test-taking contests, such as the Iowa series or the Stanford Nine. Because Arizona is seeking to improve its standing on the "Who's Who in Education Among the States" list, a great deal of emphasis has been placed on each school's standardized test scores. Double that for us unproven charter schools. So now, instead of focusing on the traditional Montessori goals of developing character, self-esteem, self-reliance, self-discipline, and on directing independent study at the student's own pace, we find ourselves "teaching to the test" so that we won't look bad when we are compared to the other schools that we have worked so hard not to imitate all these years. Having to fit our oc-tagonally-shaped peg into the traditional round hole has cost us some of our shape and, sadly, some of our distinctiveness.

New Wine in Old Wineskins

This question of fit brings me to one of my favorite analogies, a biblical parable that explains the inadvisability of putting new wine in old wine-skins. A new wineskin is soft and pliable. New (unfermented) wine, when put into a new wineskin, causes the skin to stretch as the wine ferments. By stretching, the new skin contains the juice, helping the wine reach its full potential. An old wineskin, on the other hand, has already been stretched out. If you put juice into an old wineskin, the already-stretched skin can't stretch anymore; both the skin and the wine are lost as the liq-uid ferments and the old skin bursts.

Charter schools are like a new wine. Because Arizona lacks a new model to contain and enable these schools, they have been placed into the old wineskin of the traditional public education system. Privately, many of these schools could survive, perhaps even thrive, in the form their founders envisioned. I fear, though, that forcing these schools to operate within the confines of outdated traditional system regulations will cause much of the innovation and freshness of this "new wine" to be lost. If we miss the chance at real reform, and even of renaissance, that the charter school movement represents, we may irreparably harm the only educational sys-tem we have. To use yet another analogy, remember Michael Jordan's at-tempt to succeed at baseball? The new skills required eluded him, and he performed poorly under a different set of rules. Thank heaven for the strike that year, or he might still be a second-rate baseball player instead of a bas-ketball legend. The same lesson holds for schools: Forcing a private school to operate in a public school environment can turn a great school into a mediocre one.

"Whose Idea Was This, Anyway?"
Problems with Implementing the New Law

When I get into a particularly whiny state of mind, I sometimes ask, "Whose idea was this, anyway?" Sometimes I ask it of my wife, and sometimes she asks it of me. We usually ask it right after we've opened a letter from the Department of Education. Sometimes, though, we intend it as a broader inquiry, and what we're actually asking is, "Did the folks who thought this up really think it through?" I truly don't think so.

Being what it is, the political process prevents issues from being adequately studied before they become laws. The legislative session is only so long, legislators have a number of obligations, and most terms of office in the state are only two or four years in length. When the well-meaning legislators created charter schools in Arizona, I'm convinced they did so without all the data they needed and without all the "what ifs" answered. Forget that they very possibly enacted charter school legislation to avoid dealing with the question of school vouchers. Simply consider whether they really created what they thought they were creating, and, if they did, whether they knew how much turmoil would result.

For example, I wonder if anyone thought about what the term "route mile" meant when charter schools (most of whose students are transported to school not by school buses but by individual automobiles) applied for transportation support funds.

I wonder how a school district with under 100 children (read "charter school") pays for a law-abiding special education program.

I wonder how students of a charter school, whose teachers do not have to be state certified, can participate in interscholastic sports when the sports authority requires that the teachers at participating schools be accredited, and the accrediting agency requires that all the school's teachers be state certified.

There are a lot more questions I wonder about. Sometimes I feel like wailing, "When we were private, we didn't have these problems."

The "Route Mile" Whammy

"They" tried to keep it quiet, but some enterprising charter school operator who applied to the "stimulus fund" for start-up capital discovered that the law governing transportation funding was a gold mine. Apparently, the law, which was written for school districts with school buses, said that schools would be funded for transportation on the basis of how many "route miles" were traveled getting kids to and from school.

For example, let's say you have a small school with 400 children attending. If you had ten school buses that each traveled a ten-mile route while picking up and dropping off forty children apiece each day, the district would be paid for the cost of ten buses traveling ten route miles a day, 175 days a year. The state pays $1.50 per route mile. A brief calculation shows that the state's formula suggests that $26,250 is needed to maintain the bus fleet. Enter the charter school. Most charter schools require that parents drop off and pick up their children as part of their "contract" with the school. Each of 400 children are ferried to and from school by private auto, with each car traveling an average of five miles each way. Instead of ten vehicles each traveling ten miles, you have 400 vehicles traveling an average of five miles. Calculating these costs with the state's figures shows that 400 "buses" for five route miles, 175 days a year, at $1.50 per route mile provides the charter school with $525,000 for transportation. Needless to say, this would have blown the state education budget.

The state was saved by a quick law change and by the relatively small number of charter schools who filed for the funds, but only after losing several million dollars in excess transportation costs and providing "stimulus funds" to several schools that otherwise would have done without the money.

Special Education or "The Hidden Siphon"

Private schools do *not* have to accept everybody, and they try to serve the segment of the market they can best address—those parents and students whose needs they can meet. If the private school simply cannot afford to provide complete care for children with disabilities, the private school operators explain that fact to parents of prospective students and tell them what services can be provided. Some parents still choose to enroll, whereas others choose to go to another school they believe is better suited to meet the needs of their child.

Charter schools have to accept everyone who applies, up to their capacity, and they have to provide whatever that child needs to learn in the school environment. The state fractionally supports special education. The expectation, I presume, is that its provision eventually will cover the cost of building a special education program. The state does not provide nearly enough funding to create a special education program from scratch on opening day. It does, however, legally require that one be in place. Small schools, like charter schools, that have no bonding authority or credit history can literally be put out of business by a relatively few students with special needs.

So as not to exaggerate the problem by using the example of a child with multiple physical, psychological, and emotional disabilities, simply consider the needs of a young child with Down's syndrome. The child must be evaluated by a specialist ($350). The child very likely will require ongoing speech therapy ($150/month), ongoing physical therapy ($150/month), and ongoing occupational therapy ($150/month). The child will be the subject of several progress evaluation meetings with specialists, school officials, teachers, and parents ($100/month), and will probably require special tutoring ($150/month). The child will require these services monthly, whether the school is in session or not. This child's needs will cost the school $8,750 per year over and above what it costs to educate the child. The school probably receives a total of $5,000 to educate this child and meet his or her special needs ($2,500 if the child is a kindergartner). If the school does a good job with this child and attracts several others with more severe problems, the school will not survive long enough to do any lasting good, given the current funding mechanism.

How does our school pay for special education, you ask? We cut the budget in other places. We reduce the salaries of teachers, administrators, and the business manager, and we sell chocolate. And frankly, if this section lacks the playfulness of the other parts of this chapter, it's because it's very difficult to find any humor here.

Hey Mom, Where's the Team?

"Hey Mom, why doesn't my school have a soccer/track/volleyball/etc. team?" Good question; a lot of charter high school students probably ask it. This is not a big issue with the elementary schools because younger children are just as happy to rely on Pop Warner programs. With high school students, though, athletic competition is more complicated. It's not just a game; it's a social imperative. Many charter high schools are not accredited, however, because all of their teachers are not certified. And unaccredited schools are not allowed to participate in authorized competitions with other schools.

Currently, the accrediting agency is addressing this issue. If a change in policy is made, the problem of competing with district schools may become simply one of size and funding. These issues are not easy ones, but they are more understandable. After all, why should a teacher who is fluent in five languages have to be state certified to teach Spanish? And why should an experienced biochemist have to be "state certified" to teach high school biology and chemistry? If the accreditation problem remains, charter schools may soon be numerous enough to form their own interscholastic athletic association. Alternatively, charter schools may simply continue to compete with the private schools in their surrounding area, schools that tend to be unaccredited but excellent.

The Benefits of "Going Public"

So, apart from "it sounded like a good idea at the time," why did we become a charter school?

First, as a private school in Flagstaff, we could count on receiving about $3,200 a year per child to meet all the school's expenses and put food on my family's table. As a charter school, we receive what every other public school receives from the state: In 1997–1998 that was about $4,500 per student. This additional funding enabled us to pay our teachers a good bit more and to outfit our classrooms more completely with new Montessori equipment. Given these additional outlays, the special education requirements, and the start-up expenses associated with adding new grades and new equipment every year, we are making only a bit more than we did as a private school. As operators of the school, we hope to reap a better return eventually, but only after we are finished building what we started.

Second, it's rewarding to be able to offer people something that they never had before, and even more rewarding when it's better than what they were getting elsewhere. I do believe that our charter school is a better choice for most children than the traditional public school. If I didn't believe that, I'd be running the liquor store. We take pride in what we are doing and experience a level of satisfaction that we did not experience when we relied entirely on equipment we would purchase at garage sales.

Third, it's exciting to be a pioneer. Yes, the pioneers tend to get hit by all the arrows, but they also get to be the first to cross the Rockies, see the Pacific, and raise their children in a new world. There is something to be said for dreaming, but so much more for using the dream as your blueprint when you build something tangible. We have an excellent school. Someday it will be unbelievable.

In Conclusion: Would I Do It Again?

There are days when I could go either way, but, on balance, I'd do it all again. I say this in the midst of trying to get a loan to build a 32,000 square foot facility to be home to our charter school. We've had half a dozen bankers say no, but we are still hopeful. I say this knowing that the 1998–1999 fiscal year budget forms came today from the Arizona Department of Education—they are always fun. I say this, knowing that the state supreme court may declare our latest school legislation unconstitutional, completely confusing our funding situation for the next fiscal year. And I say this knowing, even expecting, that the next arrow won't hurt any less than the last 178. Being a private school definitely had its advantages, but now that we are a charter school, I wouldn't go back.

At least, not today.

Notes

1. Author's Note: I've been told that my writing tends toward the outrageous, makes copious use of hyperbole, and is generally tongue-in-cheek. For this reason: Proceed at your own risk!

2. For more information on Montessori methods, see the American Montessori Society's web site at http://www.amshq.org. Or, for those more comfortable with the printed page, there is Maria Montessori's *Dr. Montessori's Own Handbook* (1978).

References

American Montessori Society. November 20, 1998, URL: http://www.seattleu.edu/~jcm/montessori/ano_bib.html.

Edison Project. 1998. May 10, 1999, URL: http://www.edisonproject.com/schooldesign.html.

Montessori, Maria. 1978. *Dr. Montessori's Own Handbook.* 1941. Reprint, New York: Shocken Books.

PART FOUR

Lessons

16

In Lieu of Conclusions: Tentative Lessons from a Contested Frontier

ROBERT MARANTO, SCOTT MILLIMAN,
FREDERICK HESS, APRIL GRESHAM

Tentative Lessons

Schools embody our highest hopes and our worst fears. We want them to be places where our children are raised to be virtuous and capable citizens, but we fear they may be places where our children are exposed to nefarious influences and permitted to founder. We have a mythical conception of public schools as anchors of the communities, or as places where communities together settle upon shared values and invest for the common welfare, but we too often see schools as riddled by inattention and neglect, or by conflict and gridlock.

Against a backdrop of hopes and fears, school choice plans have won widespread attention in recent years. Although numerous scholarly works have explored school choice, the work has been of necessity either theoretical or speculative, with much of the latter based on small-scale choice programs or on statistical speculations based on private school enrollments. In Arizona, for the first time, a state has implemented relatively comprehensive school choice through charter schools. The works in this volume represent the first published examination of a large-scale, comprehensive school choice system in the real world.

In Arizona and across the nation, the frontiers of school choice are sharply contested terrain. As in *Rashomon*, different observers see very different events. Still, it is our contention that a careful reading of the works in this volume presents several lessons for policy makers, educators, and citizens in other states.

First, school choice depends on political support.   As the chapters by Leal, Timmons-Brown and Hess, and Maranto and Gresham make clear, the passage of charter laws may depend on the near passage of voucher laws. Arizona came the closest of any state to passing a statewide voucher scheme and then passed the nation's most pro-charter law. Where vouchers are politically viable, choice opponents focus their attention on defeating them rather than charters. Indeed, charters may be seen as a middle way between vouchers to private schools and no educational reform whatsoever, explaining why federal appropriations to charters have increased and why nearly two thirds of states have passed charter school legislation. The exact provisions and implementation of charter laws depend on the political correlation of forces. As the Arizona–Nevada comparison shows, pro-charter laws are unlikely where teachers' unions dominate education policymaking.[1] And as Hess and his colleagues suggest in Chapter 11, on this matter teachers' unions probably represent the views of their members.

The viability of a full-scale charter system such as Arizona's may depend on the aggressive implementation of charter laws in ways favorable to charter schools. As Maranto and Gresham explain in Chapter 6, decisions by the Arizona Department of Education and the State Board for Charter Schools allowed charters to flourish by permitting multiple campuses for single charter holders, by allowing districts to charter schools (often for profit) that then served in *other* districts, and by permitting private schools to switch to charter status. The first two of these allowances, in particular, are controversial "loopholes" in the law that some feel delegitimize the chartering process.

Indeed, the aggressive implementation of charter law allowed Arizona to develop much more comprehensive school choice than proposed in any voucher scheme that has ever come near passage. As Garn and Stout explain in Chapter 9, state authorities have been very understanding about reporting deficiencies from charter schools. (District schools are not treated here.) In addition, as Maranto and Gresham and Hartley explain, the state government agreed to generous repayment plans for charters that overestimated first year enrollments. But, if Lisa Graham Keegan is replaced as superintendent of public instruction by a charter school opponent, a positive regulatory regime could turn negative. As it is, the pro-charter bias of state institutions allowed a charter sector to take off. In the long run, however, this bias may limit the administrative accountability of charters, a point discussed further below.

Second, education markets require a strong state bureaucracy.   As Garn and Stout detail in Chapter 9, in theory both parental enrollment decisions and state administrative actions keep charter schools accountable. (Hartley also notes the importance of collecting both financial and performance information.) Both parental and administrative accountability work best if a well-staffed, state-level education bureaucracy disseminates information about how individual schools perform. Without such information, it is more difficult for parents to judge schools, and more difficult for the state to close schools guilty of illegal practices. As Garn and Stout detail and as will be discussed further below, there is serious concern about whether the Arizona state-level authorities have sufficient resources to perform this role. This weakness in the Arizona bureaucracy may stem from Keegan's (and other charter proponents') concern that too much bureaucratic reporting will harm charters' freedom to innovate. Finally, a strong state level bureaucracy is required to step in the breach to assist parents and local districts when charter schools fail, as occasionally happens.

Third, a free market in education unlocks enormous energy from entrepreneurial parents and teachers. Arizona's charter school law has allowed 272 flowers (and weeds) to bloom. It seems likely that if most states had charter laws similar to Arizona's, America would soon have 10,000 or more charter schools—far more than the 3,000 called for by President Clinton. The charter school law has allowed talented and idealistic teachers, social workers, and business people to pursue their dreams. It also has allowed disaffected parents, such as the Waldorf supporters in Flagstaff, to pursue their favored curricula and methods, something the political processes governing school districts probably would not have permitted. Notably, even if Arizona's barriers to entry are the nation's lowest, they are still substantial. New operators must find an appropriate site, recruit students for a nonexistent school, hire teachers for an unknown enrollment, and somehow balance the books, all while complying with numerous state and federal regulations. Many operators and parents take enormous personal and financial risks, and it is hard not to laud their success.

Still, as Hartley details, the very freedom that has allowed capable operators to open their schools, has also allowed an unknown number of corrupt or incompetent operators. In addition, the state has not assured aggressively that charter schools will not mix church and state.

Fourth, the market model of education has proven credible, but no panacea. Clearly, the Arizona experience shows that comprehensive choice is feasible in the real world. Arizona has it, and with the possible exception of Hartley, none of the contributors to this volume would claim that the sky has fallen. In fact it is remarkable that brand new charter schools, usually starting from scratch, have been able to provide education alternatives competitive with district schools that (usually) have greater resources and decades of experience behind them. *But*, with the possible exception of

Keegan, none of the contributors to this work would claim that Arizona offers an education panacea. Although the charter sector works on many dimensions, as will be discussed below, whether charter schools on the whole "work better" than district schools remains to be seen. As Stout and Garn report in Chapter 10, the degree to which charter curricula differ from district curricula may be overstated. Finally, as the exchanges in this volume between Maranto and Halchin and Keegan and Hartley suggest, comparative evaluations of charter and district schools really depend on what "better" means, a point returned to below.

Fifth, at least in the near term, charter schools will not replace district schools. Both pro- and anti-market theorists hope and fear, respectively, that school choice will replace most or all conventional district schools with theme-based schools of choice. The Arizona experience suggests that at least in the short term, this is highly unlikely. As Maranto and Gresham report, in the fourth year of near comprehensive school choice, Arizona charter schools account for about 4.4 percent of total public school enrollment, and charter enrollment increases may be leveling off. In part this may represent supply-side changes, since the teachers and social workers who dreamed of opening their own schools have already done so. Arizona spends less on education than most states, and thus has not attracted as many for-profit operators as expected. To an even greater extent demand-side forces may be at work: Parents who desperately wanted a different option already have gone to the charters. The 95 percent who remain are probably happy with their district schools and are thus unlikely to leave.

Further, as Maranto and his colleagues suggest in Chapter 8, districts that have lost large numbers of children to charter schools make efforts to win those children back. Sometimes those efforts pay off, and sometimes charters fail for other reasons (e.g., financial mismanagement), so over the long term we do not expect the movement from districts to charters to always go in one direction. It may be that the charter school market share will stabilize at 5–15 percent of the district market share statewide, with higher percentages in school districts that are not doing a good job serving the desires of parents.

Of course, our projection may not hold for the long term. Just as few economists forecast the advent of low-cost Southwest Airlines when flying was deregulated in 1978, over the *long term* innovation fostered by school choice could replace or radically remake existing school systems—there is simply little evidence at the moment that such change is on the horizon. Rather, as Hager suggests, it is likely that charter and district schools will coexist for some time. Over time, the two sectors may work out mutually beneficial relationships.

Sixth, because charters will not replace district schools, they may have their greatest effects via impacts on district schools that are trying to compete. As Maranto and his colleagues find in Chapter 8, interviews and teacher surveys suggest that charters have forced some school districts to work harder to please parents. It seems likely that this will lead to positive impacts over the long term. But, the impacts found are relatively small in size. Further, it is not clear whether the perceived improvements reflect better outreach and marketing efforts on the part of district schools, or actual improvements in classroom instruction. In part because educational reform takes a long time and in part because the state recently changed its standardized tests, there is no way to tell if competition from charter schools is improving educational outcomes. Notably, the teacher survey data reported by Maranto and Gresham suggest that charter school teachers have more power over curricula and class schedules than do their district school peers. Possibly, the charter example could encourage district schools to empower their teachers in like fashion, though the larger size of districts may make this difficult. More research on district reactions, perhaps focusing further on dimensions of school governance and classroom instruction, is needed to assess how charters are impacting the traditional Arizona school system.

Contested Frontiers

Although we bring home some tentative lessons from works in this volume, many of the most important questions about Arizona charter schools require more research. This is particularly true regarding the education market's impacts on accountability, innovation, academic performance, and social equity.

First, are charter schools accountable to parents and taxpayers? For charter critics such as Garn and Stout and Hartley, the answer is *no*. As Hassel writes, the Arizona charter law in fact has some of the weakest accountability hooks in the nation. Garn's interviews and the media reports cited by Hartley suggest that good data on charter schools, both financial and academic, is often unavailable due to insufficient staffing at the Arizona Department of Education. The department is unable to check reports from charter schools (or district schools) for accuracy, so it is unable to hold charters accountable. Since Arizona recently changed its standardized tests, there is no solid cross-sectional data to determine whether schools are getting better. Further, Garn and Stout (as well as Maranto and Gresham) suggest that strong political support for charters on the Arizona charter board and the board of education means that those entities are reluctant to close charters. In short, administrative efforts seem unlikely to hold Arizona charter schools accountable.

In contrast, charter supporters such as Keegan and Maranto emphasize the role of parents in holding charters accountable. Keegan reports anecdotal evidence of "Ninja parents" closely monitoring their charter school's academic standards (though not school finances). Maranto predicts that the small size of charters gives parents incentives to get involved, since a single parent can make a real difference in a small school. Further, giving parents a choice of schools gives them incentives for learning about schools. In addition, Keegan suggests that it is improper to discuss the accountability of charter schools without comparing them to district schools. As of April 1999, nineteen of the 272 charter campuses had closed, either because they could not retain sufficient enrollment (market accountability), or because their charters were revoked (administrative accountability). In contrast, failing district schools never close. Although charter schools are not perfectly accountable, they may be more accountable than district schools.

In part, the disagreement between charter critics and supporters could be reconciled by additional research supplementing Garn and Stout's credible first efforts. We recommend that this research focus on the relative effectiveness of parental monitoring, as opposed to administrative monitoring. How necessary is each kind of monitoring to a viable charter system? What are the implications of parental as compared to administrative monitoring for charter schools? For parental knowledge? Is bureaucratic accountability (at least at the level of collecting and verifying standardized information) necessary for parental monitoring? Garn and Stout's findings indicate that Arizona parents receive less than adequate information from administrative sources. A next step is to ascertain if parents are able to overcome these deficiencies.

A separate but related line of research stemming from these initial efforts would focus on parental motives in choosing schools. If empowered parents select charter schools based on their academic quality, and if they take the time and effort to find out what is going on in the classroom, then market-based accountability might work better than administrative accountability, as is suggested by Chubb and Moe (1990). Maranto and Gresham's survey results suggest that charter school teachers have much closer and more positive relationships with parents than do district school teachers. If true, this could mean that the small size and market focus of charter schools fosters parental monitoring of classroom teachers.[2]

On the other hand, if parents lack the expertise to judge the quality of schools, or if they select schools based on racism, cultural solidarity, geography, or any of a number of factors other than academic quality, as is suggested by Smith and Meier (1995), then market-based accountability is highly suspect. In this regard, Maranto finds that charter elementary schools are somewhat more segregated than district elementary schools, though this is not true of charter secondaries. More research on parental decisionmaking is required to bring order to these contending claims.

Garn and Stout make a number of useful suggestions about how accountability mechanisms could be improved. In addition, perhaps the Arizona Department of Education could work to advise parents in order to improve parental monitoring of charters (and indeed all schools). Such outreach could develop a synergy between administrative and market compliance. On this score, credit is also due to state senator Hartley, who discusses ways to involve parents in charter school accountability.

A second contested question is whether Arizona charter schools are innovative. Market supporters such as Chubb and Moe (1990), Brandl (1998), and, in this volume, Keegan and Maranto expect market-based education to be innovative because competitive pressures will spur creativity and because in a market innovative ideas cannot be blocked by hostile political coalitions. As Hassel notes, to a greater degree than other charter laws, the Arizona statute gives charter schools the freedom and resources to innovate. Yet this is not enough. Schools also require sufficient numbers of parents and teachers who desire innovation.

Hassel notes that charter schools across the nation seldom introduce pathbreaking new ideas but do implement well-known (if not widely adopted) methods such as thematic instruction, team teaching, and year-round schooling in ways that foster a coherent mission. In contrast, district schools using such approaches tend to do so as add-ons to existing programs rather than in support of a coherent whole. Stout and Garn carefully examined the curricula of seventy-five Arizona charter schools and found that none of the curricula is pathbreaking, though charter schools do have a clearer focus and greater variability than district schools.

In essence, the Stout and Garn findings accord with Hassel's discussions of charter schools nationally; and whether charters are innovative depends on how one defines *innovation*. Economists see innovation as a three-stage process: invention; refinement of the invention so that it is viable; and, finally, dissemination of a new product to consumers (Greer 1984). Despite the hopes of charter proponents, Arizona charter schools have not yet invented new modes of education (according to Stout and Garn's definition of innovation). However, as Maranto and Spencer maintain (and Stout and Garn do not refute), charter schools may be making more widely available such options as Montessori schooling, programs previously available primarily to paying parents. In short, although charter schools are not inventing new forms of education, they appear to be refining and disseminating existing forms to parents (and teachers) who want them. Although worthwhile, this development is not the type charter proponents promised.

Finally, initial research suggests that charter schools are governed differently than district schools. Chapter 6 indicates that charter teachers are more "empowered," and this can be thought of as process (rather than curricular or method) innovation. Future researchers should continue Stout and Garn's line of curricular research but, as Hassel suggests, should also study other potential areas of innovation, including school governance systems.

Third, do children attending Arizona charter schools learn more than children in Arizona district schools?   Unfortunately, there is simply insufficient data to make more than very limited speculation in answer to this very important question. Since Arizona recently changed its standardized tests, baseline data is unavailable. Further, the mix of students in charter schools makes it very hard to compare their test scores with those of district counterparts. This is particularly true for charter secondary schools, which tend to educate at-risk students. For the most part, charter opponents and proponents exchange warring anecdotes.

In the most systematic attempt to divine the answer to date, Stout and Garn find preliminary indications that the performance of charter students on standardized tests is probably about the same as for district school students. Further research making use of baseline data as it becomes available should be able to compare the performance of charter and district school students. This question is the one most open to future research, since so little has been done in this area.

Finally, does market-based reform threaten social equity?   In some respects, charter schools seem likely to increase equity. After all, if they thought the public schools were failing, middle- and upper-income parents could always leave by sending their children to private schools, or by moving across district lines. Each option is far more difficult for low-income families (Maranto and Milliman 1996). As Superintendent Keegan notes, Arizona charter schools give low-income parents education options they never had before and thus promote social equity. Maranto and Gresham and Stout and Garn agree that most charter secondary schools are for at-risk children who have failed in traditional public schools. Indeed district schools often encourage such students to transfer to charters. Charter schools for at-risk students would seem to increase social equity by giving students who do not fit in district schools a second chance.

The charter school system also may increase equity in a different way by allowing political losers to win. Maranto reports that parents who find their programs blocked by opponents on their local school board can now exit to charter schools offering the curricula they desire. Finally, it is notable that most charter schools are small schools and have a single coherent curriculum, rarely practicing tracking. Thus, charter schools may be less likely to suffer the internal segregation so common to district schools, where those of different ethnic groups often take different courses, partake in different extracurricular activities, and rarely eat at the same lunch table (Greene 1998).

On the other hand, Arizona's charter schools present serious equity concerns. Interviews conducted by Maranto and Gresham (Chapter 6) suggest that relatively few charter operators have sited their schools in low-income and minority areas. Accordingly, low-income parents may have difficulty finding and transporting their children to a charter school. (Few charters offer transportation.) As Halchin speculates in Chapter 2 and as one operator cited in Chapter 6 laments, many low-income parents either do not know about charter schools or assume that charters charge tuition. Hartley notes a few cases in which charter operators have charged fees, tending to screen out low-income families. Additionally, many charters draw from informal recruiting networks. Perhaps for such reasons, charter elementary schools have somewhat greater percentages of white students than do district counterparts.

Finally, charters serve notably fewer special education students than district schools, perhaps because parents of such students choose to stay in district schools, which have the size and resources to offer superior special education. However, Hartley reports a disturbing number of anecdotes about special education students being (illegally) discouraged from attending charter schools. Given the tenuous financial status of many charters and the high expense of special education, such actions may be widespread. If true, this would represent a serious failing on the part of the charter sector.

Intensive interviews and further analyses of the racial compositions of both charter and traditional public schools should help to shed light on these serious equity-related issues. For instance, interaction between students of different races could be compared, both within charters and within district schools, continuing Greene's (1998) line of research. Other research could divine how many low-income parents exit their districts for charters, and whether their decisions are prompted by school performance. Are there barriers (real or perceived) to charter participation by low-income and minority parents? Can these barriers be overcome by parental education, or would they require fundamental restructuring of the charter school sector? Finally, does the relatively low charter enrollment among special education students reflect parental demand or illegal discrimination by charter operators?

Whereas most of this volume addresses empirical issues, many of the fundamental questions about school choice have to do with the normative purposes, or goals, of public education, as Halchin argues in Chapter 2. For choice skeptics like Halchin and Hartley, the purpose of public education is not merely to educate students but also to inculcate in students democratic values in order to make them good citizens, as well as literate and numerate ones. Key to this is assuring that all (or nearly all) American young people attend a common public school, teaching common values and mixing those of different ethnic and religious groups and social backgrounds. Because public education reflects the values of the whole society, all citizens (and not merely parents) should be involved in school policymaking. To do otherwise would risk long-term balkanization of society.

In contrast, for choice proponents like Keegan, Maranto, and Milliman, parents and teachers are at the center of the education enterprise. They have the most incentive to care about education, and only they can make schools work (or fail) on a daily basis. Further, there is no one best way to educate all students; nor is there a single best way for teachers to teach. Accordingly, the best course is to let a thousand flowers bloom, as individual teachers and parents choose their own best practices. To hold parents and teachers hostage to a slow, unwieldy, and highly bureaucratized policymaking system will merely increase frustration with public education.

These are fundamentally normative arguments not subject to easy empirical verification. Ultimately, these debates will be compromised and perhaps settled in our political system, which, over the long run, issues authoritative judgments about school policy. We can hope that the ongoing debate will be civil, measured, and will make use of the empirical research such as that presented here.

Notes

1. In Arizona the opponents of school choice—districts and teachers' unions— did not comprehend fully the breadth of the charter law passed by the state legislature in 1994. Both the supporters and (especially) opponents of school choice were caught by surprise, and this is not apt to happen again. Notably, according to the Center for Education Reform web site, eighteen of the twenty-four charter school laws passed before 1997 were strong laws, as compared to four of the eight most recent laws.

2. Although it is difficult to judge the accountability of charter schools, it can be said that since charter school teachers are "at will" employees who can be dismissed with relative ease, operators can hold their teachers accountable more eas-

ily than district schools can. However, operators themselves have much more power than principals or other bureaucratic counterparts.

References

Brandl, John E. 1998. *Money and Good Intentions Are Not Enough, or, Why a Liberal Democrat Thinks States Need Both Competition and Community.* Washington, D.C.: Brookings Institution.

Chubb, John E., and Terry M. Moe. 1990. *Politics, Markets, and America's Schools.* Washington, D.C.: Brookings Institution.

Greene, Jay P. 1998. "Civic Values in Public and Private Schools." In *Learning from School Choice,* ed. Paul E. Peterson & Bryan C. Hassel. Washington, D.C.: Brookings Institution.

Greer, Douglas F. 1984. *Industrial Organization and Public Policy.* New York: Macmillan.

Maranto, Robert, and Scott Milliman. 1996. "The Impact of Competition on Public Schools." Paper presented at the annual meeting of the American Political Science Association, San Francisco, California, September 2.

Smith, Kevin B., and Kenneth J. Meier. *The Case Against School Choice: Politics, Markets, and Fools.* Armonk, N.Y.: M. E. Sharpe.

About the Editors and Contributors

Gregg A. Garn is an assistant professor in educational leadership and policy studies at the University of Oklahoma. He received his Ph.D. in educational leadership and policy studies from Arizona State University. He earned an M.A. from Arizona State University and a B.A. in history education from the University of Northern Iowa. His articles have been published in *Educational Leadership* and the *Arizona School Boards Association Journal*. His current research interests are charter schools, vouchers, school choice issues, and superintendent and school board relations.

April Gresham is a researcher, writer, and statistician living in Villanova, Pennsylvania. She has taught social psychology at the University of Minnesota, Furman University, and Lafayette College. Her scholarly work has appeared in *Family Law Quarterly*, the *Journal of Applied Psychology*, the *Journal of Traumatic Stress Studies, Social Behavior and Psychology*, and *PS: Political Science and Politics*. She received her Ph.D. in social psychology from the University of Minnesota in 1993 and her B.A. in psychology from the University of Georgia in 1985.

Lee L. Hager, Ph.D., University of Arizona, 1981, is assistant superintendent for curriculum and instruction with the Flagstaff Unified School District. He is on the adjunct faculty for Northern Arizona University at the Center for Excellence in Education. He has authored articles and made numerous presentations on middle level education, site-based shared decisionmaking and educational innovation. He has been a member of the U.S. secretary of education's Blue Ribbon Schools panel since 1984. Lee is a member of the Ecological Futures Global (EFG) curriculum consortium founded by futurist Joel Barker and educator Barbara Barnes. He is also a board member of the Western Regional Middle Level consortium. Lee has experience in both public and private education in Arizona, New York, and Washington State. Lee is married and has three children and may be reached at lhager@flagstaff.apscc.k12.az.us

L. Elaine Halchin is a Ph.D. candidate in political science at Syracuse University. Her dissertation, "Public Education and Vouchers: The Challenges and Possibilities for Democracy," examines how parents of school-age children in Milwaukee view education and the implications thereof for democracy. Her essay "A Different Type of Civic Education" was published in *The Good Society* in 1997. In addition to education policy, her interests include citizenship, urban government, and adult civic education. Prior to beginning work on her doctorate, she served as an officer in the U.S. Air Force for eleven years.

Mary Hartley has represented the 20th legislative district in the Arizona state senate since 1995. The district encompasses portions of Phoenix, Glendale, El

Mirage, and Surprise. Prior to her election, senator Hartley served on the Alhambra Elementary School District's governing board for eight years. Her work on the board won the Arizona School Board Award of Excellence in 1995. Her work in the state senate has won awards from the American Federation of State, County, and Municipal Employees; the Sierra Club; the Audubon Council; and Mothers Against Drunk Driving. Senator Hartley received the National Association of Partners in Education Outstanding School Volunteer Award in 1992. This honor included being named one of President Bush's Points of Light. Senator Hartley has been married for twenty-seven years to John Hartley and has three children and one grandchild.

Bryan C. Hassel directs Public Impact, an education policy consulting firm based in Charlotte, North Carolina. He conducts research and consults widely on charter schools and other education policy issues. He is the author of *The Charter School Challenge* (Brookings, 1999) and co-editor, with Paul E. Peterson, of *Learning from School Choice* (Brookings, 1998). Dr. Hassel received a Ph.D. in public policy from Harvard University, an M.Phil. in politics from the University of Oxford, and a B.A. in history from the University of North Carolina at Chapel Hill.

Frederick Hess is an assistant professor of government and education at the University of Virginia. He holds his Ph.D. in government from Harvard University and has written widely on the politics of education, including *Spinning Wheels: The Politics of Urban School Reform* (Brookings, 1999). He is a former public high school teacher and holds an M.Ed. in teaching and curriculum from the Harvard Graduate School of Education. He received his B.A. in politics from Brandeis University.

Lisa Graham Keegan has been state superintendent of public instruction since 1995. As superintendent, she oversees the Arizona Department of Education, which has an annual budget of over $2 billion. Prior to her election as superintendent, Ms. Keegan served in the Arizona house of representatives from 1991–1994. She chaired the Education Committee and was a member of the Joint Legislative Budget Committee in 1993–1994. While in the legislature, Ms. Keegan co-authored many of Arizona's school reform statutes, including legislation establishing charter schools and open enrollment. Ms. Keegan holds an M.S. in communication disorders from Arizona State University and a B.S. in linguistics from Stanford University. She and her husband, John Keegan, have five children.

David L. Leal is an assistant professor in the Department of Political Science at the State University of New York (SUNY) at Buffalo. He received a Ph.D. in government from Harvard University, a B.A. in political science from Stanford University, and is a 1998–1999 American Political Science Association Congressional Fellow. His articles have appeared in *American Politics Quarterly, Political Behavior, Urban Affairs Review, Policy Studies Journal, Urban Education,* and *Hispanic Journal of Behavioral Sciences.*

Robert Maranto is an assistant professor of political science and public administration at Villanova University and has taught political science at the Federal Executive Institute, James Madison University, the University of Pennsylvania, and Lafayette College. He has written widely on bureaucratic politics, including *Politics and Bureaucracy in the Modern Presidency* (Greenwood, 1993), as well as over twenty-five articles and reviews for such journals as the *American Journal of Political Science,*

Administration and Society, Presidential Studies Quarterly, and the *American Review of Public Administration.* He is now working on one book on presidential transitions and another on administrative reform. Bob earned a B.S. at the University of Maryland and a Ph.D. in political science at the University of Minnesota. He is married to April W. Gresham and is the proud grandson of illegal immigrants from Sicily. Bob can be reached at maranto@esinet.net.

Scott Milliman is associate professor of economics at James Madison University. Trained as an environmental economist, he has published in the *Journal of Environmental Economics and Management, Land Economics,* the *Canadian Journal of Fisheries and Aquatic Sciences,* and the *North American Journal of Fisheries Management.* Scott earned his B.A. at the University of California at Santa Cruz and his M.A. and Ph.D. at the University of Wisconsin. He is married to Ellen Lucius, a public elementary school administrator, and is the father of Darby Anne Lucius-Milliman, who will begin first grade in 2003. Scott can be reached at millimsr@jmu.edu.

Jim Spencer is president of Montessori Schools of Flagstaff. Prior to starting his own Montessori school, Spencer had a successful career in business and the military. He served in the U.S. Marine Corps from 1969 to 1975, then worked in information technology for the Fluor Corporation. From 1981 to 1991, he served in executive positions for British Petroleum, culminating with a stint as director of corporate materials and contracts, a $2 billion dollar department. He left BP in 1991 and moved to Flagstaff in order to take control of his life and future in an environment more conducive to raising a family. Jim earned a B.S. from the U.S. Naval Academy, an M.S. in systems management from the University of Southern California, and an M.B.A. from Harvard.

Robert T. Stout is a Professor of educational leadership and policy studies at Arizona State University, where he served as dean of the College of Education from 1978 to 1985. He has authored or co-authored eight books and monographs and more than fifty articles and chapters on a variety of education issues, including race and gender equity, desegregation, market-based education, policy leadership, and school finance. He also has served as a consultant to a number of school districts and to the U.S. Department of Education. He earned a B.A. at Carleton College and a Ph.D. at the University of Chicago.

Stephanie Timmons-Brown is a doctoral candidate in educational policy at the University of Virginia. She received her undergraduate degree in business administration at the University of California at Berkeley. She previously worked as a senior financial analyst of nonprofit organizations at Coopers and Lybrand. She is in the process of publishing in the *American School Board Journal.* Currently, she is conducting research on urban education, school finance, and school choice.

Index